"THE LAST
OF AMERICAN FREEMEN"

"THE LAST
OF AMERICAN FREEMEN"

*Studies in the Political Culture
of the Colonial and Revolutionary South*

BY
Robert M. Weir

MERCER UNIVERSITY PRESS

ISBN 0-86554-174-4

The paper used in this publication meets
the minimum requirements of American National Standard
for Information Sciences—Permanence of Paper
for Printed Library Materials, ANSI Z39.48-1984.   ∞ ™

Library of Congress Cataloging-in-Publication Data
Weir, Robert M.
    "The Last of American Freemen"
    Includes bibliographies and index.
    1. South Carolina—Politics and government—Colonial period, ca. 1600-
1775—Addresses, essays, lectures. 2. South Carolina—Politics and government—Revolution, 1775-1783—Addresses, essays, lectures. 3. Southern
States—Politics and government—Colonial period, ca. 1600-1775—Addresses, essays, lectures. 4. Southern States—Politics and government—1775-
1865—Addresses, essays, lectures. I. Title.
F272.W465   1986   975   85-28391
ISBN 0-86554-174-4 (alk. paper)

Contents

Preface ————————————————————————————— ix

Chapter One
    "The Harmony We Were Famous for": An Interpretation
    of Prerevolutionary South Carolina Politics ——————— 1

Chapter Two
    "The Scandalous History
    of Sir Egerton Leigh" ————————————————— 33

Chapter Three
    Who Shall Rule at Home: The American Revolution
    as a Crisis of Legitimacy for the Colonial Elite ————— 63

Chapter Four
    John Laurens: Portrait of a Hero ——————————— 89

Chapter Five
    Rebelliousness: Personality Development
    and the American Revolution
    in the Southern Colonies ——————————————— 105

Chapter Six
    "The Violent Spirit," the Reestablishment of Order,
    and the Continuity of Leadership
    in Postrevolutionary South Carolina ——————— 133

Chapter Seven
    The Role of the Newspaper Press in the Southern Colonies
    on the Eve of the Revolution: An Interpretation ————— 159

Chapter Eight
    The South Carolinian as Extremist ——————— 213

Index ————————————————— 231

For Carol and Suzanne

Let us then act wisely, of two Evils *choose the* least—*JOIN with our Sister-Colonies in a determined proper Opposition to Tyranny, resolved rather to die the* last of American Freemen, *than live the* first of American slaves.

The South Carolina Gazette,
13 June 1774

Preface _____

"Between the idea and the reality . . . between the conception and the creation, falls the Shadow." Ambiguous and evocative, these words of T. S. Eliot have, in an all-too-literal sense, nagged at me for years now whenever I thought about the project that first prompted the essays collected here. It was to write a history of the American Revolution in South Carolina. The idea was a good one, but I found that to understand the subject, I first needed to know more about other things. The character of local politics during the colonial period and the behavior of South Carolinians during the nineteenth century thus became, like the Revolution elsewhere in America, absorbing topics, and the task at hand grew larger. Invitations and opportunities to write about related subjects presented themselves, and the original project remained uncompleted. It still is, despite good work by other historians who cover portions of the subject. Perhaps I shall yet write that book.

Several years ago, however, a friend of mine in the historical profession began to despair that he would never see the work and suggested that I gather together some of my essays into a single volume. Being busy at the time with another book—which, I was resolved, would be finished—and being unwilling to believe his implicit prediction, I did not pursue the matter then. But more recently I had occasion to reread some of my own work, and doing so led me to reevaluate his idea.

Several considerations suggested that collecting the essays might be worthwhile. In the first place, the various items were not quite as diverse as I had remembered. To be sure, the subjects range from the mid-eighteenth century to the antebellum period; a number also draw on evidence from disparate colonies. Yet even the selections that most explicitly treat general themes rely heavily on data from the Southern colonies and states, especially South Carolina. Furthermore, each piece deals in one way or other with the dominant political culture of the region—that is, with the body of assumptions, beliefs, customs, and ideals that conditioned political behavior among the elite—and with men whose actions exemplified or failed to exemplify this culture. Such a concern with political elites does not imply that they were intrinsically the most important part of the body politic, nor does it deny the existence of countercultures. That the restricted focus has disadvantages as well as advantages is obvious; that it would be an efficient and potentially fruitful way of approaching the politics of a region in which, as one eighteenth-century observer noted, "a Sort of Aristocracy prevails," merely seemed to be a reasonable assumption.

Unified subject matter does not necessarily constitute a book. A collection of essays should somehow add up to more than the sum of its individual parts. In this case, there was reason to think that it might. Several items are explicitly interdisciplinary in approach, others are implicitly so. My assumption in writing them was that human behavior tends to be all of one piece. This is not to say that an individual's actions are always consistent, for as Lord Chesterfield observed, any given hero might well have been a coward under slightly different circumstances. Rather the present contention is simply that an individual who seeks to act in a particular way in one situation is apt to try to behave similarly in other contexts where such behavior is appropriate—or often where it is not. In short, we study life by compartmentalizing it; we live it as a whole. Assigning a particular kind of human behavior to the domain of psychology, another to the realm of sociology, and so forth may appear to make the task of understanding each behavior somewhat easier and may in fact be necessary. But the approach risks losing the meaning of actions for people who acted without recognizing the boundaries. Thus historians, whose discipline is potentially one of the most inclusive, can least afford to be exclusive in their methodology. Borrowing, however, can be a dangerous enterprise, as many who have tried it can testify. I, therefore, offer the interdisciplinary essays here in a spirit of considerable humility, being aware that getting caught red-handed on alien turf may be embarrassing. Success, however, can be commensurately rewarding, and in one or two cases at least the effort seems to have paid off. Furthermore, because the essays are a mixed bag in methodological terms, they may well be more useful as a group.

An essay is, after all, according to *Webster's Dictionary,* a "trial; [an] attempt." The purpose of the historical genre is to see how well certain bits of evidence fit together, to discover if possible the patterns of the past. Many who write, paint, or sculpt occasionally experience a feeling that whatever is taking shape under their hands has a life of its own. The thing, the artifact or intellectual construct, lurks in the medium; their task is merely to uncover it. Anyone who has had the sensation will know what I mean. To others, let me say that the experience can be a very intense one. This does not mean that the product is necessarily accurate or true, though artists especially have been wont to attribute a metaphysical existence to their creations. Historians, realizing that time and much else has clouded the glass through which they see, have usually been more skeptical of their own work. In addition, the farther one gets from that first flash of light, the dimmer it often seems. Original insights, if they are any good at all, remain valid, but an author begins to doubt whether they explain quite as much as he had initially hoped. Making extensive revisions in an essay after it has stood for a considerable time is, therefore, intellectually dubious as well as psychologically difficult. One is apt to qualify it out of existence.

Accordingly, except for the silent correction of a few minor errors, the text of each essay appears as it was originally written. Footnote form has been standardized throughout this collection, however, and the original documentation for the sketch of John Laurens is printed for the first time. Although a number of sources have been published since the earliest essays were written, I believe that indicating each case would introduce an anachronistic element; instead, the note below identifies some important examples and gives further bibliographic guidance.[1] The arrangement of

---

[1]The most frequently cited primary source to be subsequently published is probably *The Papers of Henry Laurens,* edited successively by Philip M. Hamer, George C. Rogers, Jr., David R. Chesnutt, and others (Columbia: University of South Carolina Press, 1968-). Volume 10 (12 December 1774-4 January 1776) has just appeared. Secondary works in a similar category include, among others, Richard Maxwell Brown's paper, "Back Country Violence (1760-1785) and Its Significance for South Carolina History," now published in

the essays is roughly by date of composition, but thematic unity takes precedence over chronology whenever possible.

The first essay, "An Interpretation of Prerevolutionary South Carolina Politics," outlines the central assumptions and ideals of country ideology. Permeating the political culture of South Carolina and other Southern colonies, this conception of politics involved expectations about political behavior that some Loyalists failed to understand. The second essay accordingly describes how one official, Sir Egerton Leigh, demonstrated that he was out of step. Most local leaders found, however, that following the precepts of country ideology legitimized their role among their constituents, although they remained provincial upstarts to imperial authorities. The effects of the latter's attitude is the subject of the third essay, which examines the American Revolution as a crisis of legitimacy for the colonial elite.

The next two essays deal with related but slightly different questions. Both seek to understand how the behavior of succeeding generations was affected by the ways in which this ethos was transmitted. In the case of John Laurens, the first piece argues, schooling in virtue ultimately proved to be very costly. But among Southern patriots in general, the other essay suggests, political rebellion and a quest for order were constructively related to their experience with rebelliousness in adolescence.

The next two pieces are also something of a pair insofar as they both continue the theme of order. The first item explicitly addresses the question of how revolutionaries curbed "the Violent Spirit" of revenge; the second examines the role of the newspaper press not only in the beginning of the Revolution, but also in restoring government and maintaining the position of the elite during the postwar period.

Finally, the concluding essay entitled "The South Carolinian as Extremist" examines some ramifications of these continuities in leadership and political culture under the changing conditions of the nineteenth century.

---

his *Strain of Violence: Historical Studies of American Violence and Vigilantism* (New York: Oxford University Press, 1975), and Jerome J. Nadelhaft's dissertation, "The Revolutionary Era in South Carolina, 1775-1788" (University of Wisconsin, 1965), which has been published as *The Disorders of War: The Revolution in South Carolina* (Orono: University of Maine at Orono Press, 1981). See my *Colonial South Carolina: A History* (Millwood NY: KTO Press, 1983), for a comparatively complete bibliography.

Taken as a whole, the essays represent variations on two larger themes. The first of these is continuity over time. All history, to be sure, deals with continuities (or the lack thereof), but the subjects in this case—namely, the political culture and leadership of the Southern colonies in the revolutionary era—exhibited unusual staying power. As a result, the legacy of the eighteenth century is clearly visible in the antebellum South, but nowhere more prominently than in South Carolina. Thus, what James Banner and other historians have seen as "the problem of South Carolina"—that is, its political extremism in the nineteenth century—was partly a result of its unusual success during the late colonial period in developing a political system closely approximating prevailing ideals, and therefore resistant to change.

Yet the tragic effect of success was only one of the larger ironies to be found in the history of a state and region where putatively democratizing influences, such as the press, have often had contrary effects, even during the revolutionary era. Accordingly, the subtitle of this volume could have been "Studies in Historical Irony," for this also is a central theme of the entire book. One of my original intentions in writing and assembling the essays was to illustrate the degree to which "the irony of Southern history" had eighteenth-century dimensions as well as the more recent ramifications described by C. Vann Woodward. Only later reflection made me realize that the ubiquity of irony had unexpected implications of its own in the present context. No doubt, from some perspectives, a past replete with paradox and irony has helped to make South Carolina unique. From another point of view, however, the problem of the state may not be so idiosyncratic after all. Part of it is shared not only by other Southerners but, to some extent, by human beings everywhere. Those who make history rarely see what they have really made; death and the contingencies of life intervene. Thus the special task of historians becomes, to recall Eliot's words, one of illuminating the shadows. And in going about their business they find, more often than not, "how uncertain and unpredictable are the consequences of what men do."[2] This, to me, is the most fascinating, rele-

---

[2]Ernest R. May, *"Lessons" of the Past: The Use and Misuse of History in American Foreign Policy* (London: Oxford University Press, 1973) as quoted in *The Past before Us: Contemporary Historical Writing in the United States,* ed. Michael Kammen (Ithaca: Cornell University Press, 1980) 232.

vant, and perhaps by common consent among many historians, the real lesson of history. Certainly it is one that bears repeating.

If these essays cast any light, it is in large measure because of a number of persons who have helped directly and indirectly with this book. A master essayist, Jack P. Greene, first stimulated my interest in the history of the revolutionary period. More than one item has benefited from his incisive criticism, and all owe much to his example. Robert Calhoon was kind enough to permit me to reprint an essay which, in conception and execution, is at least half his; more important, his example has also taught me much about being a historian. Several chairmen from Allen Going at the University of Houston, to George C. Rogers, Jr., at South Carolina, presided over departments in which working was a pleasure, while the many librarians and archivists whose institutions are mentioned in the notes made the work itself feasible. At various times, grants from the American Council of Learned Societies, the American Philosophical Society, the Association for State and Local History, the National Endowment for the Humanities, the University of Houston, and the University of South Carolina helped to support research on which these essays are based. The American Antiquarian Society, *American Heritage,* the United States Capitol Historical Society, Duke University Press, the *Journal of Interdisciplinary History,* the University of North Carolina Press, and the *William and Mary Quarterly* generously permitted me to reprint copyrighted materials. Paige Fillon, Susan Giaimo, Stephanie North, Rowena Nylund, Katherine Richardson, and Carolyn Wharton helped with typing and the final preparation of the manuscript. Grants from the Institute for Southern Studies and the history department of the University of South Carolina enabled David Fischer to compile the index. And, as always, my wife Anne provided indispensable assistance and encouragement. I thank them all.

Columbia, South Carolina   Robert M. Weir
October 1985

"The Harmony We Were Famous for": An Interpretation of Prerevolutionary South Carolina Politics ⎯⎯⎯⎯⎯

This essay developed from a paper on the political culture of colonial South Carolina given at the annual meeting of the Southern Historical Association in 1966. The remarks of Gordon Wood and William Freehling, who commented on the session, and an essay by Jack P. Greene, "Changing Interpretations of Early American Politics," in The Reinterpretation of Early American History: Essays in Honor of John Edwin Pomfret, *ed. Ray A. Billington (San Marino CA: Huntington Library, 1966), which appeared at about the same time, prompted me to put my findings in a wider perspective. The present essay is the result, and is printed here by permission from Robert M. Weir, " 'The Harmony We Were Famous for': An Interpretation of Pre-Revolutionary South Carolina Politics,"* William and Mary Quarterly, *3d ser. 26 (1969): 473-501.*

South Carolinians have always intuitively felt that their state was different, that its politicians were especially virtuous, that its political system was unusually perfect. However debatable these notions are concerning most of its history, there can be little doubt that during the late colonial period political life in South Carolina closely approximated the prevailing ideal. For South Carolinians, as perhaps for many other Americans, this ideal was largely a product of what J. G. A. Pocock has termed "the country ideology,'' a body of related ideas that appeared throughout most of the British Empire at different times during the seventeenth and eighteenth centuries. Despite some local variations in its content, the distinctive feature of this ideology in South Carolina was its extraordinary ability to transform the character of politics. To describe the character of this transformation, to account for it, and to suggest some of its implications for later developments is the purpose of this essay.[1]

I

By the mid-eighteenth century South Carolinians shared a coherent body of ideals, assumptions, and beliefs concerning politics. The foundation of all their political assumptions was their conception of human nature: they deeply distrusted it. Although man was a social being, he was hardly fit for society. The daily experiences of life demonstrated that he was unreliable, subject to his passions, and motivated by self-interest. But man's capacity for rational action made him more than a mere animal; therefore freedom, defined as the ability to act in conformity with the dictates of one's own reason, was the greatest of human values.[2] As the quality that distinguished a man from a beast or a slave, liberty was the source of human dignity.

---

[1]Although it does not develop the relationship between country ideology and local politics, M. Eugene Sirmans, *Colonial South Carolina: A Political History, 1663-1763* (Chapel Hill: University of North Carolina Press, 1966), is an excellent account. For a wider perspective and stimulating suggestions about the role of country ideology in colonial politics, see Jack P. Greene, ''Changing Interpretations of Early American Politics,'' in *The Reinterpretation of Early American History,* ed. Ray A. Billington (San Marino CA: Huntington Library, 1966) 151-84; Bernard Bailyn, *The Ideological Origins of the American Revolution* (Cambridge MA: Belknap Press of Harvard University Press, 1967); and idem, ''The Origins of American Politics,'' *Perspectives in American History* 1 (1967): 9-120. That the assumptions governing political behavior in South Carolina were not unique can be clearly seen in Richard Buel, Jr., ''Democracy and the American Revolution: A Frame of Reference,'' *William and Mary Quarterly* 3d ser. 21 (1964): 165-90; and *The Diary of Colonel Landon Carter of Sabine Hall, 1752-1778,* ed. Jack P. Greene, 2 vols. (Charlottesville: University Press of Virginia, 1965) 1: esp. the intro. For the term ''country ideology,'' see J. G. A. Pocock, ''Machiavelli, Harrington, and English Political Ideologies in the Eighteenth Century,'' *William and Mary Quarterly* 3d ser. 22 (1965): 549-83.

[2]Arthur Middleton to William Henry Drayton, 22 August 1775, in ''Correspondence of Hon. Arthur Middleton, Signer of the Declaration of Independence,'' ed. Joseph W. Barnwell, *South Carolina Historical and Genealogical Magazine* 27 (1926): 134; John Mackenzie and William Henry Drayton, in *The Letters of Freeman, etc.,* ed. William Henry Drayton (London, 1771) intro., 9, 31, 76-77.

Thus, the central problem of human existence was the maintenance of freedom in the face of the manifold threats posed by man's own frailties; unless limits were placed on the exercise of passions and power, life was chaos and liberty impossible. At all times the prudent individual would therefore endeavor to order his life in such a way as to preserve his liberty. Aided by Christian virtue, education, and concern for his honor, he could practice self-discipline to avoid becoming a slave to his own passions.[3] If wise, he did not trust even himself with the possession of excessive power, lest it be a temptation to its abuse. Above all, constant exposure to the realities of slavery reminded him never to allow another man to assume uncontrolled power over him. Personal independence therefore became a nearly obsessive concern, and the absolute necessity of maintaining it meant that the possession of property was of prime importance. Economic independence was the bulwark of personal liberty.[4] The resources of the individual alone, however, were insufficient to secure the social order necessary to freedom. Therefore governments had been established to aid him by protecting his property, his freedom, and his life from the aggressions of his fellow creatures. When a government discharged its responsibility, its citizens were obligated to support and obey it. But when it threatened liberty by exceeding the limits of its authority, the people had not only the right but also the duty to resist.[5]

---

[3]H. Laurens to John Laurens, 21 February 1774, in "Letters from Hon. Henry Laurens to His Son John, 1773-1776," *South Carolina Historical and Genealogical Magazine* 3 (1902): 146; "Carolinacus," *South Carolina Gazette* (Charleston), 9 November 1769; Harriott H. Ravenel, *Eliza Pinckney* (New York: Charles Scribner's Sons, 1896) 65, 115-18.

[4]H. Laurens to Isaac King, 6 September 1764, Laurens Letter Book, 3:421-22, South Carolina Historical Society, Charleston; H. Laurens to William Fisher, 26 June 1769, Etting Manuscripts, Old Congress, 2:63, Historical Society of Pennsylvania, Philadelphia (hereafter HSP). The ideal of personal independence was common to the English-speaking world. It was, in Professor Pocock's phrase, "one of the few subjects on which the age allowed itself to become fanatical." But South Carolinians appear to have been even more concerned than most of their contemporaries. Pocock, "Machiavelli, Harrington, and English Political Ideologies," 567. See particularly William Wragg, in Drayton, ed., *Letters of Freeman, etc.*, 53.

[5]"Pro Bono Publico," *South Carolina Gazette*, 17 May 1773; H. Laurens to James Marion, 31 August 1765, Laurens Letter Book, 1762-1766, p. 312, HSP; Presentments of the Cheraw District Grand Jury, *South Carolina Gazette*, 29 May 1775; Mackenzie, *South Carolina Gazette*, 26 September 1768; "To the Printer . . . ," *South Carolina Gazette*, 2 June 1766.

Frequent recourse to such drastic measures was dangerous because it threatened to create the chaos that governments were instituted to avoid; therefore continuous effective checks on the power of government were necessary. Under the English system the constitution performed this function, and South Carolinians invoked the hallowed term frequently but ambiguously. Often they used it to refer to the limits that society placed on its rulers; power and authority were different attributes. The former represented absolute force; the latter was power sanctioned by right, and the authority of government did not include the power to invade fundamental human rights. At other times the constitution denoted the spirit and principles that men believed ought to animate government; these included the idea that free men were bound only by laws to which they had consented, that private interests ought not to be set in competition with public good, and that the welfare of the whole was the supreme law. Finally, the constitution also referred to the existing composition of government.[6]

To South Carolinians the glory of the British constitutional system was that it included institutional means to limit government and insure—as far as humanly possible—that it would act according to the principles that ought to animate it. Because the freedom of a citizen depended on the security of his property, taxes were considered voluntary though necessary gifts toward the support of government. To facilitate the grant of taxes, property holders of the nation chose representatives whose primary control over the public purse gave them an effective means to check the executive power and obtain a redress of grievances. In practice, therefore, the chief historical role of the British House of Commons had been the protection of the people. Considering their own Commons House of Assembly to be a small counterpart, South Carolinians looked upon their local representatives as the natural guardians of the liberties and properties of the people.[7]

---

[6]Mackenzie, in Drayton, ed., *Letters of Freeman, etc.,* 35, 110; Christopher Gadsden, *South Carolina Gazette,* 5 February 1763, 24 December 1764; "[To] Mr. Timothy," *South Carolina Gazette,* 15 November 1770; H. Laurens to Marion, 31 August, 1765, Laurens Letter Book, 1762-1766, p. 312, HSP; Gadsden, *South Carolina Gazette,* 30 November 1769; Speech by Governor Montagu, 10 October 1772, South Carolina Commons House of Assembly Journals, 39:5, South Carolina Department of Archives and History, Columbia (hereafter cited as SCDAH).

[7]29 November 1765, South Carolina Commons Journals, 37, pt. 1: 27; Mackenzie, *South*

The discharge of such important responsibilities required ability and the freedom to use it; therefore a member of the Commons was expected to be a relatively free agent. Theoretically he did not solicit but accepted a duty that imposed upon him an almost professional obligation to use his political expertise in behalf of his constituents, the whole people. He should therefore be able, independent, courageous, virtuous, and public-spirited.[8] Although riches did not insure that a man would exhibit these qualities, it was assumed that they made it more likely. Economic independence promoted courage, and material possessions fostered rational behavior. In addition a large stake in society tied a man's interest to the welfare of the whole. Wealth also enabled him to acquire the education believed necessary for statecraft. Finally, the influence and prestige of a rich man helped to add stature and effectiveness to government.[9] Thus a series of interre-

---

Carolina Gazette, 26 September 1768; Ralph Izard to George Livins, 7 April 1776, in *Correspondence of Mr. Ralph Izard of South Carolina from the Year 1774 to 1804,* ed. Ann Izard Deas (New York: C. S. Francis, 1844) 1:202; Charles Garth to Committee of Correspondence, 19 January 1766, in Joseph W. Barnwell, "Hon. Charles Garth, M. P., the Last Colonial Agent of South Carolina in England, and Some of His Work," *South Carolina Historical and Genealogical Magazine* 26 (1925): 78; *A Full Statement of the Dispute betwixt the Governor and the Commons House of Assembly of His Majesty's Province of South Carolina in the Americas* (London, 1763) 38; 17 November 1767, South Carolina Commons Journals, 37, pt. 2: 479.

[8]Sir Egerton Leigh, *The Man Unmasked: or, The World Undeceived in the Author of a Late Pamphlet Entitled "Extracts from the Proceedings of the High Court of Vice-Admiralty in Charleston, South Carolina &c."* with *Suitable Remarks* (Charleston SC: Peter Timothy, printer, 1769) 103. In the early period, particularly, theory and practice were not always identical—see John Dart's advertisement in the *South Carolina Gazette,* 5 April 1735, in which he successfully campaigned for election to the Commons. Drayton, *South Carolina Gazette,* 21 September 1769. In theory, voters might demand preelection pledges from a candidate as a condition for electing him and constituents might instruct their representatives, but neither practice appears to have been common. See Robert M. Weir, " 'Liberty and Property and No Stamps': South Carolina and the Stamp Act Crisis" (Ph.D. dissertation, Western Reserve University, 1966) 93-94, for a full discussion of this point. Gadsden, a Whig, and Wragg, subsequently a Loyalist, represented opposite poles of the political spectrum, but they both assumed, like almost everyone else, that although a representative might consult his constituents, in the final analysis he should use his own judgment. See *The Dispute betwixt the Governor and the Commons,* 26-27 and 43-44. "A Native," *South Carolina Gazette,* 5 October 1765.

[9]For example, militia Colonel George Gabriel Powell expected to be able to reason with the South Carolina Regulators because several of them were "men of good Property" and therefore, Powell assumed, open to "Conviction"; 26 August 1768, South Carolina Coun-

lated assumptions about the virtues thought to be associated with wealth helped to maintain the belief that members of the elite should rule.

Nevertheless, no matter how qualified and how public-spirited an individual seemed, appearances might be deceiving and human nature was prone to corruption. It was therefore necessary for a representative's constituents to retain due checks upon him. The most effective means was to harness his own self-interests to theirs.[10] In theory this usually meant that he should hold property where they did. Over a period of time, however, the interests of a representative and his constituents might diverge; to prevent such a development, the election law stipulated a maximum term of three years for each assembly. Moreover, the entire process of representation was a sham without free elections. South Carolinians, therefore, prided themselves on using the secret ballot, which provided a convenient means to undermine the efficacy of coercion and bribery.[11] In addition, collective bodies of men should be checked against each other. Everyone therefore gave at least habitual allegiance to the ideal of balanced government. Governor Lord Charles Montagu prized it as the "Palladium" of liberty, and the popular patriot Christopher Gadsden declared that he no more wished to see the power of the Commons enlarged beyond its proper limits than vice versa.[12] Not surprisingly, however, most local leaders considered those limits very wide.

---

cil Journals, 34:223, SCDAH. For the same assumption, see also Middleton to Drayton, 22 August 1775, in Barnwell, ed., "Correspondence of Arthur Middleton," 134; *South Carolina Gazette*, 8 August 1771, reprinting material from the *North Carolina Gazette* ; Drayton, *South Carolina Gazette*, 6 March 1775; Gadsden, *South Carolina Gazette*, 3 December 1764; "Carolinacus," *South Carolina Gazette*, 9 November 1769; 20 November 1767, South Carolina Commons Journals, 37, pt. 2: 482.

[10]Mackenzie, *South Carolina Gazette*, 26 September 1768. See also *South Carolina Gazette*, 20 July 1765, reprinting material from the *New York Gazette*, and Buel, "Democracy and the American Revolution," 183-89, which discusses this point.

[11]Thomas Cooper and David McCord, eds., *The Statutes at Large of South Carolina*, 10 vols. (Columbia SC: A. S. Johnston, 1836-1841) 3:135-40; H. Laurens to J. Laurens, 21 February 1774, in "Letters from Henry Laurens to His Son John, 1773-1776," 145-47; Governor James Glen to Duke of Bedford, 10 October 1748, Transcripts of Records Relating to South Carolina in the British Public Record Office, 23:242, SCDAH, hereinafter cited as Trans., S.C. Records. *The Dispute betwixt the Governor and the Commons*, 32.

[12]Izard to George Dempster, 1 August 1775, in *Correspondence of Ralph Izard*, 1:112-13; [Sir Egerton Leigh], *Considerations on Certain Political Transactions of the Province of South Carolina* (London: T. Caudell, 1774) 59-60; William Wragg, *South Carolina and American General Gazette* (Charleston), 31 October 1765; 10 October 1772, South Carolina Commons Journals, 39:5; Gadsden, *South Carolina Gazette*, 24 December 1764.

The efficacy of balanced government, indeed the validity of the whole concept of checks and balances, was predicated on the discreet identity of each element in the system. Parties or factions, or any combinations of men acting together for selfish purposes, were inherently dangerous. In the absence of factions, the self-interested politician found himself checkmated at every turn by individuals whose common attributes were personal independence and a concern for the public welfare. Factional politics, however, provided a context that allowed private interests to flourish at the expense of the public and that permitted the executive to build centers of support in the other branches of government, thereby weakening their will and subverting their ability to check the encroachments of executive power. Factionalism and corruption, especially when associated with the executive, presaged the demise of freedom.[13]

Elitist in its assumptions, this ideology envisioned the existence of a society in which the clash of economic and class interests played no role. Instead, a struggle between the executive and the united representatives of the people appeared to supply the dynamics of politics. The idealized political figure was therefore the individualistic patriot who exhibited his disinterested concern for the public welfare by rejecting factional ties while remaining ready to join with like-minded individuals in curbing arbitrary exercises of executive power.

II

The country ideal, at least in part, figured in the political life of the colony from its founding, but its dominant role represented a delayed development. Lord Shaftesbury, the man most responsible for the Fundamental Constitutions of Carolina, was also one of the progenitors of country ideology; as a result that document sought to structure society and government so that rule by an elite composed of public-spirited men of indepen-

---

[13]Greene, "Changing Interpretations," 174; Pocock, "Machiavelli, Harrington, and English Political Ideologies," 564-65; and "Cato's Letters," Nos. 16 and 17, conveniently available in *The English Libertarian Heritage,* ed. David L. Jacobson (Indianapolis: Bobbs-Merrill, 1965) 45-56. Because of the lack of factionalism in late colonial South Carolina, South Carolinians seldom articulated these points in fully developed form, but on British politics see H. Laurens to J. Laurens, 21 February 1774, in "Letters from Henry Laurens to His Son John," 142-49. The classic statement on the evil effects of party was, of course, Henry St. John, Viscount Bolingbroke, *A Dissertation upon Parties,* 2d ed. (London: H. Haines, 1735) particularly xv, 1, 2, 43, and 217.

dent property would be the natural result.[14] Often attacked as anachronistic, the Fundamental Constitutions were ahead of their time in this aspect. Of diverse origins, linked together chiefly by their common residence and economic ambitions, South Carolinians spent most of the first seventy years squabbling over religious differences and contending for the perquisites of power. A degree of order, stability, and prosperity, as well as a fairly strong sense of community, was necessary before a sophisticated and basically altruistic political ethic could have much relevance to local politics— something that eighteenth-century writers apparently realized when they assumed that chaotic factionalism was normal in small, immature colonial societies.[15] Gradually, however, during the first four decades of the eighteenth century, economic and social developments provided the prerequisites necessary for the growth of Shaftesbury's ideals.

Prosperity was the most important factor. Until the 1730s the economic history of the colony was a checkered one; thereafter, except for a relatively brief period during King George's War, ever-increasing prosperity seems to have been the rule. From 1730 to 1760 rice production almost doubled; indigo production catapulted from nothing to more than one-half million pounds per year. Annual returns on invested capital are difficult to calculate, but they may have ranged as high as thirty percent for planters and perhaps fifty percent for the luckiest merchants. Given returns such as these, it is no wonder that by the 1760s travelers marveled at the wealth to be seen in Charleston. Not surprisingly, South Carolinians were soon convinced that theirs would be the richest province in America.[16]

---

[14]Pocock, "Machiavelli, Harrington, and English Political Ideologies," 558; Sirmans, *Colonial South Carolina,* 9-15.

[15]Sirmans, *Colonial South Carolina,* chs. 2-9; Daniel Defoe, "Party Tyranny," 1705, in *Narratives of Early Carolina, 1650-1708,* ed. Alexander S. Salley, Jr. (New York: Charles Scribner's Sons, 1911) 225; "A Bahamian," *South Carolina Gazette,* 30 August 1773.

[16]David Ramsay, *History of South Carolina from Its First Settlement in 1670 to the Year 1808,* 2 vols. (Newberry SC: W. J. Duffie, 1858) 1:69; Alexander Hewatt, *An Historical Account of the Rise and Progress of the Colonies of South Carolina and Georgia,* 2 vols. (London: A. Donaldson, 1779) 2:13, 15, 127, 141, 268; Sirmans, *Colonial South Carolina,* 226; U. S. Bureau of the Census, *Historical Statistics of the United States, Colonial Times to 1957* (Washington: Government Printing Office, 1960) 762, 767. By the 1760s in South Carolina, returns on invested capital—except in special cases—appear to have been sufficient merely to make a modest profit on funds borrowed at eight-percent interest per

Economic plenty bound the community together in several ways. It not only lessened competition among groups for a portion of its benefits, but it also fostered upward social mobility by individuals. As a result, the distance between social classes was never very wide, though the contemporary historian Alexander Hewatt doubtless exaggerated when he reported that "in respect of rank, all men regarded their neighbour as their equal."[17] In addition, prosperity and social mobility homogenized interest groups. Although merchants, if rich, were considered eminently respectable, possession of land tended to connote high social status. Wealthy merchants therefore purchased plantations and in the process acquired an understanding of the planters' economic interests and problems. Significantly, by the end of the colonial period almost all of the prominent leaders among the professional men and merchants in the Assembly owned plantations. Intermarriage between planting and mercantile families also blurred distinctions. In addition, as every planter was well aware, the economic health of the province depended upon the export trade. Thus consanguinity and a consciousness of shared economic interests helped to bind together potentially disparate segments of society.[18]

---

year; but in Georgia at this time (a period in its development roughly comparable to that of South Carolina twenty to thirty years earlier), DeBrahm believed that planters could achieve a return of nearly thirty perecent a year. John William Gerard DeBrahm, "History [of] the Three Provinces of South Carolina, Georgia and East Florida," 1770, 142-43, Harvard College Library, on microfilm at SCDAH; Weir, "South Carolina and the Stamp Act Crisis," 40-42; Mackenzie, *South Carolina Gazette,* 26 September 1768; *South Carolina Gazette,* 30 November 1769.

[17]For evidence of this mobility, see Eliza Lucas to her brother, 22 May 1742, Pinckney Papers, Library of Congress; Gadsden, in Drayton, ed., *Letters of Freeman, etc.,* 180; "Twist and Company," *South Carolina Gazette,* 26 November 1772; and H. Laurens to King, 6 September 1764, Laurens Letter Book, 3:420, SCHS; Hewatt, *Historical Account of South Carolina and Georgia,* 2:294.

[18]For example, of the fourteen merchants who served in the 1762-1765 House, at least eleven had planting interests, as did seven of the eight lawyers and one of the two physicians. Weir, "South Carolina and the Stamp Act Crisis," 92 n. 18, and 454-58. See the following for genealogical information: Louis and Mary Manigault, "The Manigault Family of South Carolina from 1685 to 1886," and Myrta J. Hutson, "Early Generations of the Motte Family of South Carolina," Huguenot Society of South Carolina, *Transactions* 4 (1897): 48-84 and 56 (1951): 57-63; A. S. Salley, Jr., "Col. Miles Brewton and Some of His Descendants," *South Carolina Historical and Genealogical Magazine* 2 (1901): 128-52; Henry A. M. Smith, "Wragg of South Carolina," *South Carolina Historical and Genealogical Magazine* 19 (1918): 121-23; George C. Rogers, Jr., *Evolution of a Federalist: William Laughton Smith of Charleston, 1758-1812* (Columbia: University of South Carolina Press, 1962) 402-403.

The passage of time and waning religious zeal also contributed to a growing sense of community. Ethnic diversity and religious antagonisms had been major causes of factional strife in the early 1700s. By mid-century, the Huguenots had been completely assimilated and a broad religious toleration had replaced narrow sectarianism. Lieutenant Governor William Bull reflected the prevailing spirit when, speaking as a public official, he wrote, "I charitably hope every sect of Christians will find their way to the Kingdom of heaven," but for political reasons he thought "the Church of England the best adapted to the Kingdom of England." Thomas Smith, a merchant member of the Assembly, was even more tolerant when he privately noted that if an Anglican church were not available, he would be just as willing to take communion in a dissenting one.[19]

Geographic and demographic features of the society also unified it. In the first place, Charleston was the economic, political, social, and cultural center of the colony. As a result, urban values permeated the culture of even the most remote low-country parishes, giving substance to the common saying that as the town went, so went the country.[20] In addition, society was remarkably small, and as late as 1790 most of the low-country parishes contained less than 200 white families. In 1770 there were only 1,292 dwellings, housing about 5,030 white persons, in Charleston. The central position of the city in the life of the colony, coupled with the relatively small population, meant that members of the elite had the opportunity to know each other, communicate, and develop a community of shared values. A prominent figure like Speaker of the House Peter Manigault could realistically assert that "I am well acquainted with the Circumstances of most of our Inhabitants." In short, low-country society possessed

---

[19]"Dr. Francis Le Jau to Secretary of the Society for the Propagation of the Gospel," 30 June 1707, in *The Carolina Chronicle of Dr. Francis Le Jau, 1706-1717,* ed. Frank J. Klingberg, University of California Publications in History, 53 (Berkeley: University of California Press, 1956) 27; Sirmans, *Colonial South Carolina,* 19-222; Arthur H. Hirsch, *The Huguenots of Colonial South Carolina* (Durham: Duke University Press, 1928) passim, esp. 261-64; Bull to Lord Hillsborough, 30 November 1770, Trans., S.C. Records, 32:371; T. Smith to William Smith, 20 February 1766, Smith-Carter Papers, Massachusetts Historical Society, Boston.

[20]Carl Bridenbaugh, *Myths and Realities: Societies of the Colonial South* (Baton Rouge: Louisiana State University Press, 1952) 59-60; "The Journal of Lord Adam Gordon," in *Travels in the American Colonies,* ed. Newton D. Mereness (New York: Macmillan Co., 1916) 397; "Americanus," *South Carolina Gazette,* 2 June 1766.

many of the characteristics of a primary group, and its public mores reflected the influence of those usually enforced by the family. Perhaps this fact helps to account for much of the harmony and politeness that visitors observed in the community.[21]

In addition, strategic considerations related to geographic location and the composition of the population produced community solidarity. Even after Georgia was established as a buffer between South Carolina and Spanish Florida, Charleston remained open to assault from the sea, and throughout the colonial period South Carolinians were periodically convinced that they were the target of imminent attack. Moreover, until the Revolution, the Creek and Cherokee Indians represented a real threat to the safety of the backcountry.[22] But what tied all of these dangers together into a source of constant, deep concern was the growing slave population. Huge importations of slaves accompanied the rising prosperity; in 1710 Negroes represented less than forty percent of the population; by 1730 they outnumbered whites two to one, and by the end of the colonial period the ratio in some low-country parishes was more than seven to one.[23] Whether in the nineteenth century "Sambo" was real or a figment of wishful thinking is an open question, but South Carolinians of the eighteenth century certainly failed to recognize him. To them, the African represented "a fierce, hardy and strong race," a "Domestic Enemy" who was ever ready

---

[21]U. S. Bureau of the Census, *Heads of Families at the First Census of the United States Taken in the Year 1790: South Carolina* (Washington: Government Printing Office, 1908) 9; Bull to Hillsborough, 30 November 1770, Trans., S.C. Records, 32:387; Manigault to Charles Alexander, [Spring 1768], Peter Manigault Letter Book, 1763-1773, Old Salem, Inc., Winston-Salem, North Carolina; Hewatt, *Historical Account of South Carolina and Georgia*, 2:293; Mereness, ed., "Journal of Gordon," 397; John Hughes to Jonathan Roberts, 24 July 1770, Correspondence of John Hughes from Charleston, 1768-1771, Hughes Papers, HSP.

[22]Sirmans, *Colonial South Carolina*, 20, 44, 84-87, 126, 210-15, 320; John R. Alden, *John Stuart and the Southern Colonial Frontier . . . , 1754-1775* (Ann Arbor: University of Michigan Press, 1944) passim, particularly 101-38.

[23]South Carolina Merchants, "Memorial of Merchants, Traders and Planters and Others Interested in the Trade and Prosperity of South Carolina and Georgia to the Lords Regents of Great Britain," [1755], Loudoun Papers, Henry E. Huntington Library, San Marino, California; U. S. Bureau of the Census, *Historical Statistics*, 756; Mark A. DeWolfe Howe, ed., "Journal of Josiah Quincy, Jr., 1773," Massachusetts Historical Society, *Proceedings* 49 (1915-1916): 456.

to revolt or join any outside attackers. His presence meant that any lapse in vigilance, any failure of government, presented the white community with the threat of annihilation. South Carolinians were therefore notoriously leery of any disorders.[24] Indeed, the prevailing atmosphere approached that of a garrison state. Unity among the defenders was essential, divided command dangerous, and any momentary lapse an invitation to disaster. In part, this is no doubt why prominent leaders like Henry Laurens considered internal political discord "more awful and more distressing than Fire, Pestilence or Foreign Wars." In short, disruptive factionalism was regarded as a potentially fatal luxury and, significantly, panics over insurrection often coincided with political turmoil within the white community, as occurred during the Stamp Act crisis and the outbreak of the Revolution.[25]

By the 1730s this growing Negrophobia, as well as the social and economic changes that contributed to it, began to mute political discord. Planters who were dependent on the export trade and merchants who had sought the prestige of plantation ownership cooperated to facilitate final settlement of a long disruptive controversy over paper currency—the last major factional battle in South Carolina politics. This compromise signaled the emergence of an increasingly well-integrated society, knit together by a community of economic interests and social values. Thus the controversies associated with the land boom during Governor Robert Johnson's administration did not prove permanently divisive. In fact, the heavy acquisition of land in the 1730s satiated the appetite of a generation and thereby helped to remove land as a future source of serious conten-

---

[24]Hewatt, *Historical Account of South Carolina and Georgia*, 2:71, 85; Bull to Hillsborough, 7 June 1770, Trans., S.C. Records, 32:281; *South Carolina Gazette*, 17 October 1774; Glen to Lieut. Gov. Robert Dinwiddie, January 1755, enclosed in Glen to Board of Trade, 29 May 1755, Trans., S.C. Records, 26:221.

[25]Presentment of Charleston Grand Jury, *South Carolina Gazette*, 5 November 1737; Hewatt, *Historical Account of South Carolina and Georgia* 2:245; Richard Oswald, "Mem[orandu]m with Respect to So. Carolina," 21 February 1775, Dartmouth Manuscripts, Item 1156, p. 15, Staffordshire County Record Office, Stafford, England; H. Laurens to Christopher Rowe, 8 February 1764, Laurens Papers, HSP; 17 December 1765, South Carolina Council Journals, 32:680; Gabriel Manigault to his son Gabriel Manigault, 8 July 1775, in "Papers of Gabriel Manigault, 1771-1784," ed. Maurice A. Crouse, *South Carolina Historical Magazine* 64 (1963): 2.

tion.[26] More important, between 1738 and 1742 South Carolinians confronted a crisis in Indian affairs, the most serious slave rebellion of the colonial period, a very destructive fire in Charleston, a real possibility of Spanish invasion, and the apparent threat to order and stability posed by the Great Awakening. The result was an unprecedented willingness by local leaders to compromise and cooperate with each other. In short, the crises of the late 1730s and early 1740s tended to produce political unity at the same time that potentially divisive issues were losing much of their sense of urgency. Significantly, many of the leading planters, whose social status was already assured, soon found politics boring, and in increasing numbers they refused to accept election to the Commons House.[27]

Not everyone, however, succumbed to the prevailing political apathy. Increasing prosperity and the accompanying growth in population led to the development of a relatively large class of merchants and professional men. The departure of the leading planters created a void in political leadership that members of this group could fill. Their residence in Charleston made it convenient for them to attend sessions of the legislature and their technical knowledge proved useful when the House considered commercial and legal matters. They, in turn, undoubtedly hoped to realize benefits from their service. For the less affluent, economic and professional advancement might be one hope; for the wealthier, prestige and high social status might be more important goals; for some—and their numbers increased over the years—the feeling that one had discharged his duty to so-

---

[26]Sirmans, *Colonial South Carolina*, 159-82. For varying interpretations of these land controversies, see David D. Wallace, *South Carolina: A Short History, 1520-1948* (1951; rpt., Columbia: University of South Carolina Press, 1966) 141-48; and Richard P. Sherman, *Robert Johnson: Proprietary and Royal Governor of South Carolina* (Columbia: University of South Carolina Press, 1966) x-xi, 170-82. For evidence that thereafter competition for land was a relatively minor factor in the history of the colony, see Manigault to Alexander, 5 June 1770, Peter Manigault Letter Book, 1763-1773, Old Salem, Inc.; Hewatt, *Historical Account of South Carolina and Georgia*, 2:300; and Robert K. Ackerman, "South Carolina Colonial Land Policies" (Ph.D. dissertation, University of South Carolina, 1965) 198.

[27]Sirmans, *Colonial South Carolina*, 193-222, 231-32, 247, 255; 11, 14 December 1739, in *The Journal of the Commons House of Assembly, Sept. 12, 1739 to March 26, 1741*, ed. J. H. Easterby (Columbia: South Carolina Archives Department, 1952) ix, 97-98, 121-22. Fear that the Great Awakening would lead to a slave revolt may have been an important reason why the religious revival made a relatively small impression on South Carolina.

ciety became the chief reward.[28] These were the devotees of country ideology, and at least in the beginning they came chiefly from the ranks of the merchants and lawyers. Relatively well educated, often maintaining contacts in Great Britain, the permanent residents of Charleston were able to stay abreast of intellectual developments in the mother country; they were importers of culture as well as material goods and technical skills; they made the *South Carolina Gazette,* established in 1732, a success; they patronized the booksellers, formed discussion groups, and founded the Charleston Library Society.[29]

At the same time that Charleston was emerging as something of a center of intellectual activity, the works of two British journalists, John Trenchard and Thomas Gordon, were enjoying remarkable popularity in Great Britain and especially in America. *Cato's Letters,* as Clinton Rossiter first noted, soon became the "most popular, quotable, esteemed source of political ideas" in the colonies, and *The Independent Whig* was not far behind.[30] Like other Americans, South Carolinians found these works attractive. The *South Carolina Gazette* reprinted many of *Cato's Letters* during the first two decades of its existence, while individuals as well as the Charleston Library Society purchased collected editions. This was not a temporary fad; for more than fifty years the works of these two journalists continued to be staple reading for South Carolinians. In 1772 Laurens made a special present to a chance acquaintance of *The Independent Whig,*

[28]In 1744 the Assembly recognized the emergence of the mercantile-professional community by revising the tax laws to tap more of its wealth. Glen to Board of Trade, 25 May 1745, Trans., S.C. Records, 22:97-100. Sirmans, *Colonial South Carolina,* 247-48; "Publicola," *South Carolina Gazette,* 22 September 1766.

[29]Hennig Cohen, *The South Carolina Gazette, 1732-1775* (Columbia: University of South Carolina Press, 1953) 7, 9, 10; Rogers, *Evolution of a Federalist,* 32-33; Sirmans, *Colonial South Carolina,* 232; Frederick P. Bowes, *The Culture of Early Charleston* (Chapel Hill: University of North Carolina Press, 1942) passim. Of the seventeen individuals who established the Library Society, twelve were Charleston merchants or professional men. Anne King Gregorie, "First Decade of the Charleston Library Society," South Carolina Historical Association, *Proceedings* (1935): 5-6.

[30]Caroline Robbins, *The Eighteenth-Century Commonwealthman* (Cambridge MA: Harvard University Press, 1959) 115-25; Clinton Rossiter, *Seedtime of the Republic: The Origin of the American Tradition of Political Liberty* (New York: Harcourt and Brace, 1953) 141; Milton M. Klein, ed., *The Independent Reflector or Weekly Essays on Sundry Important Subjects More Particularly Adapted to the Province of New York* (Cambridge MA: Belknap Press of Harvard University Press, 1963) 21.

which he noted was to be found "in almost every Gentleman's Library."[31] Trenchard and Gordon presented a version of country ideology in particularly readable form, but booksellers' advertisements, inventories of personal estates, and the records of the Charleston Library Society indicate that the Whig historians of the eighteenth century and the classical republicans of the seventeenth century, as well as Henry St. John, Viscount Bolingbroke, and the members of his literary circle, were also popular writers. Content rather than form was obviously the basic cause of the popularity of the works dealing with country ideology.[32]

There were several reasons for the appeal of these ideas. First, many of them reflected the orientation of religious dissenters, and the dissenting tradition was strong in Charleston, not only among persons of Huguenot descent but also in the large Baptist, Presbyterian, and Congregational populations. Second, country ideology was the product of a group at the periphery of British political power; being in the same situation, Americans found it congenial. It justified an increasing degree of local autonomy, and South Carolinians had long felt themselves better informed about and more capable of handling local problems than imperial authorities.[33] Moreover, South Carolinians sought to emulate the English gentry in every way they could. Some retired to English country estates; others built En-

---

[31]*South Carolina Gazette*, 12 June 1736, 16, 29 July, 8 August 1748, 20 March 1749; Inventories of estates of John Ouldfield, Andrew Johnston, and Hopkin Price, Charleston County Inventories, R (1751-1753): 527; W (1763-1767): 66-71; BB (1777-1784): 248, SCDAH; H. Trevor Colbourn, *The Lamp of Experience: Whig History and the Intellectual Origins of the American Revolution* (Chapel Hill: University of North Carolina Press, 1965) 221-22, 209-10; H. Laurens to Mynheer Van Teigham, 19 August 1772, Laurens Letter Book, 5:333, SCHS.

[32]Cohen, *South Carolina Gazette, 1732-1775,* 126-56; Inventories of estates of John Lloyd, Paul Jenys, James Parsons, Thomas Middleton, and Thomas Lynch, Jr., Charleston County Inventories, CC (1732-1736): 136-37; R (1751-1753): 404-5; BB (1777-1784): 195; A (1783-1787): 186, 390; Colbourn, *Lamp of Experience,* 209-10; *A Catalogue of Books, Given and Devised by John MacKenzie Esquire, to the Charleston Library Society, for the Use of the College when Erected* (Charleston SC: Robert Wells, 1772). For a convenient description of the lexicon, see Bailyn, *Ideological Origins of the American Revolution,* 34-42. For a stimulating discussion of Bolingbroke and his literary associates, who included Jonathan Swift and Alexander Pope, see Isaac Kramnick, *Bolingbroke and His Circle* (Cambridge MA: Harvard University Press, 1968).

[33]Buell, "Democracy and the American Revolution," 167; Hewatt, *Historical Account of South Carolina and Georgia,* 2:290, 167; Debrahm, "History [of] S. C., Ga. and E. Fla.," 32. Harvard College Library, on microfilm at SCDAH.

glish country houses in the swamps of Carolina, traced their genealogies, and attempted to found families. The adoption of country ideology was one more step by which they could play what they believed to be the role of the independent English country gentleman. In addition, it has been suggested that Americans adopted this ideology in part because they discovered it to be a handy weapon against factional opponents.[34] South Carolinians found a different but related utility in these ideas.

The implications of country ideology made it particularly attractive to local leaders who were unable to become councilors. Following the institution of royal authority in 1721, the Council was at its height; and its prestige, if not its power, considerably overshadowed that of the Commons. Men coveted membership and gladly gave up a seat in the lower house to accept one in the upper. But only twelve men could sit in the Council at one time. To be one of the twelve required luck and influence.[35] For those who failed to achieve appointment, the implications of country ideology proved to be soothing to wounded egos. Obviously councilors holding office at the pleasure of the Crown could not be independent. Election to the Commons could therefore be interpreted as being more prestigious. Certainly, it represented public recognition that a man had reached a social status that entitled him to a position of public leadership.

Moreover, country ideology told him how to discharge his duties with honor. In blunting the antagonisms of the earlier period, prosperity and increasing social integration had made it less appropriate for a representative to be the champion of a particular interest group. Collectively, the Commons could model its conduct on that of the British House of Commons, and it had tried to do so at least from its early days in the 1690s.[36] But for the individual member, the problem was potentially acute. How was he to

---

[34]Ramsay, *History of South Carolina*, 2:230; Mereness, ed., "Journal of Gordon," 397-98; Rogers, *Evolution of a Federalist*, 22, 34; *South Carolina Gazette*, 28 September 1738, 27 April 1748; Bridenbaught, *Myths and Realities*, 70-72; David D. Wallace, *The Life of Henry Laurens* (New York: G. P. Putnam's Sons, 1915) 12-14; Buel, "Democracy and the American Revolution," 166.

[35]Sirmans, *Colonial South Carolina*, 139; M. Eugene Sirmans, "The South Carolina Royal Council, 1720-1763," *William and Mary Quarterly* 3d ser. 18 (1961): 378-81; *South Carolina Gazette*, 17 September 1772.

[36]Jack P. Greene, *The Quest for Power: The Lower Houses of Assembly in the Southern Royal Colonies, 1689-1776* (Chapel Hill: University of North Carolina Press, 1963) 35; Sirmans, *Colonial South Carolina*, 69

conduct himself under the changing conditions of political life? Because country ideology provided a particularly satisfactory answer, it became the contemporary *Book of the Governor*. Its precepts delimited an honorable role; by following them, an aspiring politician could justify his leadership.

In the final analysis, however, what gave country ideology its over-whelming power over political behavior was its ability to satisfy, rather than thwart, the needs and desires of local leaders. Its precepts—which made sense in the light of their experience—helped to give purpose to their lives, justified their conduct, rationalized their freedom of action, sup-ported their positions of leadership, and brought them honor, while de-priving them of little except the pursuit of private gain at public expense. But prosperity, their own increasing wealth, and the relative lack of lucra-tive patronage in the hands of either the governor or the lower house made it fairly easy to forego the lesser for the greater reward. Perhaps if the so-ciety had been larger and the turnover in membership in the Commons smaller, the pursuit of status and power might have taken forms con-demned by country ideology. As it was, a man could satisfy his ambitions without denying the same satisfaction to others.[37]

III

Country ideology therefore transformed the character of local politics well before the Revolution. "Before 1743 constitutional issues relating to

---

[37]George Dempster, a member of Parliament who urged conciliation with America, cynically but perhaps realistically believed that American legislatures were public-spirited because "the Governor's power of gratifying them is very limited." Dempster to Izard, 6 July 1775, in *Correspondence of Ralph Izard,* 1:97. In South Carolina not only the power of the governor but also that of the Commons was closely circumscribed. The only lucra-tive appointments controlled by the House were the offices of provincial treasurer and com-missary general, both of whom were barred from the Commons by law. Glen to Board of Trade, 23 December 1749, Trans., S.C. Records, 23:438. For the value of these positions, see Greene, *Quest for Power,* 228; and Henry Peronneau's case in "Examinations in Lon-don: Memorials, Schedules of Losses, and Evidence, South Carolina Claimants, American Loyalists," Audit Office Transcripts, 52:522, Manuscript Division, New York Public Li-brary, New York. Although the intangible rewards of public service were real, achieving them often proved to be very time-consuming. As Sirmans noted, "The South Carolina Commons House was probably the hardest-working assembly in the American colonies." As a result, turnover in its membership at each election never dropped below about one-third, even in the late colonial period when membership remained more stable. Sirmans, *Colonial South Carolina,* 241, 245; Weir, "South Carolina and the Stamp Act Crisis," 251-52.

the rights and privileges of the house appeared only as by-products of social and economic conflicts involving the entire population,'' M. Eugene
Sirmans noted. Once these basic conflicts were settled, he found that ''the
frequently violent constitutional struggles in the assembly stood in marked
contrast to the general political calm that prevailed outside the legislature.'' In part institutional momentum promoted the Commons' aggressive quest for power that produced these constitutional battles. Undoubtedly
the personal ambition of its members was also an important factor, and
Governor William Henry Lyttelton probably recognized a universal phenomenon when he noted that William Wragg, who at different times played
leading roles in both houses, was ''a zealous stickler for the rights and
privileges real or imaginary of the body of which he is a member because
he derives his own importance from it.'' Obviously the example of the
British House of Commons exerted a powerful influence. But what informed the quest, guided its direction, and in the final analysis gave it
meaning was country ideology. In 1739 the Commons defined its role in
terms that were a distillation of prevailing assumptions; its current position
was the result of the need to keep a jealous eye on expanding power.[38] That
the House could voice such a position during a period of crisis and could
continue to act upon its implications throughout the remainder of the colonial period—despite the psychological and social pressures toward
avoiding political controversy—is an important measure of how seriously
local leaders regarded the precepts that appeared to govern their duty. Royal
governors, however, were not in a position to give the Commons really
determined opposition, and their patronage power was sufficiently limited
to make such stock elements of country ideology as the fear of corruption—or executive influence in the House—largely irrelevant. The role of
country ideology is therefore less conspicuous, though probably fully as
important, in the Commons' attempt to acquire power at the expense of the
governor, than it is in the attack on the upper house. Nowhere is the effect
of these ideas more apparent than in the link they provided between internal changes within the Commons and its changing relationship with the
Council.

----

[38]Sirmans, *Colonial South Carolina,* 223-24; Greene, *Quest for Power,* x; Governor
Lyttelton to Board of Trade, 6 December 1756, Trans., S. C. Records, 27:202; 5 June 1739,
in *Journal of the Commons House, November 10, 1736 to June 7, 1739,* ed. J. H. Easterby
(Columbia: South Carolina Archives Department, 1951) 717, 723.

Theoretically, only a house composed of independent men of property could be counted upon to fulfill its role in checking the other agencies of government. Beginning in the mid-1730s the Commons, under the leadership of Speaker Charles Pinckney, began vigorous efforts to make the reality coincide with the theoretical ideal. Thereafter the lower house repeatedly attempted to insure that its own membership would conform to the ideals of country ideology by revising the election laws to require higher property qualifications and to exclude placemen. Imperial authorities refused to permit the exclusion of Crown officials and repeatedly disallowed these laws for various other reasons.[39] Nevertheless the passage of time achieved what the law could not; by the end of the colonial period electors usually agreed with "A Native," who noted that "men in public employments are not the properest for your choice."[40] In the meantime both the caliber and wealth of the average member rose, in part because the leading planters who had formerly refused to sit in the House gradually returned as they assimilated the new ideals and viewed the rising prestige of the lower house. In contrast, the status of the upper house declined. To the Commons it appeared that councilors, lacking the independence necessary to qualify them as members of a separate house of the legislature, were in reality nothing more than appendages of the executive. Temporarily discarding the British Parliament as a model, the members of the Commons dropped the name Commons House of Assembly in 1744 and arrogated to

---

[39] Apparently the efforts of the members of a committee appointed in December 1736 to consider revision of the election law were too vigorous for their colleagues. The committee recommended that a member be required to be worth £1,000 sterling clear of encumbrances; the House failed to approve the recommendation. In 1745 the House passed an act substantially increasing the property qualification and disqualifying officeholders. It was, therefore, disallowed. In 1748 the Assembly passed an act making elections biennial and liberalizing the qualifying oath for Protestant Dissenters. It, too, was disallowed. And another act increasing property requirements, passed 7 April 1759, was also disallowed. 2 December 1736, 12, 13 January 1737, in *Journal of the Commons House, Nov. 10, 1736 to June 7, 1739,* 23, 168, 171; Cooper and McCord, eds., *Statutes of South Carolina,* 3:656-58, 692-93, 4:98-101; Matthew Lamb to the Board of Trade, 15 July 1747, Trans., S.C. Records, 22:292-93; Order in Council, 30 June 1748; ibid., 23:148-49; Lamb to the Board of Trade, 28 January 1750, ibid., 24:18; Order in Council, 31 October 1751, ibid., 380-82; Board of Trade to the king, 29 May 1761, ibid., 29:112-13; meeting of the Board of Trade, 25 August 1761, ibid., 10.

[40] *South Carolina Gazette,* 5 October 1765. Nevertheless, as late as 1761 the popular vice-admiralty judge John Rattray was a member of the Commons. *South Carolina Gazette,* 3 October 1761.

themselves alone the title of General Assembly. In the following year they attempted to give real substance to this symbolic gesture by denying the Council any role whatever in the passage of legislation. Both force of habit and the opposition of Governor James Glen barred success; most persons continued to call the lower house the Commons, and Glen refused to sign legislation that had not been passed by the Council.[41]

Later, however, Governor Lyttelton and the Board of Trade unwittingly played into the hands of the Commons. In 1756 Lyttelton ousted William Wragg from the Council without publicly giving reasons for the action. The Board of Trade then gave the coup de grace to the already dwindling prestige of the Council by confirming Wragg's suspension and adopting a deliberate policy of appointing placemen in the hopes of obtaining a more pliant upper house. Then, when the ministry belatedly realized that the Council needed strengthening, they could find few South Carolinians of stature who would accept appointments; obviously a position held by so precarious a tenure was not compatible with the status of an independent country gentleman. By the end of the colonial period, the Council had become a cipher, its real power practically nonexistent and most of its members virtual incompetents, not only in the estimation of many South Carolinians, but also in that of a capable Crown investigator, Captain Alexander Innes.[42]

The results of the Council's actual decline, in the context of a political culture suffused with the ideals of country ideology, were far reaching. On one level, it appeared that the Crown had subverted the constitution by capturing control of a second branch of government—the upper house—as well as the executive. Moreover, its action reversed the natural order of things: councilors occupied their official position not because they be-

---

[41]5 June 1739, in *Journal of the Commons House, Nov. 10, 1736 to June 7, 1739*, 721; Sirmans, *Colonial South Carolina*, 313; 25 February 1744, in *Journal of the Commons House, February 20, 1744 to May 25, 1745*, ed. J. H. Easterby (Columbia: South Carolina Archives Department, 1955) 17; Bull to Lord Dartmouth, 18 September 1773, Trans., S. C. Records, 33:306.

[42]Lyttelton to Board of Trade, 6 December 1756, Trans., S. C. Records, 27:202-203; Sirmans, "South Carolina Royal Council," 389-90. Bull to Hillsborough, 20 October 1770, Trans., S. C. Records, 32:343-45; Gadsden, *South Carolina Gazette*, 3 December 1764; Edward Rutledge, *South Carolina Gazette*, 13 September 1773; Innes to Dartmouth, 3 July 1775, in B. D. Bargar, "Charles Town Loyalism in 1775: The Secret Reports of Alexander Innes," *South Carolina Historical Magazine* 63 (1962): 135.

longed to the class whose right and responsibility it was to govern; rather, they sought entry to that class because of their official position. As a result, the status of the Council became a tangible symbol of other imperial measures that frequently appeared to be unnatural and subversive of good government. More important yet, the increasing identification of the governor with these measures and the declining position of the Council apparently vitiated the ideal of balanced government. Everyone recognized that the composition of the upper house did not reflect a separate stratum of society comparable to that of the British Lords. The habit of thinking in terms of old concepts nevertheless tended to persist, and members of the Council such as William Henry Drayton and Egerton Leigh frequently advocated permanent appointment of councilors in order to add dignity and weight to the upper house. Outside the Council, however, men were less enthusiastic about bolstering it, and Christopher Gadsden even noted that the power of the American councils was a kind of "politico-Meter," that varied inversely with the liberty of the people. By the end of the colonial period everyone recognized that the lower house dominated local government, and most local leaders believed its position fully justified. By 1772 Speaker Manigault revealed a willing acceptance of the realities that undermined the ideal of balanced government when he noted, "I . . . Love to have a weak Governor."[43] Had he added a weak Council as well, probably few persons would have disagreed.

Nevertheless, even in its decline, the Council maintained sufficient weight to serve as a foil to the lower house. The more attached to the prerogative the upper house appeared, the more concerned the lower became about preserving the rights and liberties of the people; the more irresponsible the Council seemed to become, the more members of the Commons felt their responsibility for the public welfare, because they alone appeared to have it at heart. Moreover, rivalry between the houses contributed to the esprit that unified the lower house. By the early 1740s members were finding it politically expedient to join in and support claims to rights and priv-

---

[43]Drayton, "A Letter from 'Freeman' of South Carolina to the Deputies of North America, Assembled in the High Court of Congress at Philadelphia," 10 August 1774, in *Documentary History of the American Revolution*, ed. R. W. Gibbes, 3 vols. (New York: D. Appleton, 1853-1857) 1:17; [Leigh], *Considerations on Certain Political Transactions*, 69; Gadsden, *South Carolina Gazette*, 24 December 1764; Manigault to Daniel Blake, 24 December 1772, Manigault Letter Book, 1763-1773, Old Salem, Inc.

ileges, whether or not they privately considered these claims justified. By
the early 1770s both Governor Montagu and Lieutenant Governor Bull
noted that members who singly disagreed with steps taken by the House
would jointly approve them; moreover, Bull reported that because members felt honor-bound to support the Commons, it was practically impossible to induce one house to reverse the actions of another.[44]

The solid front that the Commons was able to present reflected the lack
of factions within the House. In the absence of roll-call votes, which are
not extant for the colonial period, it is impossible to assign a precise date
for the disappearance of factionalism or even to assert, categorically, that
no vestiges remained. Nevertheless, all available evidence indicates that
by the 1750s, if any factions still existed, few contemporaries were aware
of them and their influence on political behavior was negligible. Faction
and party were terms of opprobrium, and given an excuse, a politician
would hardly have overlooked the opportunity to accuse an opponent of
being motivated by party spirit. Certainly in the early eighteenth century,
references to faction and its evil effects were common. By mid-century such
comments were conspicuously scarce; those that did occur almost always
reflected the disgust of a Crown servant at what he considered to be the
factious opposition of the Commons.[45] In discussing the early eighteenth
century, contemporary historians like Hewatt and David Ramsay identified factions and chronicled their struggles; as they approached their own
time such references disappear from their works, although Hewatt, a Scottish Loyalist who published his history during the Revolution, was con-

---

[44]Sirmans, *Colonial South Carolina,* 249-50. Bull to Hillsborough, 23 August 1770,
Trans., S. C. Records, 22:317; Montagu to Hillsborough, 26 September 1771, ibid., 33:84;
Bull to Dartmouth, 10 March 1774, ibid., 34:17.

[45]For early attacks on factionalism and its evils—often written more in sorrow than in
anger—see Samuel Thomas to secretary of the Society for the Propagation of the Gospel,
20 April 1706, in "The Letters of Reverend Samuel Thomas, 1702-1706," *South Carolina
Historical and Genealogical Magazine,* 4 (1903): 285; John Stewart to Maj. William Dunlop, 27 April 1690, in "The Letters from John Stewart to William Dunlop," ed. Mabel L.
Webber, *South Carolina Historical and Genealogical Magazine* 32 (1931): 3; John Arch-
dale, "A New Description of That Fertile and Pleasant Province of Carolina," 1707, in
Narratives of Early Carolina, 282; Le Jau to secretary of S. P. G., 30 June 1707, 12 April
1711, 22 January 1714, in *Chronicle of Dr. Le Jau,* 27, 90, 137. For the charges of Crown
officials, see Lyttelton to Board of Trade, 11 June 1757, Bull to Hillsborough, 5 December
1770, Trans., S. C. Records, 27:280, 32:407; [Leigh], *Considerations on Certain Political
Transactions,* 78.

vinced that a "party-spirit" had reemerged in 1761 after a lapse of indeterminate length. What he referred to, however, was not political factionalism, but a local version of the anti-Scottish prejudice that became endemic throughout much of the empire during Lord Bute's ministry.[46] The testimony of local leaders is even more conclusive. Sorrowfully viewing the political struggles of the 1780s, Gadsden lamented the apparent loss of that "harmony we were famous for." Earlier Laurens, horrified at the factional alignments within the Continental Congress, noted that he "discovered parties within parties, divisions and Sub-divisions" that he compared unfavorably with the situation in South Carolina.[47]

The absence of factionalism did not mean that local leaders never differed over men and measures; it did mean that these differences, even when they involved strong personal animosities or clashes of opinion, did not lead to permanent alignments that fractured the unity of the Commons House. Potentially, the most disruptive and politically significant personal quarrel was between successive speakers, Rawlins Lowndes and Manigault, who cordially disliked each other and gave vent to their feelings in a series of newspaper polemics, in which Lowndes professed to believe that he had been ousted from the speakership by a clique surrounding Manigault.[48] Yet after Manigault resigned because of ill health, a house led by

---

[46]If Ramsay did not plagiarize Hewatt's account, portions of his *History of South Carolina* followed Hewatt closely. Nevertheless, it was written from a different perspective, and the interpretations were compatible with Ramsay's experience. Hewatt, *Historical Account of South Carolina and Georgia,* 1:77, 98, 148, 294; Ramsay, *History of South Carolina,* 1:50. Hostility toward Col. James Grant for his actions during the Cherokee War stimulated some local antagonism against Scotsmen before Bute took office; South Carolinians, therefore, readily accepted the anti-Scot diatribes that followed. Hewatt, *Historical Account of South Carolina and Georgia,* 2:254-55; Bailyn, *Ideological Origins of the American Revolution,* 122-23; J. Steven Watson, *The Reign of George III, 1760-1815* (Oxford: Clarendon, 1960) 93; Wallace, *Life of Henry Laurens,* 102-105, 119.

[47]Gadsden to the Public, 17 July 1784, in *The Writings of Christopher Gadsden,* ed. Richard Walsh (Columbia: University of South Carolina Press, 1966) 207; H. Laurens to John Lewis Gervais, 5 September 1777, in *Letters of Members of the Continental Congress,* ed. Edmund C. Burnett, 8 vols. (Washington: Carnegie Institution, 1921-1938) 2:476-77.

[48]"Bobbedel," *South Carolina Gazette and Country Journal* (Charleston), 28 February 1769; "Demosius," *South Carolina Gazette and Country Journal,* 7 March 1769; "Friendless," *South Carolina Gazette and Country Journal,* 23 March 1769. For identification of the authors, see Richard J. Hooker, ed., *The Carolina Backcountry on the Eve of the Revolution: The Journal and Other Writings of Charles Woodmason, Anglican Itinerant* (Chapel Hill: University of North Carolina Press, 1953) 268-69.

substantially the same men reelected Lowndes to the post. Moreover, there is no evidence that there was any important difference in the way the two men handled the Commons. The general policy pursued under the leadership of each was the same; neither did committee assignments change significantly. From the beginning of the century it had been customary to elect the speaker unanimously; by mid-century what had begun as a symbol of wished-for unity had become the expression of real unanimity.[49]

Paradoxically, however, this unanimity concealed—even in large measure arose from—the independence upon which each member of the Commons prided himself. In essence the House remained an aggregate of individuals. Wragg, a universally admired but cantankerous figure who was unable to cooperate with anyone, nevertheless voiced a sentiment to which everyone subscribed when he declared, "He must be a very weak or a very wicked man, and know very little of me, who thinks me capable of surrendering my judgment, my honor and my conscience upon any consideration whatever."[50] Drayton declared that he had made it a "first principle not to proceed any farther with any party, than I thought they travelled in the Constitutional highway." Laurens phrased the same sentiment only slightly differently: "I am for no Man nor for any Party—you see—one Minute after they depart from Principles of Honesty."[51] This spirit—the epitome of the local version of country ideology, altruistic yet intensely

---

[49]28 October 1772, South Carolina Commons Journal, 39:17; Edward McCrady, *The History of South Carolina under the Royal Government, 1719-1776* (New York: Macmillan Co., 1899) 699. The key figures under both Rawlins Lowndes and Manigault were Gadsden, H. Laurens, Thomas Lynch, Isaac Mazyck, James Parsons, Charles Pinckney, and John Rutledge. Greene, *Quest for Power,* 475-88. Unanimous election of the speaker apparently began in the first decade of the eighteenth century. In the 1690s it was still by majority vote.

[50]"American Loyalists," *Southern Quarterly Review* 4 (1843): 145. Wragg became a Loyalist, and it is quite ironic that the statement quoted above—a distillation of prevailing attitudes—was Wragg's justification to the General Committee for not signing the Revolutionary Association. His career warrants further study, but for a perceptive evaluation of his personality that helps to account for his extremism and his singularity, see George C. Rogers, Jr., "The Conscience of a Huguenot," Huguenot Society of South Carolina, *Transactions* 67 (1962): 1-11.

[51]Drayton, "Letter from 'Freeman' to Deputies of North America Assembled in Philadelphia," 10 August 1774, in *Documentary History of the American Revolution,* 1:12; Laurens to Alexander Garden, 24 May 1772, Laurens Letter Book, 5:291, SCHS. It is worth noting that neither man referred to a specific party in South Carolina, but rather used the term in a general sense.

individualistic—suffocated factions. It even put strict limits on the influence of family connections. In contrast to contemporary British politics and later conditions in South Carolina, family relationships apparently counted for surprisingly little on the local scene at this time. British placemen thought in terms of connections, and frequently claimed to see their operations; by mid-century South Carolinians seldom did. Indeed, Laurens could effectively refute a charge of being disloyal to his family by noting that so meager a consideration as family connection alone would never influence him where the public welfare was concerned.[52]

Because local leaders shared similar interests and a common code of political behavior, their hypertensive individualism did not prevent cooperation with one another. Like Manigault, they preferred "to sail with the Stream, when no Danger or Dishonour, can attend it." Under the prevailing circumstances, neither honor nor fear often prompted them to take singular positions, even in matters pertaining to their own constituents. Members of the Commons took seriously the admonition to remember that though they were elected as representatives of a particular area or group, once they took their seats, their responsibility was to the welfare of the whole.[53] Thus on the one hand, except in matters of unusual importance, it was of no great consequence whether an elected representative actually owned property or resided in the parish that elected him, and prominent members of the Commons frequently represented constituents with whom they had no direct material connection. On the other hand, in matters of more importance or where different geographical areas or interest groups could be presumed to be unequally affected by public measures, equity required that each entity be separately represented. Perhaps it was only coincidence, but the twelve men who performed most of the committee business in the Commons in the early 1760s included four lawyers, four

<hr>

[52]For the opinion of British placemen, see Chief Justice Charles Shinner's report enclosed in Montagu to Board of Trade, 6 August 1766, Trans., S. C. Records, 31:127; and Searcher George Roupell to Commissioners of the Customs, 11 July 1768, enclosed in Commissioners of Customs in America to Lords Commissioners of the Treasury, 25 August 1768, Treasury Papers, Class 1, Group 465, Photostats, Library of Congress. Henry Laurens, *Extracts from Proceedings of the High Court of Admiralty,* 2d ed. (Charleston SC: David Bruce, 1769) appendix, 33.

[53]Manigault to Daniel Blake, 10 March 1771, Manigault Letter Book, 1763-1773, Old Salem, Inc.; "The Free Thinker, No. 67," reprinted in the *South Carolina Gazette,* 25 September 1762.

merchants, and four planters; the three delegates to the Stamp Act Congress represented the same three economic groups. In 1769 the committee that drafted and enforced the nonimportation agreements included thirteen mechanics, thirteen planters, and thirteen merchants. In addition, local representatives consistently discharged most of the Commons' business that affected their constituents.[54] Ideological consensus and social homogeneity made localism and particularism compatible with the unity of the whole.

Being human, South Carolinians neither created a utopia nor achieved absolute political harmony through universal dedication to the public weal. During the recession caused by King George's War, deep fissures appeared between different economic groups, and it became difficult to make a quorum in the Commons because many prominent men were too concerned about the welfare of their private interests to incur the expense, and sacrifice the time, that service in the House required.[55] Moreover, after the war, opportunists occasionally found their way into the Commons, and even the most conscientious members were not exempt from what Reinhold Niebuhr has called an effect of original sin—the inability of human beings to use power entirely disinterestedly. Nevertheless, by the time that Charles Pinckney sailed for England in 1753, the *South Carolina Gazette* clearly recognized that he and his contemporaries had transformed the character of public life. He was, in the words of the *Gazette,* "a true Father of his Country."[56]

---

[54]"Craftsman," *South Carolina Gazette,* 4 April 1774. Rutledge, a lawyer, Gadsden, a merchant, and Lynch, a planter, attended the Stamp Act Congress. Of the twelve most-active members, the four lawyers were Rutledge, Parsons, Pinckney, and Manigault; the merchants were Gadsden, Mazyck, Laurens, and Benjamin Smith; the planters were Lynch, Lowndes, Wragg, and Thomas Wright. *South Carolina Gazette,* 27 July 1769.

[55]"An Overture and Proposal Concerning Carolina," *South Carolina Gazette,* 23 August 1746; Testimony of Col. Alexander Vander Dussen before the Board of Trade, 25 May 1748, Trans., S. C. Records, 23:15; Glen to the Board of Trade, 10 October 1748, ibid., 222.

[56]*South Carolina Gazette,* 9 April 1753. An interesting example of the way in which old habits of thought persist in the face of changing reality can be seen in Pinckney's acceptance of a seat on the Council. Perhaps as much as any single individual, he was responsible for raising the prestige of the lower house to the point where it eclipsed that of the upper, yet in 1741 he was willing to leave the Commons to accept appointment to the Council. 28 October 1741, in Easterby, ed., *Journal of the Commons House, May 18, 1741, to July 10, 1742,* 260, 264.

During the thirty years before the Revolution in South Carolina, ideas had increasingly become the dominant force in local politics; by the end of the colonial period, the intangible ideal had found expression in the realities of everyday politics. The majority of political leaders actually were the independent men of property revered in country ideology and, to an amazing extent, generally accepted ideals, assumptions, and normative expectations about political conduct governed their behavior. Upholders of the prerogative excepted, there was virtually unanimous agreement that social and political harmony prevailed in what was an unusually well-governed colony.[57] Perhaps one of the reasons for the proverbial pride of South Carolinians, and the high esteem that they have traditionally accorded to politicians, can be found here. Certainly, colonial South Carolinians believed that they had achieved an unusually successful political system that safeguarded a freedom which they were morally obligated to bequeath to posterity.[58]

IV

Modern sociological investigations tend to show that the more homogeneous a society is, the more integrated its culture, and the more adapted

---

[57]The median wealth—exclusive of land holdings—of Commons members in a sample drawn from the 1762-1765 and 1765-1768 Houses proved to be nearly £7,000 sterling. Weir, "South Carolina and the Stamp Act Crisis," 50. For typical statements that reveal the sense of responsibility that local leaders felt for the public welfare, see Laurens to James Penman, 26 May 1768, Laurens Letter Book, 4:216, SCHS; Pinckney's will in Ravenel, *Eliza Pinckney*, 185; Wragg, *South Carolina Gazette*, 8 December 1758; Gadsden to William Samuel Johnson, 16 April 1766, in *Writings of Gadsden*, 71; and, from a slightly later period, Edward Rutledge's letter to his son, 2 August 1796, ed. Marvin R. Zahniser in *South Carolina Historical Magazine* 64 (1963): 65-72. The favorable assessment of local politics by DeBrahm, Hewatt, and Ramsay helps to confirm that these professions of concern were more than pious platitudes. DeBrahm, "History [of] S. C., Ga. and E. Fla.," 33; Hewatt, *Historical Account of South Carolina and Georgia*, 2:105-106; Ramsay, *History of South Carolina*, 1:69. Undoubtedly, the character of the rule provided by the local elite buttressed its position of leadership in a society where the populace shared both wide access to the franchise and deferential attitudes. Sirmans, *Colonial South Carolina*, 239-40. For convincing evidence that even the Regulator discontent of the late 1760s did not represent a serious exception to these generalizations, see Richard M. Brown, *The South Carolina Regulators* (Cambridge MA: Belknap Press of Harvard University Press, 1963) 62, 137-41.

[58]Committee of Intelligence, *South Carolina Gazette*, 7 September 1775; "A Native," *South Carolina Gazette*, 5 October 1765; 2 May 1766, 3 February 1775, South Carolina Commons Journals, 37, pt. 1:117-18, 39:191.

that culture is in coping with its environment, the more resistant that society may be to cultural change.[59] By these criteria, the political culture of
mid-eighteenth-century South Carolina ought to have been extremely stable. This was the case. South Carolinians, who enjoyed unusual material
advantages within the empire, were in the forefront of resistance after 1763
to what many considered to be threatening imperial measures. Moreover,
the Revolution in South Carolina has usually been considered to have involved comparatively little social and political change. In fact, the public-
spirited, independent man of property remained a political ideal throughout the antebellum period, and John C. Calhoun's views on patronage and
political corruption were in large measure the familiar elements of eighteenth-century country ideology.[60]

If, as seems to have been the case, the political culture of the eighteenth century persisted into the nineteenth in South Carolina with relatively little modification, it may be worthwhile to emphasize a few aspects
of prerevolutionary politics, and to suggest what some of their wider implications may have been.

First, for almost a generation before the Revolution, very little internal
conflict existed in South Carolina. As imperial authorities made more vigorous attempts to enforce policies that appeared inimical to the welfare of
South Carolinians, and as the Council increasingly became the preserve of
British placemen, the constitutional struggle took on aspects of a contest
between the united representatives of one society and the representatives
of an outside power. Insofar as the Revolution represented the means by
which local leaders ultimately disengaged themselves from a conflict with
external authority, it represented the culmination of a process that had been
developing for thirty years as the locus of conflict gradually moved toward
the periphery of local society.

---

[59]For a convenient introduction to these findings, see Bernard Berelson and Gary A.
Steiner, *Human Behavior: An Inventory of Scientific Findings* (New York: Harcourt, Brace
and World, 1964) 615-16.

[60]See Harold Schultz, *Nationalism and Sectionalism in South Carolina, 1852-1860*
(Durham: Duke University Press, 1950) 3-25; and William W. Freehling, "Spoilsmen and
Interests in the Thought and Career of John C. Calhoun," *Journal of American History* 52
(1965): 25-42. In fact, the contortions and contradictions of Calhoun's political thought,
analyzed by Professor Freehling, can be seen as the result of attempts to adapt eighteenth-
century assumptions to the changing political conditions that the diversities of nineteenth-
century America produced. Wallace, *South Carolina: Short History*, 344.

Indeed, the intense cultivation of the country ideal in the presence of real internal conflict would have been incompatible with the maintenance of an ongoing political system. To the extent that the imperatives of country ideology actually governed behavior, the political success of the society depended upon a shared homogeneity of interests and a consensus about values. The trading of interests, the engineering of political compromises by any means except the power of reason alone, was incompatible with the status of an independent man of honor who accepted public office because of his dedication to the public weal. More fundamentally, by idealizing personal and political independence, the prevailing political culture risked equating individualism with patriotism. Perhaps this is one explanation of why so many of South Carolina's revolutionary leaders pursued apparently erratic political courses that are impossible to classify accurately under traditional rubrics. In view of the general harmony that prevailed before the Revolution, it is also ironic that cultivation of an individualistic political ethos sanctioned an abrasive individualism that could easily lead to personal friction between political leaders. Unity in the face of external (imperial) pressure therefore camouflaged characteristics of the system that could have made it a spawning ground for an unusually contentious group of political individualists. But cultivation of the local version of the country ideal created powerful and potentially dangerous centrifugal forces. Given a breakdown of the basic consensus and the injection of real conflict into the system, these forces could become explosively destructive.

Equally ominous for the future, South Carolina politics lacked during the late colonial period features that would have contributed to the development of techniques for handling basic political conflicts; the result may well have been a fateful heritage that left South Carolinians unprepared to cope with the political realities of a developing American society. Elsewhere in the colonies only Virginia enjoyed a comparable freedom from factionalism, but the position of its Council was far more important and secure.[61] At the end of the colonial period South Carolina, alone among the original thirteen colonies, appeared to be neither blessed with a useful upper house nor cursed with factions. Although the ideal of balanced government was not realized anywhere in America, this was less significant

---

[61]Greene, "Changing Interpretations of Early American Politics," 177; Jackson Turner Main, *The Upper House in Revolutionary America, 1763-1788* (Madison: University of Wisconsin Press, 1967) 43-49.

for later developments than that the concept itself embodied an institutional means by which a viable political system could be maintained in a pluralistic society. Like many other Americans, James Madison realized that the traditional tripartite division of society into king, lords, and commoners did not fit America and that, contrary to the assumed ideal, factionalism was a fact of life in the new nation. Unlike most, he saw that under American conditions a balance of competing factions might be institutionalized and thereby made to safeguard liberty. By the mid-nineteenth century, most Americans had in fact followed Madison; South Carolinians apparently took a different road.

Because the prevailing political system had arisen from the cultivation by a homogeneous society of a particular version of the liberal tradition, which tended to recognize the political influence of conflicting interests only insofar as it condemned it, the political experience of colonial South Carolinians not only lacked internal conflict, but their assumptions and ideals even failed to encompass the possibility that it might exist. The essence of politics, as they knew it, involved not the resolution of conflict within the body politic, but a constitutional struggle between extraordinarily able men, representing a unified local society, and the agents of another power. When the actions of such a power seemed to become excessively hostile, the logical response was to withdraw; when internal divisions threatened, the natural response was to extend the consensus.

Noting that in 1855 the opinions of South Carolinians were "so unanimous on most questions of policy and of public interest, that the game of party politics furnishes no excitement whatsoever to its votaries," Professor F. A. Porcher asked, "By what process was this perfect amalgamation effected?"[62] Clearly, the means were varied and complex, and it is possible to underestimate both the effects of the revolutionary era and the impact of antebellum social, economic, and political developments; it is equally possible to overestimate the political harmony of the late colonial period. But it is impossible not to wonder if there was a direct connection between the politics of the 1750s and the 1850s, between the pattern of the Revolution and that of secession. Perhaps it is significant that the *Southern Quarterly Review* published the writings of William Wragg in 1843. It is

---

[62]F. A. Porcher, "Address at the Inauguration of the South Carolina Historical Society," 28 June 1855, South Carolina Historical Society, *Collections* 1 (1857): 8.

also hard to imagine that Calhoun, who believed that there could be no conflict between capital and labor because the slave owner unified the interest of both, who believed that he had found in the device of the concurrent majority a homeopathic remedy that would restore a lost consensus, could have come from any state but South Carolina. Perhaps it is one of the tragic ironies of history that South Carolinians succeeded too well in the late colonial period, that they realized Shaftesbury's ideal a century too late and thereby bound themselves to a political system that was fast becoming an anachronism.

"The Scandalous History of Sir Egerton Leigh" _____

Robert M. Calhoon,* who was interested in Loyalist thought during the revolutionary era, first outlined Leigh's ideas in a separate paper that arrived while I was thinking about the character of politics in colonial South Carolina. Intrigued by Leigh's combination of perceptivity and blindness toward the local situation, I suggested that Calhoon and I collaborate. The result was the present article, which raises questions about the Loyalists' understanding of colonial political culture. Reprinted by permission from Robert M. Calhoon and Robert M. Weir, " 'The Scandalous History of Sir Egerton Leigh,' " William and Mary Quarterly, 3d ser. 26 (1969): 47-74.

"I am a down-right *Placeman*," Egerton Leigh declared in 1773. Shortly thereafter, with equal candor, Thomas Lynch, a delegate from South Carolina to the First Continental Congress, and a man of sound judgment, described him as the greatest "Rascall among all the Kings Friends."[1] That South Carolinians of Lynch's stature had come to regard

_____

*Mr. Calhoon, who is a member of the Department of History and Political Science, University of North Carolina at Greensboro, wishes to thank the university's Research Council for financial assistance in the preparation of this article.

[1][Sir Egerton Leigh], *Considerations on Certain Political Transactions of the Province of South Carolina* (London, 1774) 2; entry of 31 August 1774, *The Diary and Autobiography of John Adams,* ed. Lyman H. Butterfield, Leonard C. Farber, and Wendell Garrett, 4 vols. (Cambridge MA: Belknap Press of Harvard University Press, 1961) 2:118. The authors wish to thank Miss Wylma Wates of the South Carolina Department of Archives and History (hereafter cited as SCDAH) for calling their attention to the latter reference.

the terms *placeman* and *rascal* as virtually synonymous was largely because Leigh appeared to share both roles, and his notorious quarrel over
vice-admiralty matters with the merchant Henry Laurens, though not always fully understood, has long been familiar to students of early American history.[2] What has hitherto been generally overlooked, however, is
that Leigh was one of the most able Crown servants in the colony prior to
the Revolution and that his early achievements appeared to establish firmly
his position in local society. Indeed, the contrast between his early promise and later disgrace has the fascination of classical tragedy as well as considerable historical significance.

Certainly, Leigh was not the only Crown officeholder to find the difficulties of the prerevolutionary period insurmountable, but his unique
vantage point and qualifications made him an unusually perceptive inter-
preter of the forces that helped to destroy him. His career, his awareness
of the political hostility that he aroused, and his introspective contempla-
tion of his own dilemma illustrate the complexity of Loyalist motivation
and, in addition, illuminate several facets of the prerevolutionary period in
South Carolina.

In 1753, at the age of twenty, Leigh arrived in South Carolina with his
father, the newly appointed chief justice. Doubtless under the latter's be-
nign aegis, Leigh quickly launched a brilliant career. He began to practice
law immediately and, aided by a short term as clerk of the Court of Common Pleas—a position that gave him valuable contacts among the legal
profession—he rapidly built up a very successful private practice.[3] With
equal speed, he accumulated public honors and offices. In January 1755

---

[2]For standard treatments of this affair, see David D. Wallace, *The Life of Henry Laurens* (New York: G. P. Putnam's Sons, 1915) 137-49, and Oliver M. Dickerson, *The Navigation Acts and the American Revolution* (Philadelphia: University of Pennsylvania Press,
1951) 224-31. Two more recent works, Thomas C. Barrow, *Trade and Empire: The British
Customs Service in Colonial America, 1660-1775* (Cambridge MA: Harvard University
Press, 1967) 206-10, 234-35, and Carl Ubbelohde, *The Vice-Admiralty Courts and the
American Revolution* (Chapel Hill: University of North Carolina Press, 1960) 107-14, provide brief accounts that anticipate some points that we emphasize.

[3]H. Hale Bellot, "The Leighs in South Carolina," *Transactions of the Royal Historical
Society,* 5th ser. 6 (1956): 175; 12 August, 6 November 1754, Miscellaneous Records,
KK:76, 113, SCDAH, Columbia; Governor William Henry Lyttelton to Board of Trade,
14 April 1759, Transcripts of Records Relating to South Carolina in the British Public Records Office, 28:188, SCDAH; hereafter cited as Trans., S. C. Records.

he was elected to the Commons House of Assembly by St. Peter's parish; reelected in 1757, he retained this position until January 1760 when he took a seat on the Council.[4] In the meantime, on 3 November 1755, he was appointed surveyor general of the province. Six years later he became judge of the Charleston Vice-Admiralty Court, and in 1765 he became the attorney general.[5]

Wealth and social position accompanied his professional rise. From 1756 to 1765 his private law practice yielded between £1,000 and £1,200 sterling per year, and his official positions probably more than doubled this amount. As a result his income was among the largest in the colony.[6] Although somewhat more aggressive in acquiring offices than land, between 1757 and 1763 he accumulated grants totaling 1,800 acres, bought a 500-

---

[4]It is not clear that at the time of his election Leigh held property in St. Peter's, a rural district relatively remote from Charleston. Indeed on 24 January 1755, he purchased the first real estate he is known to have owned in South Carolina, two lots in Charleston, for which he paid £2,000 South Carolina currency. Less than one week later he was elected to the Assembly. It hardly seems a coincidence that the election law stipulated that a member of the Commons House must possess a freehold of five hundred acres and ten slaves or £1,000 worth of buildings, lands, or town lots. Two other men had been elected for the parish and failed to qualify; Leigh, who was elected unanimously, was therefore the third choice. In all probability voters turned to him because, as a resident of Charleston and a man of ability who was willing to serve, he represented an available candidate. See Charleston County Deeds, PP: 236-37, microfilm, SCDAH; Thomas Cooper and David McCord, eds., *The Statutes at Large of South Carolina*, 10 vols. (Columbia: A. S. Johnston, 1836-1841) 3:137; 13 November 1754, 8 January, 6, 7 February 1755, South Carolina Commons Journals, 30, pt. 1:28-29, 60, 62, 216-18, 226, SCDAH; 6 October 1757, South Carolina Commons Journals, Colonial Office Group, Class 5, Piece 474, Public Record Office; and 11 January 1760, South Carolina Council Journals, 28:154, SCDAH.

[5]3 November 1755, 2 October 1761, 31 January 1765, Miscellaneous Records, KK:402, LL:405, MM:277, SCDAH.

[6]Egerton Leigh, Memorial to Lord Dartmouth, 2 March 1775, Dartmouth Papers, 2:1174, Staffordshire County Records Office, Stafford, England. Although it is impossible to give a precise figure for the worth of each of Leigh's offices, a rough idea can be obtained from the fact that James Simpson, who replaced Leigh as attorney general in 1771, claimed to have received more than £2,000 sterling per year from a private practice worth 700, the attorney generalship, and the office of clerk of the Council. The vice-admiralty position was not considered lucrative. See James Simpson's case in Examinations in London: Memorials, Schedules of Losses, and Evidence, South Carolina Claimants, American Loyalists, Audit Office Transcripts, 54:213, Manuscript Division, New York Public Library, New York (hereafter cited as Loyalists' Trans.); and Lieutenant Governor William Bull to Lord Hillsborough, 16 October 1768, Trans., S. C. Records, 32:55.

acre plantation on the Santee River, and purchased more than 2 acres in
Ansonboro, a rapidly developing northern suburb of Charleston.[7] In 1756
he married Martha Bremar, the daughter of Martha and Francis Bremar.
The elder Martha was Henry Laurens's sister; Francis had been a merchant
associate of Laurens and a member of the Commons House.[8] If the marriage to Laurens's niece did not bring immediate wealth to Leigh—which
it probably did not—it did help to cement a friendship between the two men
and thereby insure that for more than a decade, Leigh would handle much
of Laurens's legal business.[9] Leigh, a cultured man whose versatile talents
included considerable ability as a musician as well as a poet and prose
writer, rented a house in Charleston and furnished it with an extensive library, which soon totaled more than 800 volumes, a large organ, and a
magnificent collection of paintings, including works by Veronese and
Correggio.[10] The parishioners of St. Philip's elected him a vestryman, and
he became a commissioner of the provincial free school in Charleston. In
1765 the local Masons elected him deputy grand master and heir apparent
to the provincial grand master, Benjamin Smith, the respected speaker of
the Commons House of Assembly.[11]

[7]In 1770 he added an additional one hundred acres. See grants on 21 May 1757, 5 De-
cember 1759, 18 May 1763, 9 November 1770, Royal Grants, 8:4, 480; 11:62; 21:283,
SCDAH; 30 September 1758, 2 July 1775, 9 September 1757, 27 July 1761, Charleston
County Deeds, TT:338-39, SS:52, 114, XX:288-91, microfilm, SCDAH. See also M. Eu-
gene Sirmans, "The South Carolina Royal Council, 1720-1763," *William and Mary
Quarterly,* 3d ser. 18 (1961): 373-92.

[8]Bellot, "Leighs in South Carolina," 175; Joseph W. Barnwell, ed., "Correspondence
of Henry Laurens," *South Carolina Historical and Genealogical Magazine* 29 (1928): 103;
entry of 17 January 1744/45, in *The Colonial Records of South Carolina: The Journals of
the Commons House of Assembly, 1744-1745,* ed. James H. Easterby (Columbia: South
Carolina Archives Department, 1955) 277.

[9]See Laurens to Francis Bremar, 27 March 1748, in "Correspondence of Henry Laurens," ed. Joseph W. Barnwell, *South Carolina Historical and Genealogical Magazine* 31
(1930): 222, and will of Francis Bremar, 16 May 1760, Charleston County Wills, Works
Progress Administration Transcripts, 8:482-83, SCDAH. For Leigh as Laurens's lawyer,
see Henry Laurens to Lachlan McIntosh, 19 May 1763, Laurens Letter Book, 1762-1766,
47, Historical Society of Pennsylvania, Philadelphia (HSP); Laurens to Elias Ball, 5 October 1765, ibid., 331-32; and Laurens to Inglis and Hall, 12 December 1767, Laurens Papers, 4:89, South Carolina Historical Society, Charleston.

[10]*South Carolina Gazette* (Charleston), 3 December 1772, 28 February 1771; "Historical Notes," *South Carolina Historical and Genealogical Magazine* 11 (1910): 133-34.

[11]*South Carolina Gazette,* 21 April 1759, 16 December 1760; *South Carolina Gazette
and Country Journal* (Charleston), 31 December 1765.

It was an amazing performance. In a dozen years Leigh, at the age of thirty-two, had vaulted into the very top ranks of local society. Only a fortuitous combination of circumstances could account for such phenomenal success. A relative lack of competition helped, for there was a dearth of educated men to fill public offices in the colony. Family connections certainly contributed: Egerton's father, Peter, had been high bailiff of Westminster before becoming chief justice of South Carolina. Despite later stories of misconduct as high bailiff—none of which were proved—the elder Leigh seems to have retained sufficient influence at Whitehall to further his son's advancement, and his name was usually mentioned in solicitations in behalf of the young Leigh.[12]

Hard work also furthered Egerton Leigh's career. He allocated his time carefully and therefore paid more attention to his private law practice and the lucrative duties of the surveyor generalship than he did to responsibilities that he discharged gratis, such as service in the Commons. During his term in the House he seldom appeared when attendance was voluntary, though he performed required duties conscientiously enough to become a relatively prominent figure.[13] Somewhat surprisingly, although his power to appoint deputy surveyors—and he had squadrons of them—gave him control of considerable patronage, Leigh does not appear at this time to have been interested in using this power to advance his career.[14] Perhaps he did not need to, or rather aimed at goals where popular support was of little value. Certainly he succeeded in impressing men who had the political and economic power to help him. High regard for his ability and character seems to have been the most important cause of his rapid professional

---

[12]Bull to Hillsborough, 7 August 1771, Trans., S. C. Records, 33:80; Bellot, "Leighs in South Carolina," 169-74; Lyttelton to Board of Trade, 14 April 1759, Trans., S. C. Records, 28:188; Leigh, Memorial to Dartmouth, 2 March 1775, Dartmouth Papers, 2:1174.

[13]For his attendance in the House, see 7 February 1755 to 13 October 1759, South Carolina Commons Journals, vols. 30-33, passim. On the basis of the importance and amount of committee work that he performed, Leigh reached the second rank of leadership in the 1757-1758 session. Jack P. Greene, *The Quest for Power: The Lower Houses of Assembly in the Southern Royal Colonies, 1689-1776* (Chapel Hill: University of North Carolina Press, 1963) 481. For Leigh's most important committee assignments, see 5, 7 March, 11, 12 April 1755, 22 June 1756, 16 May, 8 December 1758, 31 January 1759, South Carolina Commons Journals, 30, pt. 1:293, 314, 449, 457; 31, pt. 1:204; 32:220, 38, 97-98.

[14]For a listing, see entries for Leigh in the manuscript index to the Miscellaneous Records, SCDAH.

advancement. Governor William Henry Lyttelton's enthusiastic recommendation of him as a rising young lawyer of "unblemished reputation," not influential family connections, secured Leigh's appointment to the Council.[15] Even after the break between the two friends, Laurens continued to respect Leigh's natural ability, although he vigorously condemned his judgment and his morals. For example, during the admiralty affair Laurens, a sternly moral but shrewd judge of men, noted that "if he had resolution enough to with stand the temptations of high Life [he] would be an admirable Man." What Laurens probably realized was that Leigh had mortgaged his future income for present consumption. Nevertheless, Laurens had earlier trusted his friend implicitly. When Leigh went to England in 1764, Laurens wrote merchant correspondents there, recommending him as a worthy man "for whome I bear the highest regard" and authorizing them to lend him whatever sums he might need, up to the limits of Laurens's own credit.[16]

The Stamp Act crisis, however, triggered severe financial and political problems for Leigh. Its most immediate impact was to cut off practically all of his income for nearly six months. The inability to obtain stamps brought business in the Court of Common Pleas to a standstill, closed the Vice-Admiralty Court, and prevented the granting of lands. But a sense of duty, or perhaps the hope of future reward, influenced Leigh more than concern over his immediate loss of income. Alone among the lawyers of Charleston, in the spring of 1766 he argued against reopening the Court of Common Pleas without stamped paper. When Chief Justice Charles Shinner reported to the ministry on the conduct of local officials during the crisis, he censured virtually everyone except Leigh.[17] But opposition to opening the court endeared him to few. When the nature of Shinner's re-

---

[15]Lyttelton to the Board of Trade, 14 April 1759, Trans., S. C. Records, 28:188; Privy Council, 26 June 1759, ibid., 28:201-202; 11 January 1760, South Carolina Council Journals, 28:154.

[16]Laurens to Edward Pierce, 31 March 1773, Laurens Papers, 7:82; Laurens to William Fisher, 1 August 1768, Letters and Papers Regarding the Ship *Ann,* Etting: Large Miscellaneous Manuscripts, 24, HSP; Laurens to Isaac King, 3 April, 7 May 1764, Laurens Papers, 3:345, 363.

[17]For an account of the effects of the crisis, see Robert M. Weir, " 'Liberty and Property and No Stamps': South Carolina and the Stamp Act Crisis" (Ph.D. dissertation, Western Reserve University, 1966). For Shinner's comments, see his report enclosed in Governor Lord Charles Montagu to the Board of Trade, 6 May 1766, Trans., S. C. Records, 31:134.

port became public knowledge, gossip quite naturally (and probably correctly) marked Leigh as the instigator of Shinner's accusations and dealt his popularity another serious blow. Leigh's private law practice never recovered.[18] Consequently, he became dependent upon his Crown offices for financial rewards and a sense of importance. The need to retain these pursuits, therefore, obsessed him, but his tenaciousness increasingly appeared to put private interest before the public welfare, thus further estranging him from the local community. In short, he was caught in a vicious circle.

The next step in Leigh's downfall was also a by-product of the Stamp Act crisis. In the spring of 1766 the Commons, hoping that the Rockingham ministry might be willing to make further concessions to the colonies, undertook a comprehensive review of various problems confronting South Carolina. Leigh's recent role had made him and his offices conspicuous. Among other sources of concern, the House therefore noted that Leigh and some of his fellow royal officers held positions that were partly designed to check each other. A man who sought to occupy simultaneously all of Leigh's offices risked entangling the colony, as well as himself, in many unnecessary difficulties—Laurens warned his friend against the pitfall. The Commons House, always wary of power that did not appear properly limited, took more direct action by ordering Charles Garth, its agent in London, to ask the ministry to remove Leigh from some of his offices.[19] Leigh ignored the friendly advice, attributed the actions of the Commons purely to resentment at his conduct during the Stamp Act crisis, and mobilized his friends in London in his behalf. They apparently succeeded. Lord Shelburne, who actually sympathized with the attitude of the House, informed Garth that Leigh could not be deprived of any of his offices because no charges of misconduct had been brought against him. It was, however, a Pyrrhic victory for Leigh.[20]

---

[18]Laurens to John L. Gervais, 1 September 1766, Laurens Letter Book, 1762-1766, 451, HSP; Leigh, Memorial to Dartmouth, 2 March 1775, Dartmouth Papers, 2:1174.

[19]24 June 1766, South Carolina Commons Journals, 37, pt. 1:175; Laurens to William Fisher, 1 August 1768, Letters and Papers Regarding the Ship *Ann,* 24; Committee of Correspondence to Garth, 2 July 1766, Garth Letter Book, 1766-1775, 2.

[20]Garth to Committee of Correspondence, 26 September 1766, 31 January, 12 March 1767, Garth Letter Book, 1766-1775, 14, 25, 28.

In the spring of 1767 a new customs collector, Daniel Moore, a former member of Parliament for the borough of Great Marlow, arrived in Charleston and opened Pandora's box. It is possible that Moore was primarily dedicated to serving his country by tightening up the customs service in South Carolina, but it is probable that he was more interested in enriching himself by the same means.[21] At any rate, he adopted questionable practices that may have actually violated the law. Enraged local merchants responded with an avalanche of suits, complaints, and information against him in the Courts of Common Pleas, General Sessions, and Vice-Admiralty. Within six months Moore fled to England, but not before his activities brought into the Vice-Admiralty Court what the *South Carolina Gazette* correctly termed "as difficult causes as perhaps ever came before that court in America."[22] In all likelihood no one could have coped with them successfully. Certainly Leigh failed, although within the limits set by the desire to protect his position he tried to render just and equitable verdicts.

Four cases marked Leigh's progress into an ever-deepening morass. On 19 June 1767, he released the *Active,* a coasting vessel seized for failing to clear properly. The crux of Leigh's decision was his statement that because the navigation acts were not intended to "lay any unnecessary Restraint" on legitimate commerce, they should not be rigidly applied to intracolonial trade.[23] The decision was certainly reasonable and Leigh believed it to be praiseworthy, but officialdom thought otherwise. Concerned about the precedent that the decision might set, the Lords of the

---

[21]*South Carolina Gazette,* 23 March 1767. For a brief biography of Moore—which omits his service in South Carolina—see Sir Lewis Namier and John Brooke, *The History of Parliament: The House of Commons, 1754-1790,* 3 vols. (New York: Oxford University Press, 1964) 3:160-61. For a more sympathetic treatment of Moore than ours, see Barrow, *Trade and Empire,* 204-209; for a more hostile account, the South Carolina merchants' version of his activities, see *A Representation of Facts, Relative to the Conduct of Daniel Moore, Esquire; Collector of His Majesty's Customs at Charles-Town, in South Carolina* (Charleston: Charles Crouch, 1767).

[22]*A Representation of Facts,* passim; Montagu to Lord Shelburne, 5 October 1767, Trans., S. C. Records, 31:414; *South Carolina Gazette,* 19 September 1768.

[23]"Case," Treasury Group, Class 1, Piece 465, Photostats, from the British Public Record Office, Library of Congress, Washington, D. C.

Treasury referred the matter to the British attorney and solicitors general who considered the verdict much too lenient.[24] Leigh had overreached himself, and even before he learned of the full reaction to his decision, he realized that unless he gave more support to customs officials he would jeopardize his judgeship.[25] In the next case he, therefore, relied upon a technicality to acquit Moore of a charge filed by local merchants that he had demanded illegal fees. Leigh, however, believed that Moore's under-handed conduct merited a sharp reprimand.[26] The remaining cases involved the *Broughton Island Packet* and the *Wambaw,* two coasting schooners belonging to Henry Laurens, which had been seized under almost identical circumstances because they had not cleared as Moore had demanded. But the ballast in the *Wambaw* was saleable; that aboard the *Broughton Island Packet* was not. This difference enabled Leigh to engineer a compromise by condemning the former vessel and releasing the latter. But Leigh neglected to declare "a probable cause of seizure," meaning that reasonable grounds had existed for believing that the discharged schooner had been operating in violation of the law.[27] The omission opened the way for Laurens to recover his losses on the one vessel by suing for damages in the case of the other—something that Laurens's lawyers immediately recognized. Given the context of the whole affair and the fact that Leigh was an experienced judge, it is difficult to believe that his apparent oversight was unintentional.[28]

Leigh's attempt to make his compromise as equitable as possible proved to be a fatal mistake. Laurens sued George Roupell, the customs searcher who had made the actual seizure. Although Roupell had been a member of the Commons House and for nearly twenty years a respected customs

---

[24]Sir Egerton Leigh, *The Man Unmasked: or, the World Undeceived in the Author of a Late Pamphlet entitled "Extracts from the Proceedings of the High Court of Vice-Admiralty in Charlestown, South Carolina &c." with Suitable Remarks* (Charleston: Peter Timothy, printer, 1769) 96; "Case," T. 1:465.

[25]For complaints against Leigh, see Barrow, *Trade and Empire,* 318.

[26]See Laurens to James Habersham, 5 September 1767, Laurens Papers, 4:7-12.

[27]Ibid.

[28]Laurens to George Appleby, to James Habersham, 24 May 1768, 5 September 1767, ibid., 4:204, 9.

official,[29] he was now unable to find a private lawyer to defend him, and Leigh, as attorney general, consequently acted for his fellow Crown officer. However, as Roupell later complained to the customs commissioners, "he had left such an opening when Judge, that the attorney general could not close it again," and the jury awarded Laurens a judgment that Roupell was unable to pay. Nor did the temporary collector who succeeded Moore, Roger Peter Handaside Hatley, feel free to pay the sum from customs funds without the authorization of his superiors. Roupell thus faced going to jail,[30] but on 17 June 1768 Hatley deliberately delayed receiving a bond for goods already aboard the *Ann,* a large vessel belonging partly to Laurens, so that Roupell could seize it. Acting through intermediaries, Roupell then offered to release the ship if Laurens would surrender his demand for damages. Laurens refused, and Leigh faced a serious dilemma.[31] On the one hand, because local customs officials had been filing a stream of complaints against him,[32] he could not hope to retain his office unless he protected Roupell. On the other hand, because the officers had so obviously resorted to subterfuge, it was extremely difficult to justify declaring a probable cause of seizure. The problem appeared almost insoluble, but Leigh devised a rather ingenious way out. He forced Roupell to take the seldom-used oath of calumny, a declaration that his actions were not motivated by malice. The bond had not been posted; the vessel was technically in violation of the law; Roupell swore that he had acted in good faith; *ipso facto* there was a probable cause of seizure; and on 11 July 1768, Leigh so certified when he discharged the vessel, noting that he had a "Strong

---

[29]26 February 1755, South Carolina Commons Journals, 30, pt. 1:249-50. Roupell was also an artist of considerable local renown. See Anna Wells Rutledge, "Artists in the Life of Charleston through Colony and State to Reconstruction," *Transactions of the American Philosophical Society* 39, pt. 2 (1949): 118-19; Carl Bridenbaugh, *Myths and Realities: Societies of the Colonial South* (Baton Rouge: Louisiana State University Press, 1952) 107.

[30]George Roupell to Commissioners of the Customs, 11 July 1768, enclosed in Commissioners of the Customs in America to the Lords Commissioners of Treasury, 25 August 1768, T. 1:465, Photostats, Library of Congress; 12 May 1768, Charleston County, Records of the Court of Common Pleas, 1763-1769, WPA Transcripts, 244.

[31]Transcripts of Proceedings in the Case of the *Ann,* T. 1:465, 7, 14, 16, Photostats, Library of Congress; Henry Laurens, *Extracts from Proceedings of the High Court of Admiralty,* 2d ed. (Charleston SC: David Bruce, 1769) passim; Henry Laurens, *Extracts from the Proceedings of the Court of Vice-Admiralty in Charles-Town, South Carolina* (Philadelphia: W. and T. Bradford, 1768) 9.

[32]For citations to this correspondence, see Barrow, *Trade and Empire,* 318.

Suspicion that there was more of design and Surprise on the part of some officers than of any intention to commit fraud on the part of the Claimant."[33]

Throughout the whole series of cases Leigh had really acted as an arbitrator and, considering the pressures on him, a reasonably fair one. At the time many South Carolinians may have understood this, and the *South Carolina Gazette,* a newspaper not noted for its partiality to officers of the Admiralty Court, reported that the "equitable decree" regarding the *Ann* "seems to have given general satisfaction."[34] But in attempting to protect himself while extricating everyone else from their own difficulties, Leigh had succeeded chiefly in making himself vulnerable, for, as Roupell put it in a complaint to the customs commissioners, "no Judge of Admiralty can make a Court of Equity of it upon all occasions, which for this year past has been the case."[35]

Laurens understood the situation as well as Roupell and was equally dissatisfied. He attacked Leigh in a pamphlet entitled *Extracts from the Proceedings of the Court of Vice-Admiralty.* Leigh defended himself with *The Man Unmasked,* a personal attack on Laurens, who in turn countered with a new edition of the *Extracts,* which contained an appendix in reply to Leigh. These pamphlets cannot be dismissed as mere scurrilous polemics. In a sense both Leigh and Laurens were fighting for professional and political survival. Each took the matter with utmost seriousness, and the pamphlets, therefore, reveal much about the men involved.

Leigh clearly expected that Laurens would understand the pressures that he was under and make allowances for them: that, given the circumstances, he had done the best he could for him and that the part of a relative and a friend was to help one through a difficult situation by remaining quiet. Knowing full well that he was vulnerable—throughout the entire proceedings he had tried to stifle complaints against his decisions—and knowing that Laurens knew this, Leigh was not only panic-stricken at being pilloried in the press, he was also horrified at Laurens's apparent ingratitude

---

[33]Transcripts of Proceedings of the *Ann,* T. 1:465, 10, 24-25, 28.

[34]*South Carolina Gazette,* 11 July 1768. Robert Wells, the publisher of the leading rival newspaper, *South Carolina and American General Gazette,* was marshal of the Vice-Admiralty Court. See Wells's case in Loyalists' Transcripts, 56:548.

[35]Roupell to Commissioners of Customs, 11 July 1768, enclosed in Commissioners of Customs in America to Lords Commissioners of Treasury, 25 August 1768, T. 1:465.

and Iago-like betrayal. He had, Leigh declared, violated their long friend-ship and family ties and cruelly endangered the livelihood of Leigh's wife, seven children, and mother-in-law. "Every man who reads this book, must perceive the motive," Leigh explained. "Under the specious shew of an *exalted kind of virtue,* which regards no law, no friendship, no alliances, no ties of blood," Laurens had attempted "to gain a *popular name*" and to sacrifice "the fame of a man in the meridian of his days."[36]

It was true that Laurens, for various reasons, had found himself out of step with a good part of the community during the early 1760s; he also re-alized that his conduct during the admiralty affair redeemed him in the eyes of many persons.[37] Nevertheless, in attributing Laurens's behavior to a lust for popularity, Leigh considerably oversimplified the matter. Laurens had been unfairly treated by the customs officers; the whole affair had been very expensive and time-consuming; it had forced him to postpone an intended trip to England; and he was a busy man whose attitude toward the use of time was the essence of the Puritan ethic. Equally important, while the *Ann* was loading, he left Charleston for his Georgia plantations after writing to his correspondents in England, "As I have been very attentive to the gen-eral Interest I beg you will not be under any apprehensions of mismanage-ment on Account of my absence." While he was gone, goods were put aboard the ship that led to its seizure. Moreover, Laurens had earlier lost his temper at Moore, who was an elderly man, and twisted his nose on a crowded street—a widely publicized episode that mortified Laurens after he had cooled down.[38] In short, he had good reason to be irate over the whole business and to feel that both his reputation as a merchant and his self-respect as a man of honor were at stake. Most important, all of these personal considerations contributed to his willingness to perform what he considered to be his duty. There can be no doubt that throughout his entire

---

[36]Transcripts of Proceedings of the *Ann,* T. 1:465, 25-26, 28; Laurens to William Fisher, 1 August 1768, Letters and Papers Regarding the Ship *Ann,* 24; Leigh, *The Man Un-masked,* 20-21, 27-28.

[37]For Laurens's difficulties during the Cherokee War and the Stamp Act crisis, see Wallace, *Life of Henry Laurens,* 103-106, 116-20, and Laurens to James Habersham, 5 September 1767, Laurens Papers, 4:11-12.

[38]Laurens to William Fisher, 1 August 1768, Letters and Papers Regarding the Ship *Ann,* 24; Laurens to William Cowles & Co., to Ross and Mill, to James Habersham, 7 June 1768, 8, 14 October 1767, Laurens Papers, 4:226, 35-38, 54-56.

career Laurens possessed an amazingly deep commitment to the public welfare and a heroic sense of duty, though like other human beings he could only interpret the one and exercise the other from his own limited vantage point. He and his contemporary South Carolinians were profoundly skeptical of the ability of fallible mortals to use power wisely. Because neither kings nor commoners were divine, their power had to be hedged by proper limits. As a single judge in a court without a jury, Leigh's powers were potentially dangerous. That he had placed his own self-interest above his duty in failing to curb the customs officers proved that he could not be trusted with these powers. Thus self-interest and personal considerations combined to reinforce Laurens's belief that the admiralty jurisdiction as it was constituted in America invited arbitrary exercises of power. Friend or no friend, Leigh and his court had to be attacked for the sake of the commonweal.[39]

It would be a mistake to dismiss Laurens's point of view as a mere rationalization. It would be equally erroneous to see Leigh's reaction as entirely a matter of wounded feelings or as a tactical maneuver designed to discredit Laurens. Fundamentally, what was at issue were two basically different conceptions of what constituted morality in a public officeholder. To Leigh, morality was something personal, intimate, almost clannish. The preservation of family ties and the protection of friends took precedence over abstract considerations of right and wrong, while ingratitude was the most heinous of sins. For Laurens, the priority was reversed: virtue, duty, and the common good transcended all other considerations, even the obligations of friendship and family.

Irrespective of which might be considered a higher form of ethics, Leigh's system was poorly adapted to the glare of publicity, and the episode of the vice-admiralty quarrel proved a disaster to him. Laurens made a point of demonstrating the inherent conflicts between Leigh's multiple roles, which involved him at various times in the same cases as a private lawyer, as attorney general, and as judge. Roupell made the same point in complaints to the customs commissioners and succeeded where the whole Commons House had earlier failed. The ministry directed Leigh to resign

---

[39]Laurens to William Cowles & Co. and William Freeman, 8 August 1768, Laurens Papers, 4:254-57; Wallace, *Life of Henry Laurens,* passim; Laurens, *Extracts,* 1st ed., passim; Laurens to William Fisher, 1 August 1768, Letters and Papers Regarding the Ship *Ann,* 24.

either as Vice-Admiralty judge or attorney general. Leigh resigned the less lucrative judgeship and did his best to make the resignation appear voluntary, but without much success.[40] Two years later Leigh also gave up his private practice in the Court of Chancery, on which he sat as a member of the Council. The reason for his action is not entirely clear, but it is worth noting that one of the parties in his last case was another Crown officer, George Saxby, the receiver general of quitrents. Perhaps Leigh was forced to resign; perhaps, remembering the admiralty affair, he thought it prudent. Whatever the reason, he did not give up much—his chancery business was already very small.[41]

More important than the loss of the judgeship was his increasing isolation from the community, which his declining private practice reflected. Part of this alienation was the result of his stand during the Stamp Act crisis, and part came from his questionable conduct during the adverse publicity suffered as a result of the admiralty cases. Part was largely a matter of personality. Insecure and therefore hypersensitive, flamboyant, witty, erudite, and arrogant, he possessed an unfortunate knack for unnecessarily irritating people. For example, while he was presiding over the cases of the merchants against Moore, a rumor reached him that the merchants had acted as a group in order to intimidate him by using their combined wealth and influence. Infuriated, Leigh unleashed a barrage of sarcastic accusations before checking the accuracy of his information, which proved to be false. Understandably, the merchants were offended.[42]

Whatever its causes, the growing hostility toward Leigh increasingly meant that his sins were magnified and his good deeds overlooked. Although by the late 1760s the road was not entirely downhill, Leigh was now so estranged from the local leaders that his minor triumphs—unlike his earlier successes—often appeared to be victories of an outsider, achieved

---

[40]Laurens, *Extracts,* 2d ed., passim; Commissioners of Customs in America to Lords Commissioner of Treasury, 25 August 1768, and enclosure of George Roupell to Commissioners of Customs, 11 July 1768, T. 1:465; Commissioners of Customs in America to Lords Commissioner of Treasury, 16 December 1768, T. 1:465; Bull to Hillsborough, 16 October 1768, Trans., S. C. Records, 32:54; Leigh, *The Man Unmasked,* 100.

[41]Bull to Hillsborough, 30 November 1770, Trans., S. C. Records, 32:376; A. K. Gregorie and J. N. Frierson, eds., *Records of the Court of Chancery of South Carolina, 1671-1779* (Washington: American Historical Association, 1950) 577 and passim.

[42]Laurens to James Habersham, 5 September 1767, Laurens Papers, 4:9-10.

at the expense of the community. While still judge, he had responded to complaints against supposedly exorbitant charges in the Vice-Admiralty Court by reducing fees, but he received little credit for his action. Conversely, although the Commons House seemed to begrudge him every penny, he forced it to more than double the salary first offered him, in lieu of fees, under a new court system planned for the backcountry. The reason for his success as a negotiator here was his credible threat to secure disallowance of the act establishing the courts unless he were more adequately compensated. The price of his victory was a conviction among many South Carolinians that he did indeed put his private interest before the public welfare.[43] A success of a different kind, for which he paid a different price, was his purchase in 1767 of a fine 553-acre plantation, 7 miles up the Cooper River from Charleston. Significantly, he seems to have named it "The Retreat." However, it proved to be more of a headache than a consolation. Its purchase price put a severe strain on his dwindling income, and he sold it within four years.[44] Even his election as grand master of the local Masons in January 1768 was less of an achievement than it might have appeared to be, for as deputy provincial grand master since 1765 Leigh was already in line to succeed Benjamin Smith when he retired in 1767 because of ill-health.[45]

Despite these apparent successes, Leigh was only too well aware that his fortunes had suffered an amazing reversal since 1765. Quite understandably he blamed Laurens for many of his troubles, but Leigh was too intelligent not to realize that the source of his difficulties went much deeper: that the tensions of the last few years had made it impossible for Crown officers to function effectively unless they had the power to command respect. Impotent threats only brought contempt, as Leigh had painfully dis-

---

[43]16 March 1768, 1 August 1769, *South Carolina Commons Journals,* 37, pt. 2:588; 38, pt. 1:102; Bellot, "Leighs in South Carolina," 181; Laurens, *Extracts,* 2d ed., appendix, 20-22.

[44]Henry A. M. Smith, "Charleston and Charleston Neck: The Original Grantees and the Settlements along the Ashley and Cooper Rivers," *South Carolina Historical and Genealogical Magazine* 19 (1918):59.

[45]In January 1768, before the pamphlet war with Laurens, the local lodge petitioned the Duke of Beaufort to appoint Leigh grand master; his official installation did not come until two years later. "Historical Notes," *South Carolina Historical and Genealogical Magazine* 4 (1903): 313; *South Carolina and American General Gazette,* 1 January 1768; *South Carolina Gazette,* 8 March 1770.

covered when he had futilely tried to block publication of Laurens's *Extracts* by threatening to cite him for contempt of court and sue for libel.[46] Public support made Laurens impregnable; the lack of it rendered Leigh vulnerable.

Leigh sought refuge behind the mysteries of the law. He maintained that Laurens had revealed his ignorance of the law when he had accused the Vice-Admiralty judge of inconsistent rulings in the cases of the *Wambaw* and the *Broughton Island Packet*. The difference between the cases, Leigh replied, was perfectly apparent to his trained legal eye. If Laurens could not see the difference, it only proved that he was "in a strange element, clearly out of his depth, perplexed by an enquiry foreign to the whole study and labour of his life." Leigh's definition of his craft involved more than mere technical knowledge and practice. Law was a calling requiring an elaborate initiation. Outsiders could never be expected to comprehend its wisdom. Laurens's attacks on Leigh only reassured him how "every departure, from that regular system to which we are bred . . . from that track which nature or our parents chose for us . . . will only involve us in a . . . perplexity of inextricable mazes."[47] Leigh's plea for the higher wisdom of lawyers revealed major weaknesses that he most wanted to disguise. In his eyes, indecision became judicial deliberation. The contempt with which men viewed his conduct became the ignorance of laymen about legal processes. The widespread sympathy among South Carolina leaders for Laurens's plight became blindness to Leigh's right as a royal official to deference and respect.

Laurens's criticisms, Leigh argued further, were not merely personal differences; they undermined the whole structure of law and the administration of justice. Sheltering himself within legal tradition, he tried to explain how judicial processes worked. The king was the source of justice, distributing it through the realm by the work of judges, all fallible men. The system of appeal—as well as precedent and procedure—served to correct judges' human errors. Inevitably, he explained, defeated parties accused the judge of bias. When they did so, they set themselves above the law and subverted the constitution. Attacks on judges endangered the

[46]Laurens to William Cowles & Co., and William Freeman, 8 August 1768, Laurens Papers, 4:255; Leigh, *The Man Unmasked*, 70-71.

[47]Leigh, *The Man Unmasked*, 7-10, 40-41.

community because slandered jurists had no means of retaliation. Laurens, Leigh concluded, misunderstood both the relation between the courts and society and the actual merits of his own case. Actually, he had been treated very well, Leigh observed. He, therefore, had no real grounds for complaint, and his accusations were "wild, inconsistent, irregular, and strange."[48]

In the final analysis, however, Leigh's defense rested on a plea that his professional dignity entitled him to a special construction of his actions. "When seizures are made," he explained, "the [Vice-Admiralty] judge is presumed to be totally indifferent to the parties in the dispute; charity supposes likewise that he is influenced only by his sense of duty."[49] If he had made errors, they were errors of judgment, not of evil intent. Brought before the bar of public opinion, he could, in effect, only avow that his intentions had been good and plead for mercy. Such impotence must have been a humiliating, frustrating experience for a proud and sensitive man.

What was so galling was that he could not bring most South Carolinians to recognize his own wise and constructive propensities. The trouble seemed to be that most persons did not understand the principles of human behavior. Men were difficult to analyze because they were a "mixture of so much *goodness* and so much *baseness* . . . a compound of opposite *qualities, humours,* and *inclinations.*" When faced with this problem, the average man, Leigh believed, simply counted a person's good and bad qualities, deducting one total from the other "as we do in vulgar arithmetic." Leigh proceeded differently: "I . . . sift out . . . the first ruling principle of the man, and then . . . carry in my eye his leading passion, which I separate from the other parts of his character, and then observe how far his other qualities, good and bad, are brought to support *that*."[50]

Recognition from the Crown, he hoped, would help him command respect because it would compel men to take seriously his "leading pas-

---

[48]Ibid., 12-19.

[49]Ibid., 43-44, 77-89, 100-101, 122-23.

[50]Ibid., 19-25. The concept of a "ruling passion" was fairly common in eighteenth-century literature, but Leigh cited Laurence Sterne as the source of his own sophisticated version of the doctrine. Sterne's most famous work, and the one to which Leigh was probably referring, was *The Life and Opinions of Tristram Shandy.* For an introduction to Sterne and his use of Lockean psychology, see Albert C. Baugh, ed., *A Literary History of England* (New York: Appleton-Century-Crofts, 1948) 1022-26.

sion'' of service to the king and thereby dissuade them from simply compiling his alleged misdeeds. Perhaps the triumph of a peerage could redeem everything. In the spring of 1771 he therefore set sail for England where he pestered the king's advisor, the Earl of Rochford, to recommend him. Receiving little encouragement, he finally resorted to a presumptuous maneuver. He told Rochford that if the king did not grant him a royal honor before his ship sailed for South Carolina in ten or twelve days, he would then return to Charleston ''under a patient Expectation that Royal Favour will be extended to me in due time.'' The twelve days passed without a summons from the palace, but Rochford did not disabuse Leigh of the presumption that he could force the king's hand in this manner. Six weeks later, on 14 September 1772, George III granted his hard-pressed servant a baronetcy, though not a peerage.[51]

While in England Leigh also seems to have received other favors. He made pregnant a girl in his household, an orphan who was his own ward, his wife's sister, and Henry Laurens's niece. Who seduced whom is a question that will probably always remain unanswerable.[52] Nevertheless, two points can and should be made. First, a kind of poetic injustice was involved: Leigh believed that Laurens had attempted to destroy his reputation and thereby violated family ties, while Leigh's incestuous conduct violated family ties and struck at the reputation of Laurens's family. Second, Leigh's attempts to hide the affair were astonishingly clumsy. He and the girl returned separately to South Carolina. When her time to deliver was near, he put her aboard a vessel bound for England whose captain was

---

[51]Leigh to [the Earl of Rochford], 29 July 1772, State Papers, Domestic, Class 37, Piece 9, folio 63, and Class 44, Piece 379, folios 384-85, Public Record Office, London. Leigh's patent as baronet indicated that he had made a sizable contribution to the Crown that was a major factor in his receipt of the honor. The patent said nothing of his service in South Carolina but commended him for contributing a sum sufficient to support thirty troops in Ulster for three years. Leigh Family Papers, CR 162/576, Warwick Record Office, Warwick, England.

[52]Although the girl changed her story several times and Leigh at first denied his complicity, he eventually confessed during a face-to-face confrontation with Laurens and offered to make a monetary settlement, an offer that Laurens did not accept. Henry Laurens to Leigh, to James Laurens, 30 January 1773, 15 September 1774, Laurens Papers, 7:36-39, 357-58. Historians have always chivalrously assumed that Leigh was the aggressor; nevertheless there is reason to suspect that the girl was something of a hellion in her own right. See Henry Laurens to James Laurens, postscript of 10 February 1772, to letter of 6 February 1772, ibid., 5:179.

an acquaintance of Laurens. Although Leigh enjoined the girl under threat of dire penalties not to contact her uncle, it seems almost incredible that a man of his intelligence did not realize that Laurens would learn of the affair. Indeed, Laurens himself realized as much when he wrote, "Nothing is too Wicked for him to *attempt,* even when Detection and Judgement are at his Threshold—He is the most Wicked Man and the greatest Fool that ever I heard or Read of, in a Man of tolerable Education and Sense."[53]

Not only Laurens but all of Charleston soon discovered what had happened. Before the vessel was out to sea the girl went into labor. When the captain attempted to put her ashore, Leigh prevented it. She gave birth with no midwife in attendance, and the baby died within the week. Laurens termed it murder and suspected that Leigh had hoped that without proper care the mother would die as well.[54]

Whether or not Laurens's suspicions were justified, Leigh's conduct was indefensible, and he became a social pariah, reduced to associating chiefly with Fenwick Bull, another recently fallen Crown officer who had been horsewhipped and ostracized for attempting to bribe a jockey into fixing a horse race.[55] No baronetcy could help Leigh now—it could only further intensify the disgust that South Carolinians felt for the administration that appeared to honor him. (Laurens correctly suspected that Leigh had probably purchased his title, but by this point in the prerevolutionary controversy, most colonial observers simply regarded the title as a genuine expression of the Crown's esteem for Leigh.) Thus John Adams recorded in the diary that he kept during the First Continental Congress: "He [Thomas Lynch] entertained us with the Scandalous History of Sir Egerton Leigh—the Story of his Wife's Sister, . . . and all that. There is not says Lynch a greater Rascall among all the Kings Friends. He has great Merit, in this Reign."[56]

---

[53]*South Carolina Gazette,* 2 July, 22 October 1772; Laurens to Leigh, to Edwards Pierce, 30 January, 31 March 1773, Laurens Papers, 7:36-39, 82.

[54]Laurens to Leigh, 30 January 1773, Laurens Papers, 7:38.

[55]Henry Laurens to John Laurens, 28 January 1774, ibid., 7:202. Bull, who had been a notary public and register of mesne conveyances until his disgrace, was apparently not related to Lieutenant Governor William Bull; the latter was a native of South Carolina, the former of England. *South Carolina Gazette,* 9 February 1769.

[56]Henry Laurens to James Laurens, 5 October 1772, Laurens Papers, 7:11; Butterfield, *The Diary and Autobiography of John Adams,* 2:117-18.

Whatever merit he possessed, Leigh had become ineffectual, and—certainly in South Carolina—a positive liability as a servant of the Crown. Although the powers and prestige of the Council had been waning for more than a decade, it had been a consistent source of support for royal officers who tried to uphold imperial measures. When Leigh became the senior member and president, the Council and its measures were identified with a man who was already considered to be beyond the pale. Moreover, because he led the upper house into imprudent, if not irresponsible, actions, there appeared to be some foundation for the charge that Council "business is generally done by a small Junto, under the Direction of a man desperate in Fortune, abandoned in Principle, and ruined in Reputation."[57] Leigh's presidency therefore materially accelerated the complete eclipse of the South Carolina Royal Council.

The final round of the battle between the Commons House and the Council stemmed from the Wilkes fund controversy that arose in 1769 when the Commons dispatched a donation from provincial funds to the Society of Supporters for the Bill of Rights in England, a group supporting John Wilkes. Again, Leigh found himself drawn into controversies begun by other men. In 1773 he tried to take the initiative after the Crown and successive governors had failed to induce the Commons to relinquish its claim to sole control of provincial expenditures. For nearly four years the Crown had forbidden governors to assent to a tax bill unless it included a clause prohibiting the treasurer from transmitting public funds out of the province.[58] On his return from England, Leigh took matters into his own hands. Acting on information supplied by Henry Perroneau, one of the public treasurers, he prodded the Council to prepare a report that blamed the depleted state of the provincial treasury on the Commons for its refusal to enact an acceptable money bill. Somewhat later, two members of the Council—John and William Henry Drayton—prepared a report criticizing

---

[57]The most recent and best available synthesis of material about the South Carolina Royal Council after 1763 is found in Jackson Turner Main, *The Upper House in Revolutionary America, 1763-1788* (Madison: University of Wisconsin Press, 1967) 11-20. [Arthur Lee], *Answer to Considerations on Certain Political Transactions of the Province of South Carolina* (London: J. Almon, 1774) 60. On Leigh as a liability to the Crown by 1773, see also Marvin R. Zahniser, *Charles Cotesworth Pinckney* (Chapel Hill: University of North Carolina Press, 1967) 29.

[58]Jack P. Greene, "Bridge to Revolution: The Wilkes Fund Controversy in South Carolina, 1769-1775," *Journal of Southern History* 29 (1963): 19-52.

the recent conduct of the upper house and, in effect, praising the Commons for its stand. The Draytons' manifesto appeared in the *South Carolina Gazette*. Infuriated at this opposition, Leigh, as president of the Council, ordered the arrest of the paper's printer, Thomas Powell, for violating the privileges of the upper house.[59] The Commons exploded in protest, and two local justices of the peace—both members of the Commons—immediately ordered Powell's release on the grounds that because the councillors held their positions at the pleasure of the Crown, the Council was in reality an appendage of the executive and, therefore, not an independent house of the legislature possessing the power of commitment for contempt. Powell and one of his supporters then sued Leigh but lost when the chief justice, a member of the Council, ruled that that body was an upper house of the provincial legislature and within its rights in enforcing its privileges.[60] But the Commons House transmitted a vigorous denunciation of the Council's actions to the ministry and most South Carolinians continued to believe that the justices of the peace had the better of the argument. As a result of its apparently unwarranted and arbitrary behavior, the Council sank even lower in public estimation.[61]

In the meantime, the Powell affair had made Leigh's own position completely intolerable. During a meeting of the upper house the volatile William Henry Drayton reportedly called Leigh a damn fool to his face—a remark that the journal does not record. It does show, however, that the members felt it necessary at this time to adopt a series of "Remembrances for Order and Decency to Be Kept in the Upper House of Assembly," one of which stipulated that "all personal sharp and taxing Speeches [ought to] be forborn." Worse yet, Edward Rutledge, who made his name as a patriotic lawyer by representing Powell during the proceedings, denounced Leigh unmercifully in open court. On top of all these difficulties, in the spring of 1773 the ministry ordered a temporary embargo on the granting of lands in all royal colonies, and Leigh's income as surveyor general van-

---

[59]South Carolina Council to Bull, 23 August 1773, C.O. 5/395:117-20; Leigh's warrant for Powell's arrest, 31 August 1773; Bull to Lord Dartmouth, 18 September 1773, ibid., 151, 133-38.

[60]South Carolina Council to George III, 9 September 1773; Leigh to Bull, 18 September, 16 October 1773, ibid., 163, 179-82.

[61]8 September 1773, South Carolina Commons Journals, 39:88; Committee of Correspondence to Garth, 16 September 1773, Garth Letter Book, 1766-1775, 153-54.

ished.[62] What was to be gained by remaining in South Carolina was obviously no longer worth the price. Therefore, Leigh arranged for an allowance of £500 sterling per year from James Simpson, who would act as attorney general in Leigh's absence. Then, having apparently delayed his departure in an unsuccessful attempt to avoid encountering Laurens in London, Leigh sailed for England on 19 June 1774.[63]

While waiting to depart he wrote an account of political events in South Carolina and sent the manuscript to London, where in January 1774 it was anonymously published as a pamphlet entitled *Considerations on Certain Political Transactions of the Province of South Carolina*. Leigh's defense of the Council and attack on the conduct of the lower house enraged Henry Laurens, who correctly guessed the author's identity. Laurens and Ralph Izard, also then in London, therefore enlisted Izard's friend, Arthur Lee, to compose an *Answer to the Considerations on Certain Political Transactions of the Province of South Carolina*.[64]

Even Dr. Alexander Garden, who was relatively unsympathetic to the Commons in the Wilkes fund controversy, thought that Lee's *Answer* was an effective rebuttal, though he considered Egerton Leigh the better literary stylist.[65] Nevertheless, even though his position was too extreme for a future Loyalist like Garden, Leigh's analysis of the situation in South Carolina was shrewd and perceptive. There was good reason for the quality of his observations. While he was a member of the Commons House it had been engaged in one of its periodic controversies with the upper house, and Leigh had served on a committee appointed to report whether or not the Council ought to be considered an upper house.[66] His service on this com-

---

[62]Henry Laurens to John Laurens, 19 November 1773, Laurens Papers, 7:126; 1 September 1773, South Carolina Upper House Journals, C.O. 5/478:20; 31 May 1773, South Carolina Council Journals, 37:178-79; Leigh, Memorial to Dartmouth, 2 March 1775, Dartmouth Papers, 2:1174.

[63]James Simpson's case, Loyalists' Transcripts, 54:240; Laurens to Edwards Pierce, 6 December 1773, Laurens Papers, 7:155; *South Carolina Gazette,* 20 June 1774.

[64]Greene, ''Bridge to Revolution,'' 45.

[65]Laurens to Ralph Izard, 20 September 1774, Laurens Papers, 7:367.

[66]For an account of this controversy, see M. Eugene Sirmans, *Colonial South Carolina: A Political History, 1663-1763* (Chapel Hill: University of North Carolina Press, 1966) 301-309. The committee, after requesting more time to study the matter, was eventually discharged without making a final report. 25, 27 November 1755, 22 April 1756, South Carolina Commons Journals, 31, pt. 1:10, 15-16, 192.

mittee, his general experience in the Commons, and his membership in the Council gave him unusual insight into the workings of the political system in the colony. As a result, his analysis of the Wilkes fund controversy contained a highly sophisticated study of the nature of political change in South Carolina, and in particular, it went to the heart of the matter in its discussion of the Commons's ascendancy from the 1720s to 1770s. Stripped of Leigh's attempts at self-justification, his pamphlet presented an analytical explanation of how the Commons House expanded its power. He took pains to delineate specific elements in the collective behavior of the assemblymen: the steady accumulation of power throughout the history of the legislature; the careful nurturing of precedents by the Commons; the tenacity with which assemblymen performed their functions and clung to their powers; the gratification they derived from the common endeavor; the absolute impasse between the Commons and the Crown, which the additional instruction on provincial finance imposed on their struggle; the dependence of the Council's status as an upper house upon form rather than function; the hopeless tactical position of the Council once Powell had been released; and the supreme importance that the Council placed on its dignity after the basis for that dignity had disappeared.

As an opponent of the Commons, Leigh, significantly, acknowledged primacy of constitutional principle as a motivation for the House's actions in the Wilkes fund controversy. He based his case on the undesirability and impropriety of the Commons's extension of its fiscal powers "beyond the original . . . intention of those from whom they derive their whole authority." Every political power, he reminded the assemblymen, had in its nature some limit beyond which it ought not to be extended. The constant temptations of men "to be misled by passion, fancy, or caprice" made these limits necessary and justified the Crown and Council in opposing the Wilkes fund grant or any repetition of it.[67] Neither conspiracy nor self-interest had any central place in Leigh's indictment. Rather the Commons's action had proceeded from folly, ignorance, and childish fascination with "a *factious* Club of Men . . . at the London Tavern"—as he styled the pro-Wilkes society. Leigh readily conceded the legitimacy of the Commons's body of precedents—dating back to 1737—that entitled it to appropriate public funds. "In order to combat these Facts," he argued, "let us . . . reflect

---

[67]Leigh, *Considerations,* 18-20.

what slow advances *Infant Societies* of Men make towards Regularity or Perfection.'' The feeble efforts of early provincial government to cope with its problems scarcely justified subsequent attempts by the Commons to spend public funds on any purpose whatever. These admitted ''Precedents, therefore, of new Communities are of very little weight.'' Most early examples of spending by the Commons dealt with mundane matters like the salaries of the clergy or the encouragement of silk production.[68] By admitting the legalistic nature of the Commons's appeal to its early development, Leigh recognized the central fact about the province's political history, and he thereby deprived himself of grounds for strong rebuttal. He denounced the exercise of the Commons's power; he could not, however, deny the existence of that power.

Leigh not only comprehended the constitutional ingredients of the Commons's ascendancy; he also understood its dynamic character. The success of its efforts and the sheer pleasure of maneuver and struggle reinforced the ambitions of its members and produced ''baneful effects.'' Noting the constant agitation of provincial politics since the Stamp Act crisis, he explained that ''human nature . . . cannot bear a constant Tide of flattering Successes without becoming Insolently Saucy, and Arrogantly Vain.'' This emotional dimension of politics explained why the Wilkes fund controversy had proceeded from one impasse to another in *''Geometric Progression.''* As it developed, both the Commons and Council, he recalled, held tightly to their commitments. The Council insisted that as an upper house it could refuse assent to money bills, while the assemblymen remained ''tenacious in their Rights as they conceived them.'' The additional instruction, prohibiting the governor from assenting to any money bill that did not forbid the treasurer to send money out of the province, prevented any compromise and reinforced the Council's intransigent position. The additional instruction confirmed a situation to which men on both sides were already committed. Thus the issue became ''whether the King is to recall . . . his Instruction; or the People submit to a check for an unconstitutional Application of the Public Treasure.'' ''Justice as well as Prudence,'' he declared, ''require us to yield the point.'' A gesture of

---

[68]Ibid. On the actual composition and character of the society, see Ian R. Christie, *Wilkes, Wyvill, and Reform: The Parliamentary Reform Movement in British Politics, 1760-1785* (London: Macmillan and Co., 1962) 33-49. Leigh, *Considerations,* 26-27.

obeisance by South Carolina, Leigh realized in 1773, was needed to restore the vigor of British authority in the province.[69]

Leigh derived his accurate assessment of the changes in South Carolina politics—which, in part, had destroyed his career and would contribute substantially to the coming of the Revolution there—from the same self-centered and rigid quality of mind that blinded him to his opponents' values. He realized that the protests against the Council's arrest of Powell were also a personal attack against his exercise of the Council's power. Vainly seeking the support of Lieutenant Governor William Bull, he called the suit by Powell and one of his supporters against him "the unprecedented Insult which is intended to be cast on the Second or Middle branch of the Legislature [the Council] . . . for an Act done by me as President."[70] Leigh insisted that his chief motive in arresting Powell was to uphold the dignity of the Council and thereby preserve the constitution of the province. That dignity, apart from an admittedly shadowy similarity with the British House of Lords, stemmed from the sacrifices made by its members. The lack of emoluments, public scorn of its proceedings, danger of arbitrary dismissal—and now the Wilkes fund controversy completed the sacrificial process in which Leigh took such pride. The Council, he pleaded, could not hope to maintain itself as a viable institution much longer if men in the province could publicly violate its prerogatives, if no court would enforce its decisions, and if men looked on it as an agent of oppression. "What security can such a Branch of the Legislature have," he demanded, "when . . . General Opinion proclaims, that a Place in Council is a kind of alienation from the concerns and interest of the People?"[71] He was incredulous that South Carolinians should consider him as alienated from their society, but at the same time he retained an especially acute awareness that in performing what he considered an honorable function in the politics of the province he had helped place himself, the Council, and the interests of the Crown directly in the way of the consuming flame of political opposition.

In part, Leigh had written his pamphlet in the hope of vindicating the Council and himself against the accusations of the Commons House. He also doubtlessly hoped that his performance would attract the favorable at-

---

[69]Leigh, *Considerations,* 3, 17, 30.

[70]Leigh to Bull, 18 September 1773, C.O. 5/395:163.

[71]Leigh, *Considerations,* 54.

tention of the ministry, but his success was meager. Everyone was preoccupied by the chain of events that followed the Boston Tea Party and neither the *Considerations* nor its author aroused much interest.[72] Languishing in London, he petitioned Lord Dartmouth, secretary of state for American affairs, for a position in one of the middle or northern colonies. Long residence in South Carolina, he claimed, had "so effected the state of his Nerves" that his return there would be fatal. Nevertheless, along with other councillors then in England, he was given the choice of returning or resigning his position. He resigned.[73] After the conquest of Charleston, however, he went back to South Carolina, and became a member of the military commandant's advisory council, the Board of Police, and an intendant of the city.[74] He also recommended to the ministry that civil government be reestablished as soon as possible and that, because of his experience, he be appointed governor. Neither event occurred; instead Leigh, who had been ill for some time, died in Charleston on 15 September 1781.[75]

The pathos and scandal in Leigh's career should not be allowed to obscure its historical significance. Clearly, his actions and, ultimately, his mere presence helped to disenchant South Carolinians with imperial authorities and their policy. Eventually, through the circulation of pamphlets and by word of mouth, Leigh became notorious throughout the colonies. As a result, he contributed significantly to the growing American hostility toward the Vice-Admiralty Courts and to the increasing feeling that Great Britain and her servants were corrupt.

The obvious question, however, is how a man of Leigh's ability, to all intents and purposes firmly entrenched in local society, could have gotten himself into such a predicament. One plausible explanation might be that

---

[72]Greene, "Bridge to Revolution," 48.

[73]Leigh, Memorial to Dartmouth, 2 March 1775, Dartmouth Papers, 2:1174; John Pownall to Leigh, 16 May 1775, Trans., S. C. Records, 35:114; Leigh to Dartmouth, 26 June 1775, Dartmouth Papers, 1339.

[74]20 February 1781, Miscellaneous Records, SS:382-83, SCDAH; Miscellaneous Proceedings of the Board of Police, 1780-1781, C.O. 5/520:62ff.

[75]Leigh to Hillsborough, 25 February 1781, Trans., S. C. Records, 36:112; Mabel L. Webber, ed., "Death Notices from the *South Carolina and American General Gazette,* and Its Continuation, the *Royal Gazette,* May 1766-June 1782," *South Carolina Historical and Genealogical Magazine* 17 (1916): 160.

events beyond their control placed all Crown servants in untenable situations; another might stress Leigh's apparent immorality. Neither interpretation is quite adequate. Leigh was not merely a passive victim of forces beyond his control. Rather, as the prerevolutionary movement embroiled him in difficulty, he seems almost suicidally to have rushed to meet his fate. Nor was he entirely immoral. It is difficult to believe that Laurens and others would have trusted him initially if he had been an unmitigated scoundrel. Apart from his relationship with his sister-in-law—an aberration more deserving of the clinical compassion of a psychiatrist than condemnation by a historian—none of Leigh's actions could be termed iniquitous by an impartial observer. He did occasionally use poor judgment and in a few cases violated propriety—something to which he seemed oblivious. This quality of ethical obtuseness is indeed a key to explaining much of Leigh's behavior. Like his self-destructiveness, to which it was closely related, this trait manifested itself chiefly in Leigh's inability to project an appropriate public image in a society where image and reputation mattered enormously. Being a perceptive man, he recognized that his difficulties, as well as those of other Crown officials, arose fundamentally from a lack of public support. Being something of an intellectual, he sought to resolve symbolically those dilemmas that he could not resolve in actuality. So when his actual power failed him, he loved to replay the scene on paper—a medium in which he had more control. In the process, of course, he hoped that his pamphlets would vindicate him, shame his detractors, and thereby regain for him the power that he believed he deserved to possess. However, the results of his efforts were exactly the opposite of what he intended.

These attempts at self-justification were more than the self-pitying afterthoughts of a discredited officeholder. Throughout the prerevolutionary controversy, Leigh struggled in his own tenacious way to understand the political culture of South Carolina and, in the light of the reverses he had suffered there, to understand himself. He could not help but broadcast the conclusion that he was a uniquely gifted bureaucratic and judicial operator. His presumption to a special legal insight (which was denied to laymen) regarding matters of vice-admiralty law, his belief that only his intelligence and sense of the dramatic could save the Council from further degradation, and his conviction that attacks upon himself were attempts to destroy the institutions that he served were not only defense mechanisms, they were also expressions of his pride as a placeman and the products of his sustained effort at political analysis and self-examination. His pride and intellectual determination thus drove him to accentuate the very presumptions about himself and about British authority that South Carolina most detested and impelled him to equate their resulting hostility with a leveling process that he alone could diagnose and denounce.

Although his approach was hardly calculated to win applause in South Carolina, Leigh was correct in realizing that profound changes had occurred in the character of local politics during the preceding quarter of a century. What he did not realize was that the dominant position of the Commons House of Assembly was associated with the development of a particular climate of opinion in which his own political instincts were unreliable. His success, and that of the family in which he was brought up, had depended on the ability to impress a small number of individuals who possessed the power to grant or withhold preferment. Ability, good intentions, and loyalty to one's patron were qualities that enabled one to navigate this political world successfully. Leigh's apologia, then, condemned ingratitude and disloyalty to family and friend as the greatest of sins; purity in those areas, he seemed to think, excused admitted lapses in judgment. Where political power was controlled by small factional groups, such a defense was at least relevant and might have been effective.

In South Carolina it was worse than irrelevant. Effective political power depended less on imperial than upon local popular support, and for nearly a generation, though the prerevolutionary period accelerated the trend, South Carolinians had reserved their esteem for those politicians who put the public welfare above all else. Laurens, a product of the local political environment, understood this; Leigh, a product of a different system, never did. Consequently, when the tensions of the 1760s undercut the position of Crown officers, he had no effective way to protect himself. In fact, his attempts to defend himself, instead of confounding his critics, merely served to condemn him by his own words, for they revealed that he subscribed to a different set of political mores. Lest anyone should miss these implications, Laurens hammered the point home when he replied to the charge of family disloyalty. "As far as human Strength will assist me," he wrote, "I am never influenced in Favour of any Man contrary to the publick Good, from so poor a Consideration *only* as his *Alliance to me*." These words could well serve as Leigh's political epitaph, for if, as he charged, Laurens was not at home in the technicalities of the law, Leigh was equally out of his element in the political atmosphere of prerevolutionary South Carolina.[76]

The point here is not to draw an invidious distinction between differing sets of political ethics, but rather to demonstrate that a difference did exist.[77] When rents began to appear in the fabric that bound royal officials and local leaders together into a coherent whole, it became clear that in many cases these men spoke a different language. Thus attempts at communication often failed. Instead of resolving differences, moral considerations frequently accentuated them. Isolated and introspective, Leigh sensed more acutely than most of his contemporaries that this failure of communication had occurred. As a result, his writings depict the anguish of a misunderstood villain in a complex moral struggle and provide poignant, illuminating insight into facets of the personal and intellectual dilemma of many Loyalists on the eve of the Revoution.

[76]Laurens, *Extracts,* 2d ed., appendix, 33.

[77]See also John Higham's suggestion that the Revolution be reinterpreted "as a problem in political ethics," in "Beyond Consensus: the Historian as Moral Critic," *American Historical Review* 67 (1962): 623.

Chapter Three _____

Who Shall Rule at Home: The American Revolution as a Crisis of Legitimacy for the Colonial Elite* _____

This essay had its beginnings in a request to review James Kirby Martin, Men in Rebellion: Higher Governmental Leaders and the Coming of the American Revolution *(New Brunswick: Rutgers University Press, 1973), which deals with some effects of the general reluctance of British authorities to appoint Americans to the most prestigious posts in the colonies. If, as Robert Calhoon and I believe, some Loyalists failed to understand the imperatives of colonial politics, Martin demonstrated that colonial leaders were themselves unable to meet British standards for preferment. It seemed to me, however, that no one had explored some of the ramifications of this failure. The resulting paper, which someone facetiously suggested entitling "The Founding Fathers as Juvenile Delinquents," drew upon the insights of social psychologists. Given at a conference on Interdisciplinary Approaches to the American Revolution held at Harvard University in 1975, it is reprinted from the* Journal of Interdisciplinary History 6 *(1976): 679-700, by permission of the* Journal of Interdisciplinary History *and the MIT Press, Cambridge, Massachusetts. Copyright ©1976, by the Massachusetts Institute of Technology and the editors of the* Journal of Interdisciplinary History. *Library of Congress Catalog Card Number: 77-120540.*

*The author would like to thank friends, colleagues, and especially Jack P. Greene, Pauline Maier, and John Murrin for many helpful criticisms and suggestions.

Emotions, historians are well aware, had much to do with the coming of the American Revolution. Bernard Bailyn has recently suggested that the impact of Thomas Paine's *Common Sense* in 1776 was partly due to the way in which it expressed and crystallized American anger. Furthermore, many scholars have long suspected—as Gordon Wood put it ten years ago—that the "revolutionary character of the Americans' ideas . . . indicates that something profoundly unsettling was going on in the society." With a few notable exceptions, however, most students of the Revolution have taken the emotional element for granted, and that oversight has accentuated some artificial divisions among them. For the difficulty of disentangling the complex relationships between socioeconomic developments and ideology has created an "either-or" situation in which individuals have been drawn into studying—and consequently emphasizing the primacy of—one element or the other. The resulting debate has been fruitful in the past, but it probably cannot be resolved.[1] The time has come, therefore, to give more attention to the emotional matrix through which contemporary ideas were linked to social phenomena.

Clearly, as two scholars who have studied the emotional roots of rebellion note, Americans were "boiling mad" on the eve of the Revolution, and there was a myriad of reasons for their anger. But an examination of the situation in South Carolina indicates that the precarious position of the American political elite deserves more attention than it has hitherto received. To a greater extent than has been commonly recognized, subordinate status within the empire jeopardized the security of indigenous leaders. The threat was most apparent in colonial South Carolina, where the pattern of preferment under British authority generated a great deal of resentment among aspiring natives. Yet preliminary evidence indicates—and it is the assumption of this essay—that the predicament of South Carolinians was merely a particularly visible example of a more general phenomenon. Everywhere in America after the mid-eighteenth century, British ties unsettled colonial politics, and local leaders often found themselves

---

[1]Bernard Bailyn, "*Common Sense,*" in *Fundamental Testaments of the American Revolution* (Washington: Library of Congress, 1973) 20-22; Gordon S. Wood, "Rhetoric and Reality in the American Revolution," *William and Mary Quarterly 3d ser. 23 (1966):31.* Two articles by Jack P. Greene provide an excellent survey of historiography: "Flight from Determinism: A Review of Recent Literature on the Coming of the American Revolution," *South Atlantic Quarterly* 61 (1962): 235-59; "The Social Origins of the American Revolution: An Evaluation and an Interpretation," *Political Science Quarterly* 88 (1973): 1-22.

unable to meet the criteria for leadership prevailing in the metropolitan culture. One result of this failure was a crisis of legitimacy for much of the indigenous colonial elite—that is, for members of the broad, amorphous, and continually changing category of individuals who possessed sufficiently high socioeconomic status to feel eligible for political office but who were unable to command the patronage of imperial officials.[2] Without attempting to reify a fictive and highly problematical group mind, it is suggested that this crisis aroused emotions and attitudes that contributed not only to the willingness to rebel but also to the transformation of American values during the revolutionary era.

I

Historians, like the Loyalists, have frequently assumed that the tie with Britain had a stabilizing effect for well-established persons in the colonies, but by the 1760s the opposite was often the case. As many who would become Whig leaders increasingly realized, disruptive imperial measures complicated their tasks and threatened their status. To be sure, British norms and institutions lent a modicum of form and order to colonial society. Trading privileges within the empire also helped to preclude greater instability by contributing to colonial prosperity. Yet rapid economic growth may itself have been an unsettling element. More important, imperial of-

---

[2]Edwin G. Burrows and Michael Wallace, "The American Revolution: The Ideology and Psychology of National Liberation," *Perspectives in American History* 6 (1972): 294; James Kirby Martin's *Men in Rebellion: Higher Governmental Leaders and the Coming of the American Revolution* (New Brunswick: Rutgers NJ: University Press, 1973) represents the most ambitious and stimulating attempt yet made to study the effect of prevailing patterns of preferment which, he contends, "caused stress in the colonial political systems and underlay much of the tensions giving motion to the developing American Revolution" (24). But because he failed to ask why colonial leaders might have desired appointment to royal or proprietary offices, the emoluments and real powers of which could be less than those of local posts that they already occupied, Martin did not explore important implications of his own intriguing hypothesis. Clues to some of these ramifications can be found in three other works which, though different in approach and conclusions, have contributed much to the present essay: Jack P. Greene, "An Uneasy Connection: An Analysis of the Preconditions of the American Revolution," in *Essays on the American Revolution,* ed. Stephen G. Kurtz and James H. Hutson (Chapel Hill: University of North Carolina Press, 1973) 32-80; Jack P. Greene, "Search for Identity: An Interpretation of the Meaning of Selected Patterns of Social Response in Eighteenth-Century America," *Journal of Social History* 3 (1970): 189-220; Thomas C. Barrow, "The American Revolution as a Colonial War for Independence," *William and Mary Quarterly* 3d ser. 25 (1968): 452-64.

ficials appeared to be directly or indirectly responsible for most of the up-
heavals that occurred in America after 1763.

Part of the trouble arose from ministerial instability and the hazards of
transatlantic communication that frequently led to countermanded orders
and disallowed legislation. Ignorance of colonial conditions and rigid assumptions on the part of imperial authorities, coupled with real conflicts
of interest between Britain and the colonies, further exacerbated difficulties to the point where a royal governor came to expect new instructions to
cause problems; his superiors, in contrast, often expected him to plunge
his "province into confusion" rather than violate their orders. Attempts to
circumscribe the power of the local assemblies by limiting the number of
representatives contributed directly to the lawlessness and discontent that
led to the South Carolina Regulator movement. Similarly, the Currency
Act of 1764, passed by Parliament to curb colonial emissions of paper
money, helped to produce the Regulators of North Carolina, where western residents lacked the cash to pay taxes. By precluding the flexibility
necessary for stability, directions from London frequently undermined colonial governments. Even imperial patronage, which might have helped to
stabilize local politics, possessed a contrary effect, as increasing control
of appointments by superior officials robbed governors of one of their most
useful tools, offended the native elite, and often resulted in poor choices.
In turn, martinetism, corruption, incompetence, and rivalries among royal
officials eroded respect for government. A low point came in 1772 when
two collectors, each claiming a different authority for his appointment,
halted business in the port of Charleston while they struggled for possession of the customs office. In sum, British men and measures seem to have
prompted nearly as much rioting during the last fifteen years of the colonial period as had occurred in the entire preceding century and a half.[3]

---

[3]John Wentworth of New Hampshire, quoted in Robert M. Calhoon, *The Loyalists in
Revolutionary America, 1760-1781* (New York: Harcourt Brace Jovanovich, 1973) 132;
Lieutenant Governor William Bull to Lord Dartmouth, 3 May 1774, Transcripts of Records
Relating to South Carolina in the British Public Record Office, 34:42, South Carolina De-
partment of Archives and History (hereafter cited as Trans., S.C., SCDAH), Columbia;
Richard Maxwell Brown, *The South Carolina Regulators* (Cambridge MA: Belknap Press
of Harvard University Press, 1963); Marvin L. Michael Kay, "The Payment of Provincial
and Local Taxes in North Carolina, 1748-1771," *William and Mary Quarterly* 3d ser. 26

However patriotic the mobs, or self-disciplined their actions, many members of the colonial elite regarded their appearance as an ominous sign. Established leaders may already have been under pressure because of economic developments, population movements, growing religious diversity and, perhaps, the increasing politicization of the lower classes—although the extent of the threat was not yet entirely clear.[4] But they obviously did perceive dangers in the mounting disorders. Most dreaded was anarchy. Even if such extreme fears proved groundless, extralegal protests, by their very nature, were potentially corrosive of the patterns of deference through which colonial elites reinforced their tenuous sense of social superiority. When Henry Laurens, son of a self-made saddler and himself a wealthy Charleston merchant, was visited by a mob during the Stamp Act crisis, he found that the "Jacks . . . not knowing me & dreading no body were zealous to execute the business . . . & would for some time admit to no *'Parleys'* nor *'Palabres,'* [they] not only menaced very loudly but now & then handled me pretty uncouthly." And Colonel George Gabriel Powell felt compelled to resign his commission in the militia because his men re-

---

(1969): 218-40; Joseph A. Ernst, *Money and Politics in America, 1755-1775* (Chapel Hill: University of North Carolina Press, 1973) 199-207; Bernard Bailyn, *The Origins of American Politics* (New York: Alfred A. Knopf, 1970) 74; James A. Henretta, *"Salutary Neglect": Colonial Administration under the Duke of Newcastle* (Princeton: Princeton University Press, 1972) 243; Oliver M. Dickerson, *The Navigation Acts and the American Revolution* (New York: Perpetua, 1963) 208-56; Edward McCrady, *The History of South Carolina under the Royal Government, 1719-1776* (New York: Macmillan Co., 1899) 465-68. The controversy between R. P. H. Hatley (who was appointed by Governor Charles Montagu) and George Roupell (commissioned by the customs commissioners in Boston) may be traced through the correspondence in Treasury 1/492, Public Record Office, London. R. M. Brown, "Violence and the American Revolution," in *Essays on the American Revolution,* 117-20.

[4]For these developments, see Pauline Maier, "Popular Uprisings and Civil Authority in Eighteenth-Century America," *William and Mary Quarterly* 3d ser. 27 (1970): 3-35; Richard L. Bushman, *From Puritan to Yankee: Character and the Social Order in Connecticut, 1690-1765* (Cambridge MA: Harvard University Press, 1967) 235-66; Rhys Isaac, "Religion and Authority: Problems of the Anglican Establishment in Virginia in the Era of the Great Awakening and the Parsons' Cause," *William and Mary Quarterly* 3d ser. 30 (1973): 3-36; idem, "Evangelical Revolt: The Nature of the Baptists' Challenge to the Traditional Order in Virginia, 1765-1775," *William and Mary Quarterly* 31 (1974): 345-68; Gary B. Nash, "The Transformation of Urban Politics, 1700-1765," *Journal of American History* 60 (1973): 605-32, esp. n. 53; Kenneth Lockridge, "Social Change and the Meaning of the American Revolution," *Journal of Social History* 6 (1973): 403-39.

fused to aid in arresting a leading South Carolina Regulator.[5] Not surprisingly, members of the local elite also saw the captains of the mob as potential rivals. Repeatedly, they expressed doubts that those who had been ''made men of consequence'' by leading protest movements would be willing to resume their former obscurity. Personal fears were reinforced by the broader intellectual belief that there were always the ''idle, the dissolute and abandoned'' in any society that would find disorder to be an avenue for personal advancement. That it becomes somewhat easier to identify the protest leaders as time goes on suggests that this fear was no chimera. Disassociating themselves from obnoxious British measures to lead the opposition became as much a matter of practical and social necessity as a question of ideological or political conviction for local leaders. The folly, the irresponsibility, the oppression of imperial authorities, it seemed, threatened to drag all down in the wreckage of royal government.[6]

But the widening rift between provincial patriots and the Crown possessed even more direct threats for the colonial elite. Repeated prorogations and dissolutions might render the lower houses impotent, while direct taxation of Americans by Parliament could obviously make all of the colonial assemblies ''useless in a moment.'' British authorities also tried to circumvent established leaders by filling colonial offices with British placemen and by promoting the fortunes of favorably disposed factions. Neither tactic was new, but as the prerevolutionary debate intensified, the struggle increasingly assumed a triangular character. Long before war became the medium for politics, British officials vied with local elites for the allegiance of the Southern backcountry as each side sought to outdo the other with concessions. When hostilities became imminent, Tory populism culminated in a royal proclamation pardoning all but one of the North Carolina Regulators, as well as promises of rewards for influential back-

---

[5]The letter of Henry Laurens to James Grant, 1 November 1765, with extract of letter to Joseph Brown, 26 October 1765, TD 73/63, Bundle 359, Scottish Record Office, Edinburgh, was discovered by Daniel Littlefield. George C. Rogers, Jr. kindly called my attention to it. R. M. Brown, *Regulators,* 55-58.

[6]Benjamin Smith, speaker of the South Carolina Commons House, in George C. Rogers, Jr., *Evolution of a Federalist: William Laughton Smith of Charleston, 1758-1812* (Columbia: University of South Carolina Press, 1962) 46. For similar opinions, see Arthur M. Schlesinger, *The Colonial Merchants and the American Revolution, 1763-1776* (New York: Atheneum, 1968) 307-308; *South Carolina Gazette* (Charleston), 8 August 1771, reprinting materials from the *North Carolina Gazette,* 26 July 1771.

countrymen who would rally to the Crown. It is, therefore, not surprising that well before news arrived of attempts by John Murray, earl of Dunmore and governor of Virginia, to raise Virginia blacks, Whigs in the South believed that royal officials planned to instigate slave insurrections; past British policy had prepared many Americans to assume that imperial authorities would not scruple at inverting colonial society to undercut the position of provincial leaders.[7]

This abbreviated discussion by no means exhausts the ways in which imperial officials undermined the American elite on the eve of the Revolution, but it is sufficient to make the point. The tie with England had also complicated life for local leaders throughout the colonial period. Thomas Barrow has suggested part of the reason: "By its very nature, a colonial society must be, in certain vital ways, unstable. Unable to exercise complete political control, subject to continual external intervention and negative interference, a colonial society cannot . . . create and control a political system that will be suited to the requirements of the interests indigenous to that society."[8] Prior to the era of the Revolution, this fact was perhaps most evident during the late seventeenth century when imperial authorities launched a vigorous effort to tighten up the colonial system, one of the chief results of which was turmoil in the colonies. But if the Glorious Revolution enabled American politicians to free themselves from the

[7]John Joachim Zubly of Georgia in Jack P. Greene, *The Quest for Power: The Lower Houses of Assembly in the Southern Royal Colonies, 1689-1776* (Chapel Hill: University of North Carolina Press, 1963) 377; Thomas Barrow, *Trade and Empire: The British Customs Service in Colonial America, 1660-1775* (Cambridge MA: Harvard University Press, 1967) 187; M. Eugene Sirmans, "The South Carolina Royal Council, 1720-1763," *William and Mary Quarterly* 3d ser. 18 (1961): 389-90; Patricia V. Bonomi, *A Factious People: Politics and Society in Colonial New York* (New York: Columbia University Press, 1971) 265-66; Charles Woodmason, *The Carolina Backcountry on the Eve of the Revolution: The Journal and Other Writings of Charles Woodmason, Anglican Itinerant,* ed. Richard J. Hooker (Chapel Hill: University of North Carolina Press, 1953) 184; Allan J. McCurry, "The North Government and the Outbreak of the American Revolution," *Huntington Library Quarterly* 34 (1971): 154; Gary D. Olson, "Loyalists and the American Revolution: Thomas Brown and the South Carolina Backcountry, 1775-1776," *South Carolina Historical Magazine* 68 (1967): 204; John R. Alden, *The South in the Revolution, 1763-1789* (Baton Rouge: Louisiana State University Press, 1957) 194, 195, 199.

[8]Barrow, "The American Revolution as a Colonial War," 454. See also Greene, *The Quest for Power,* 453; George A. Billias, "The First Un-Americans: The Loyalists in American Historiography," in *Perspectives in Early American History,* ed. Alden T. Vaughan and George A. Billias (New York: Harper and Row, 1973) 318.

Dominion of New England, it did not provide an escape from continued attempts to curb their provincial assemblies, or from dependence upon England, nor, ultimately, from the fears that derived from that dependence. Always remote from the center of real power, they were forced to develop uncertain transatlantic connections by which they attempted to control and predict decisions in London; when these failed, as they often did, anything from the prestige of a politician to the economy of a province might suffer.[9] Throughout much of the period after 1690 an uneasy peace of mind was possible only because imperial authorities were willing to leave America alone.

The values and imperatives of British political life may have represented a greater threat to members of the American elite than the specific actions of their superiors in London. The truism that political stability and the security of an elite depend upon a consensus supporting its status caused problems for those Americans who assiduously sought to model themselves after the British upper classes. Being colonials, they frequently found metropolitan ideals unattainable. As a result, self-made men, or those (like most colonial leaders) who remained middle class by British standards, at first experienced difficulty in commanding the authority—evident in public recognition and deference—enjoyed by the English gentry.[10] Nevertheless, provincial growth and the passage of time permitted the development of a social and economic elite that appeared increasingly legitimate as the relative isolation of the colonies modified recalled values

---

[9]R. M. Brown, "The Anglo-American Political System, 1675-1775: A Behavioral Analysis," in *Anglo-American Political Relations, 1675-1775,* ed. Alison Gilbert Olson and R. M. Brown (New Brunswick NJ: Rutgers University Press, 1970) 20.

[10]Ted Robert Gurr, *Why Men Rebel* (Princeton: Princeton University Press, 1970) 137; Jack P. Greene, "Search for Identity," 205-206; Bernard Bailyn, "Politics and Social Structure in Virginia," in *Seventeenth-Century America: Essays in Colonial History,* ed. James Morton Smith (Chapel Hill: University of North Carolina Press, 1959) 94-98, 102. An analogous situation seems to have prevailed in the professions where "European ways of securing the ability to practice were unsettling. The prestige of a transatlantic education seemed to lessen the value of the colonial forms of preparation for the vocations of law and medicine." Oscar Handlin and Mary F. Handlin, *Facing Life: Youth and the Family in American History* (Boston: Little, Brown, 1971) 40. For the continuing middle-class character of the American elite, see Carl Bridenbaugh, *Myths and Realities: Societies of the Colonial South* (New York: Atheneum, 1963) 12-13; Richard Hofstadter, *America at 1750: A Social Portrait* (New York: Alfred A. Knopf, 1971) 134, 138-39; Jackson Turner Main, *The Social Structure of Revolutionary America* (Princeton: Princeton University Press, 1965) 239, 275-77.

to fit observed realities. Increasing stability was the consequence. Yet this stability depended upon a separation of the provincial and metropolitan worlds. British neglect was indeed salutary: close contact with English values might have undermined the position of the colonial elite. By the mid-eighteenth century, however, colonial economic and demographic growth prompted imperial authorities to take a more active interest in America. Soon thereafter the French and Indian War brought colonials into whole-sale contact with transient visitors from the British Isles for the first time.[11] Abrupt juxtaposition of the metropolitan culture and provincial subcultures dramatized the differences between them, and the experience appears to have been as painful for many local leaders as adolescence is for some twentieth-century youths.

II

The analogy between adolescence and the crisis of the colonial elite at mid-century is a restricted one. Provincial leaders frequently exhibited extraordinary political, cultural, and personal maturity. Nor is adolescence the only possible model for encounters between a dominant culture and the often deviant subcultures that mark its boundaries. But in this case two considerations make it appropriate. First, our theoretical understanding of the dynamics underlying such marginal cultures is most advanced in regard to those developed by juveniles; and, second, men on both sides of the prerevolutionary debate frequently turned to the parent-child relationship as a metaphor for the one between the mother country and the colonies.[12] That the analogy applied to collectivities and not to individuals does not impair its present usefulness in symbolizing the cultural relationship between the metropolis and the provinces. England provided Americans with models of behavior, standards by which success or failure could be measured, and authoritative evaluations of performance. Furthermore, if these elements made the situation of the colonial elite roughly analogous

---

[11]Although American isolation was always relative, and a reasonable case can be made for its absolute decline throughout the eighteenth century, much recent work associates stability in the colonies with increasing isolation during the first half of the period. See Clarence L. Ver Steeg, *The Formative Years, 1607-1763* (New York: Hill and Wang, 1964) 129-51; David Alan Williams, "Anglo-Virginia Politics, 1690-1735," in *Anglo-American Political Relations,* 88; Greene, "An Uneasy Connection," 65-74.

[12]Burrows and Wallace, "The American Revolution," 167-306.

to that of adolescents vis-à-vis their parents, the parallel can be carried one step further; by the middle of the eighteenth century it was becoming increasingly clear that the offspring were frequently falling short of expectations.

In modern urban societies adolescence tends to confront individuals with a dramatic juxtaposition of the hitherto relatively separate worlds of child and adult. Adolescents often find that they cannot consistently conform to norms and expectations that they at least partially share. Thus they may go through periods of great tension characterized by alternating feelings of abject worthlessness, supreme self-confidence, and ambivalence toward adult norms.[13] An adolescent may attempt to ease his tensions by seeking emotional support from a peer group within which he "is able to acquire the status often denied him in the adult world—a status which is more predictable and based upon values and expectations he understands and can fulfill." Most adolescents find only temporary sanctuary in peer-group subcultures, which usually reinforce the values of adult society; but such is not always the case. Individuals who have been rejected by members of the dominant culture may adopt values that invert those of the parent culture in a process involving a "particular kind of dynamic linkage between norms and personality: the creation of a series of inverse or counter values . . . in [the] face of serious frustration or conflict." Not infrequently, such contracultures are associated with teenage gangs; indeed, "the very existence of the gang," some students believe, "is a sign, in part, of blocked ambition. Because tensions set in motion by this blockage cannot be resolved by achievement of dominant values, such values are repressed, their importance denied, counter-values affirmed. The gang member is often ambivalent. Thwarted in his desire to achieve higher status by the criteria of the dominant society, he accepts criteria he can meet."[14]

[13]John Demos and Virginia Demos, "Adolescence in Historical Perspective," *Journal of Marriage and the Family* 31 (1969): 637; Paul A. Osterrieth, "Adolescence: Some Psychological Aspects," and Fritz Redl, "Adolescents—Just How Do They React?" in *Adolescence: Psychosocial Perspectives,* ed. Gerald Caplan and Serge Lebovici (New York: Basic Books, 1969) 17, 82.

[14]Bernard C. Rosen, "Conflicting Group Membership: A Study of Parent-Peer Group Cross-Pressures," *American Sociological Review* 20 (1955): 161; Redl, "Adolescents— Just How Do They React?" 83; Denise B. Kandel and Gerald S. Lesser, *Youth in Two Worlds: United States and Denmark* (San Francisco: Jossey-Bass, 1972) 168, 185; J. Milton Yinger, "Contraculture and Subculture," *American Sociological Review* 25 (1960): 627, 632.

The findings of the behavioral sciences permit us to isolate the following elements in the development of a rebellious contraculture: (1) attempts to conform to the norms of the dominant culture; (2) assessment of these attempts as unsuccessful and rejection by authority figures of those who make them; (3) tension, an unstable self-image, and ambivalence toward the dominant culture on the part of the rejected; (4) increasing reliance on their fellow "outcasts" for emotional support and status; (5) the concomitant affirmation of attainable norms and values that provide a means of relieving the psychological tension and achieving social status within the deviant group.

Although early American elites were not composed of juvenile delinquents, the purpose of the preceding discussion is to suggest that the two categories share *some* significant similarities. In particular, members of each characteristically appear to have sought to conform to the norms of a dominant society whose authority figures rejected them. Americans believed that "in crossing the Atlantic Ocean, we have only changed our climate, not our minds, our natures and dispositions remain unaltered"[15]— that is, they clearly assumed that they retained all the rights, virtues, and other essential attributes of Englishmen. Just as plainly after mid-century, however, British policy often appeared to be predicated upon the assumption that Americans represented a lesser breed without the law.

The French and Indian War first brought this fact home in the attitude expressed by General James Wolfe, who wrote that "the Americans are in general the dirtiest, most contemptible, cowardly dogs that you can conceive." A "New Englandman" reported the results: "Unhappy *provincials!* If *success* attends where you are joined with the regulars, they claim all the honour, tho' not a tenth part of your number. If *disgrace,* it is all yours, though you happen to be but a small part of the whole, and have not the command." The last point was a particularly tender one with the American elite, for Crown officials drew an invidious distinction between regular and provincial officers. The former, they believed, were competent to command both kinds of forces; the latter were not. Although imperial authorities soon sought American cooperation by more equal treatment, their concessions were too halfhearted to be entirely effective, and friction persisted over the status of regulars and Loyalists in the British

---

[15]George Mason of Virginia to the Committee of London Merchants, 6 June 1766, in *Prologue to Revolution: Sources and Documents on the Stamp Act Crisis, 1764-1766,* ed. Edmund S. Morgan (Chapel Hill: University of North Carolina Press, 1959) 160.

Army during the Revolution.[16] That British officers serving under Cornwallis abused and physically mistreated Loyalist militiamen reveals how
difficult it was for Englishmen to divest themselves of the notion that
Americans were inferior upstarts. Even the most deserving could not escape the stigma of their origin. Thus Richard Davis, a baker who had gone
to Georgia where he became a minor official, found that the commission
established to consider Loyalist claims not only denied him compensation
for the loss of his offices, but also expected him to resume his trade as a
baker. In short, a maxim coined by a British officer during the French and
Indian War symbolized the perennial problem of American leaders who
sought recognition of their status: "A planter is not to be taken from the
plough and made an officer in a day." Given prevailing English assumptions, he might have added, nor in many days.[17]

These assumptions spilled over into adjacent areas as well. British authorities were reluctant to grant colonial judges tenure for good behavior.
Although other considerations were involved, this policy was in part predicated upon—and justified by—the belief that colonials lacked the professional competence of their British counterparts. However realistic this
notion was, it unmistakably implied that the American political elite was
qualified to rule only in the absence of men possessing genuine qualifications. The appointment of British placemen to colonial office in response to the exigencies of imperial patronage and a desire for pliant
subordinates conveyed the same message. Prior to mid-century, appointment to the royal councils had been the capstone of an individual's social
and political ascent: it represented the formal recognition—the legitimi-
zation—of his claims to elite status. The changing pattern of preferment
robbed the position of its significance, particularly in South Carolina where
natives already on the council actually began resigning after 1756. More-

---

[16]Wolfe to Lord George Sackville [July 1758], *Report on the Manuscripts of Mrs. Stop-
ford-Sackville,* Historical Manuscripts Commission, Fifteenth Report, Appendix 15 (London: His Majesty's Stationery Office, 1910) 2:266; *The Gentleman's Magazine* 29 (1759):
224; Douglas Edward Leach, *Arms for Empire: A Military History of the British Colonies
in North America, 1607-1763* (New York: Macmillan Co., 1973) 354-55; William B. Will-
cox, *Portrait of a General: Sir Henry Clinton in the War Of Independence* (New York:
Alfred A. Knopf, 1962) 285-86.

[17]Charles Stedman, *The History of the Origin, Progress and Termination of the American War,* 2 vols. (Dublin, Ireland: Wogan and Byrne, 1794) 2:225; Wallace Brown, *The
Good Americans: The Loyalists in the American Revolution* (New York: William Morrow,
1969) 187; *Gentleman's Magazine* 29 (1759): 173.

over, to add insult to injury, Scotsmen figured prominently among the placemen, though Scotland was in many ways as provincial as America. Its inhabitants, especially those willing to seek their fortunes in the colonies, scarcely possessed more of the traditional qualifications for political leadership than Americans, and jealousy doubtlessly contributed to the hostility Scotsmen encountered in America. Certainly, the conspicuousness of fortune hunters, racketeers, and incompetents among royal officeholders seemed to indicate that in the estimation of imperial authorities even the refuse of "greater" Britain was more qualified to govern America than the members of its native elite.[18]

Only men who felt that they had been snubbed could have adopted such an extreme view, but many obviously believed that they had been unfairly deprived of deserved rewards. Furthermore, they recognized that such deprivation could undermine their local status. Certainly, British-born officeholders and other recent immigrants took pains to remind Americans that their native elite deserved little respect when measured against British standards. Thus Charles Woodmason, an Anglican itinerant minister in the Carolina backcountry, contemptuously outlined the career of Rawlins Lowndes: "He was originally a Parish Orphan Boy, nor knows his own Origin—Taken from the Dunghill by our late Provost Marshal—Made his Valet—then learn'd to read and write—Then became Gaoler—Then Provost Marshal—Got Money—Married Well—Settled Plantations—became a Planter—A Magistrate—A Senator—Speaker of the House and now Cheif [sic] Judge." What was true for Lowndes was also true for most other local leaders, Woodmason noted. The "illegitimate" character of their origins called into question their capacity to govern. As Robert Wells, a Scots newspaper publisher and bookseller in Charleston, said in 1765, "I wish to be under the direction of the British Parliament and not our little Provincial Senate aping the grandest Assembly in the World without Knowledge, skill, power or any other requisite almost."[19]

---

[18]Bernard Knollenberg, *Origin of the American Revolution, 1759-1766,* rev. ed. (New York: Free Press, 1965) 73; Henretta, *"Salutary Neglect,"* 130-34; Sirmans, "The South Carolina Royal Council," 389-90; John Clive and Bernard Bailyn, "England's Cultural Provinces: Scotland and America," *William and Mary Quarterly* 3d ser. 11 (1954): 200-13.

[19]For the effects of relative deprivation, see Gurr, *Why Men Rebel;* Woodmason, *Carolina Backcountry on the Eve of the Revolution,* 269, 273; Robert Wells to [?], 13 August 1765, South Carolina Miscellaneous, Box 1, New York Public Library, New York.

Such scornful rejection of their attempts to adopt British models contributed to an unstable self-image among members of the provincial elite. At one extreme, their self-confidence suffered. In South Carolina Lieutenant Governor William Bull reported in 1770 that fortunes were moderate, educated men rare, and the ''Arts and Sciences'' utilitarian. His words betray a pervasive feeling of colonial inferiority that at times undermined the actual performance of local leaders. Being men of lay education, provincial judges were often reluctant to exert their authority, Bull noted, because they felt ''great mortification and timidity from a sense of their being not well acquainted with their power and their duty.'' In 1774 John Adams vividly expressed the emotional state that could accompany this sense of inferiority: ''I muse, I mope, I ruminate.—I am often In Reveries and Brown Studies.—The Objects before me, are too grand, and multifarious for my Comprehension.—We have not Men, fit for the Times. We are deficient in Genius, in Education, in Travel, in Fortune—in every Thing. I feel unutterable Anxiety.''[20] Given such a crisis of confidence on the part of colonial leaders, it is understandable that on the eve of the Revolution American society seemed to be sadly deficient.

At the other extreme, American leaders compensated for their feelings of inferiority by moments of exaggerated praise of self and denigration of others. Burgeoning economic and demographic growth, colonials believed, made America the most important part of the empire; indeed, some thought, only its existence conferred the imperial title upon Great Britain. Thus Adams could later remember Colonel James Otis: ''Our English cousins by Adam and Eve may laugh at our uneducated sages and heroes; but what then?'' His foresight ''was as sure and his bravery as great and his education as classical, for anything that I know, as the Duke of Marlborough's.'' Claiming moral superiority, Americans also contrasted their own pure and virtuous political practices with a conception of British corruption resembling that of the eccentric baron who eventually asserted that ''no one . . . has seen *real life,* or can know it, unless he has taken an active part in a contested election for Westminster.'' There he could find ''human nature in her basest attire; riot, murder, and drunkenness are the order of the day, and bribery and perjury walk hand in hand.'' Colonials

---

[20]William Bull to Lord Hillsborough, 30 November, 5 December 1770, Trans., S.C., 32:392, 410, SCDAH; *Diary and Autobiography of John Adams,* ed. L. H. Butterfield, 4 vols. (Cambridge MA: Belknap Press of Harvard University Press, 1962) 2:97.

also considered the often-noted proliferation of "luxury" in Britain to be a certain sign of moral decline.[21]

But by the late 1760s many Americans feared that they too might fall prey to the same vices. To be sure, jeremiads by the dissenting ministry had always made it difficult to overlook the pell-mell pursuit of gain, but renewed attention to an old phenomenon may have arisen partly because "luxury" was coming to symbolize the ambivalence of mid-eighteenth-century Americans. Although many had feared that an English education might make them discontented with their lot, others like Benjamin Franklin, Arthur Lee, and Ralph Izard succumbed to the attractions of London and preferred to live abroad. As John Shy suggests, a considerable number of Americans—including Adams—appear to have experienced difficulty "in distinguishing between urbanity and debauchery" among British army officers. Ambivalence toward English and Englishmen reflected the ambiguities under which colonials labored. If the specter of their own depravity helped to make them British, its exorcism would ultimately help to make them American.[22]

British authorities might have relieved some of the tension caused by these mass ambivalencies by recognizing—and institutionalizing—the status of the colonial elite. According to a wide range of contemporary observers, to have done so at the proper time would have bolstered the self-confidence of the American upper class, consolidated its position of leadership within the colonies, and reinforced its loyalty to the empire. Al-

---

[21]Richard Koebner, *Empire* (New York: Grosset and Dunlap, 1965) 86, 89, 118; John A. Schutz and Douglass Adair, eds., *The Spur of Fame: Dialogues of John Adams and Benjamin Rush, 1805-1813* (San Marino CA: Huntington Library, 1966) 256; Bernard Bailyn, *The Ideological Origins of the American Revolution* (Cambridge MA: Belknap Press of Harvard University Press, 1967) 34-54; George Hanger, *The Life, Adventures, and Opinions of Colonel George Hanger, Written by Himself,* 2 vols. (London: J. Debrett, 1801) 2:452-53.

[22]Edmund S. Morgan, "The Puritan Ethic and the American Revolution," *William and Mary Quarterly* 3d ser. 24 (1967): 3-18; Jack P. Greene, *Landon Carter: An Inquiry into the Personal Values and Social Imperatives of the Eighteenth-Century Virginia Gentry* (Charlottesville: University Press of Virginia, 1967) 36, 55; Lawrence A. Cremin, *American Education: The Colonial Experience, 1607-1783* (New York: Harper and Row, 1970) 475-76; William L. Sachse, *The Colonial American in Britain* (Madison: University of Wisconsin Press, 1956) 16-31, 68, 154, 201-203; John Shy, *Toward Lexington: The Role of the British Army in the Coming of the American Revolution* (Princeton: Princeton University Press, 1965) 385.

though these beliefs produced some baronetcies for imperial officials, several schemes to create a colonial nobility, and many recommendations that royal councillors be appointed for life,[23] individuals as diverse as Joseph Galloway and Josiah Quincy, Jr. realized that such measures required wider implementation to be effective.

Galloway, a Loyalist who had been speaker of the Pennsylvania Assembly, drew a lesson from ancient history. Perceiving colonials "as an inferior class of mortals," Romans began depriving them of the possibility of sharing "in the emoluments, honours, or dignities of office." Until the policy changed, revolts were endemic to the Roman colonies. The Roman experience, he concluded, strongly suggested the desirability of removing "as much as possible, all distinction in respect to power, rights and privileges, which have too long subsisted between a subject in Britain and one in America." Quincy, an American patriot from Massachusetts who visited South Carolina in 1773, was even more explicit on the subject. "At present," he noted, "the house of Assembly are staunch Colonists. But what is it owing to? Bad policy on the other side of the water." Suppose, he asked, British officials were to "compose the Council of the first planters, fill all the Public offices with them, give them the honours of the State, . . . introduce Baronies and Lordships—their enormous estates will bear it—and what will become of Carolinian freedom?" The answer, he implied, could be found in the complaints of several planters whom he heard say "none of us, when we grow old, can expect the honours of the State— they are all given away to worthless poor rascals."[24] Although he seems to have underestimated the scope of discontent among South Carolinians,

---

[23]Edmund S. Morgan and Helen M. Morgan, *The Stamp Act Crisis: Prologue to Revolution,* rev. ed. (New York: Collier, 1963) 35; Sir Egerton Leigh, "Considerations on Certain Political Transactions of the Province of South Carolina," in *The Nature of Colony Constitutions: Two Pamphlets on the Wilkes Fund Controversy in South Carolina by Sir Egerton Leigh and Arthur Lee,* ed. Jack P. Greene (Columbia: University of South Carolina Press, 1970) 113; Leonard Woods Labaree, *Conservatism in Early American History* (New York: New York University Press, 1948) 135-36; Anthony Stokes, *A View of the Constitution of the British Colonies* (1783; London: Dawsons, 1969) 137-38.

[24]Joseph Galloway, *History and Political Reflections on the Rise and Progress of the American Rebellion* (1780; rpt., New York: Johnson Reprint, 1972) 112-13, 124-25; Ronald Syme, *Colonial Elites: Rome, Spain, and the Americas* (London: Oxford University Press, 1958) 5, 12; Josiah Quincy, Jr., "Journal of Josiah Quincy, Jr., 1773," ed. Mark A. DeWolfe Howe, Massachusetts Historical Society, *Proceedings* 49 (1915-1916): 454-55.

Quincy clearly understood one of its important elements, and there can be no doubt that William Henry Drayton's lust for Crown office was conspicuous enough to give reasonable grounds for attributing his later rebelliousness to the effect of thwarted ambition. Nor was the desire for such recognition limited to Carolinians. George Washington himself remained loyal to the Fairfax family throughout the Revolution, apparently in part because the baron had helped to legitimize all of the local gentry by residing in Virginia; and Richard Henry Lee persistently—though futilely—sought appointment to the royal council.[25]

III

Receiving less than token recognition from imperial authorities, members of the colonial elite turned to their own kind for reinforcement and validation. In the process they developed what can legitimately be termed a contraculture. By mid-century their attention, as revealed in the colonial press, was increasingly focused upon themselves and those like them, their fellow colonials. Shared problems and feelings of rejection gave them a sense of common identity that would ultimately provide a basis for national unity. Ironically, it was also their real but limited success in imitating British models that enabled American leaders to share the fellowship of failure. As John Murrin has put it, "each colony had to become self-consciously more English before collectively they could all become American." That is to say, they became conscious of belonging to a common subculture before their growing estrangement from Britain transformed that subculture into a contraculture. Traveling the road of increasing alienation together, they developed a sense of group loyalty not unlike that of other marginal groups. Although perhaps apocryphal, the remark attributed to the septuagenarian Franklin upon adoption of the Declaration of Independence, that "we must all hang together, or most assuredly we shall all hang separately," has something characteristically boyish about it. So does the

---

[25]William M. Dabney and Marion Dargan, *William Henry Drayton and the American Revolution* (Albuquerque: University of New Mexico Press, 1962) 57-58. For Fairfax's role, see Rowland Berthoff and John M. Murrin, "Feudalism, Communalism, and the Yeoman Freeholder: The American Revolution Considered as a Social Accident," in *Essays on the American Revolution,* 270. Lee to James Abercrombie, Thomas Cummings, and William Lee, 27 August 1762, 9 July 1770, in *The Letters of Richard Henry Lee,* ed. James Curtis Ballagh, 2 vols. (New York: Macmillan Co., 1911) 1:1-3, 52.

comradery of war as remembered by Sergeant Joseph Martin: "The soldiery . . . were as strict a band of brotherhood as Masons, and I believe as
faithful to each other." That their leaders shared the same feeling is one
of the reasons that they were able to call a convention, and draft and secure
adoption of the Federal Constitution. But if the esprit exhibited by the young
men of the Revolution is reminiscent of the behavior of some youthful
groups, so too was the patriots' treatment of Loyalists; tar and feathers were
the visible marks by which a larger clique ostracized nonconformists.[26]

Because those who failed to go along with the changing mores cast
doubt upon the morality of the enterprise, their presence was especially
disquieting. Psychological pressures, as well as political considerations,
hence dictated that deviants leave, remain silent, or be converted. Con-
version was the most reassuring, for it affirmed the rectitude of group behavior. Thus the extraordinary leniency that the rebel elite often exhibited
toward those who might yet see the light is as understandable as the occasional harshness toward the unreconstructed. The questions that the
committees of safety in Massachusetts put to a suspected Tory were usually "designed to extricate him from 'suspicions and jealousies' ''; the object was not so much to discover Loyalists as it was to "persuade suspected
opponents of resistance [to Britain] to endorse a body of principles that
united them with the rest of the community." Moreover, the principles that
increasingly provided the rationale for the existence and behavior of the
group demanded the adherence of all, as American revolutionaries justified their actions by appeals to the authority of the people; group approval
became the standard by which actions were judged.[27] Increasingly, solidarity necessitated a conscious affirmation of indigenous substitutes for
British values. Thus, whatever else it was, the American Revolution became a normative revolution that fashioned new standards of legitimacy.

---

[26]Richard L. Merritt, "The Colonists Discover America: Attention Patterns in the Co-
lonial Press, 1735-1775," *William and Mary Quarterly* 3d ser. 21 (1964): 270-87; Murrin,
"The Myths of Colonial Democracy and Royal Decline in Eighteenth-Century America:
A Review Essay," *Cithara* 5 (1965): 65; Carl Van Doren, *Benjamin Franklin* (New York:
Viking, 1957) 551-52; George F. Scheer and Hugh F. Rankin, *Rebels and Redcoats*
(Cleveland: World, 1957) 503; Stanley M. Elkins and Eric L. McKitrick, "The Founding
Fathers: Young Men of the Revolution," *Political Science Quarterly* 76 (1961): 181-216.

[27]Calhoon, *Loyalists in Revolutionary America,* 302; Gordon Wood, *The Creation of
the American Republic, 1776-1787* (Chapel Hill: University of North Carolina Press, 1969)
329, 363, 375.

The change took time. Conditioned by the notion that specific British measures were illicit, Americans found it relatively easy to brand them as subversive. Significantly, the Declaration of Independence charged not merely that the actions of the Crown had been illegal, but also that they had made good government—in fact, any government—impossible; having dissolved colonial assemblies and having delayed the election of their replacements, royal authorities had exposed the colonies "to all the dangers of invasion from without, and convulsions within." But accustomed to regarding English cultural values as authoritative, the colonists found it more difficult to recognize that norms might be as subversive as measures. Yet both the popularity of radical British thinkers long before the Revolution and the growing mistrust of English education reveal an increasingly conscious rejection of dominant English values. Perhaps a suspicion that Britain was responsible for much of the turmoil in American society helped to induce the rage that made Americans respond so positively to Paine's *Common Sense*. Certainly, by reversing earlier presumptions about politics, and by rejecting the entire concept of monarchy, he implicitly urged them to shed the burden of values that had plagued them as colonials and "to begin the world over again." By the time of the Constitutional Convention Charles Pinckney could voice what many of his contemporaries had come to understand. "We have, " he declared, "unwisely considered ourselves as the inhabitants of an old instead of a new country. . . . No two people are so exactly alike in their situation or circumstances as to admit the exercise of the same Government with equal benefit: . . . a system must be suited to the habits and genius of the people it is to govern, and must grow out of them."[28]

That it took more than 150 years of colonial experience and a revolution to confirm this insight, as well as at least another half century to realize many of its implications, suggests that the process by which Americans came to terms with the conditions of the New World was lengthy and painful. The optimism, the visions of boundless possibilities that came with the Revolution itself, were the result both of the cathartic effect of rebellion and the relief of liberation from unattainable standards. That long, figur-

---

[28]Bailyn, *"Common Sense,"* 14-15; Thomas Paine, *Common Sense and the Crisis* (Garden City: Doubleday, 1960) 59; Pinckney, Debate on Representation, 25 June 1787, in *Confederation and Constitution, 1781-1789,* ed. Forrest McDonald and Ellen Shapiro McDonald (Columbia: University of South Carolina Press, 1968) 148-49.

ative moment when Americans looked about them, blinked, and decided
that those deviations from British practices which they had formerly considered badges of inferiority were in reality signs of superiority was one of
the central climaxes of the Revolution.[29]

At the center of the new legitimacy was the espousal of republicanism.
In some ways the most radical of all revolutionary innovations, it was also
one of the most conservative. For republican governments and republican
ideology ratified American conditions. Many Loyalists and imperial officials had long suspected that the colonists were "republican in . . . Government" before the Revolution, and modern historians have agreed.
"Once the colonists had opted for independence there simply was no other
available alternative."[30] For Americans, accepting this fact was one of the
first steps in accepting themselves. Despite long habituation to decrying
endemic factionalism and political partisanship, some men soon came to
realize that competition between factions might safeguard liberty and that
an opposition party might be to a republic what a House of Commons was
to a monarchy, a check upon the executive. Only sporadically foreshad-
owed earlier in the eighteenth century, and somewhat more commonly articulated in the 1780s, such ideas nevertheless became increasingly
dominant in the period between publication of Madison's tenth *Federalist*
and the rationalization of party behavior that occurred in the group around
Martin Van Buren. Webster's attempt to establish American English was
part of the same process. So too was Emerson's American Scholar: aspiring young men should realize, he claimed, "that if the single man plant
himself indomitably on his instincts, and there abide, the huge world will
come round to him." And that, many of his followers believed, is pre-

---

[29]Bernard Bailyn, "The Central Themes of the Revolution: An Interpretation," *Essays
on the American Revolution,* 19-20; Bernard Bailyn, "Political Experience and Enlightenment Ideas in Eighteenth-Century America," *American Historical Review* 67 (1962): 349-
51.

[30]Cecelia M. Kenyon, "Republicanism and Radicalism in the American Revolution:
An Old-Fashioned Interpretation," *William and Mary Quarterly* 3d ser. 19 (1962): 153-
82; Robert E. Shalhope, "Toward a Republican Synthesis: The Emergence of an Understanding of Republicanism in American Historiography," *William and Mary Quarterly* 29
(1972): 49-80. Charles Martyn to Bishop of London, 20 October 1765, Fulham Palace
Manuscripts, No. 230, Microfilm, Library of Congress; Jack P. Greene, "The Preconditions for American Republicanism: A Comment," in *The Development of a Revolutionary
Mentality* (Washington: Library of Congress, 1972) 120.

cisely what Old Hickory did. By the 1830s American leaders could thus feel reasonably confident that they would be judged by indigenous criteria.[31]

What this last point suggests is that in developing a contraculture that inverted many traditional British norms, Americans traded the habit of deference for standards of leadership that they could meet. Although deference to the elite was the accepted norm during the colonial period, it was not always easy to recognize one's betters in a society that, by English standards, was essentially middle class. Only the ignorance of isolation could perpetuate the illusion that the colonial elite was qualified to rule by virtue of its social status. Closer contact with Britain undermined the illusion. Thus the Revolution involved a crisis of legitimacy for the personnel as well as for the institutions and actions of government. If, as was increasingly clear, American leaders were not very different from those they led, what then was to clothe these ordinary mortals with sufficient authority to discharge their responsibilities? One of them, John Rutledge, understood the most important part of the answer as early as 1774. Noting that the members of the First Continental Congress possessed "no legal Authority," he observed that obedience to their decisions would only follow the "reasonableness, the apparent Utility, and Necessity of the Measures" adopted.[32]

The dilemma of the Continental Congress represented the larger dilemma of the colonial and revolutionary elite. Shorn of the traditional attributes of leadership, they had to justify their position by other means.

---

[31]Bailyn, *Origins of American Politics*, 125-30; Pauline Maier, "The Charleston Mob and the Evolution of Popular Politics in Revolutionary South Carolina, 1765-1784," *Perspectives in American History* 4 (1970): 192-96; Wood, *Creation of the American Republic*, 503, 608; Hofstadter, *The Idea of a Party System: The Rise of Legitimate Opposition in the United States, 1780-1840* (Berkeley and Los Angeles: University of California Press, 1970) 35-39, 251-52; Ralph Waldo Emerson, *Selections from Ralph Waldo Emerson: An Organic Anthology,* ed. Stephen E. Whicher (Boston: Houghton Mifflin, 1957) 79; John William Ward, *Andrew Jackson, Symbol for an Age* (New York: Oxford University Press, 1962) 211-12. Although one result of the Revolution was an increased willingness on the part of Americans to come to terms with their collective existence, what was accepted differed with variations in local circumstances. The paragraph above sketches some broad outlines of a general trend in most of the nation; the specific peculiarities of South Carolina are reserved for detailed examination elsewhere.

[32]Bailyn, "Political Experience and Enlightenment Ideas," 349; Butterfield, ed., *Diary and Autobiography of John Adams,* 2:125.

Local leaders turned to the sovereign people and found that popular approval supported their position more reliably than all of the traditional trappings of authority. Thus, despite the turmoil of the revolutionary era and the erosion of deference that it produced, the native political elite—that is, the *category* of men occupying positions of leadership—finished the Revolution with its credentials more securely established than ever before. Membership in the category changed as new men sought and attained political office; new demands for greater responsiveness confronted older leaders; and new ideas gradually undermined the very notion of leadership by a social and economic elite. In the long run these developments posed an even greater challenge to the members of the old colonial elites and their descendants than that previously engendered by the British connection, and the fate of these specific groups varied widely in different parts of America. But the Revolution helped to insure that performance and conformity to norms within reach, not ascriptive status based on unattainable values, would henceforth provide the criteria for leadership in the developing contraculture. The American Revolution could therefore involve "fundamental changes in norms and values" but surprisingly little disruption of the existing society.[33] To a remarkable degree, in fact, it represented a confirmation rather than a repudiation of the previous 150 years of American social development.

IV

In closing it is worthwhile to say something about the scope of the present hypothesis. This essay has suggested not only that Gordon Wood was correct in surmising that most of the colonies "were experiencing their own forms of social strain that . . . sought mitigation through revolution and republicanism," but also that insights derived from the behavioral study of marginal groups can help to alert historians to the nature of the process.[34] From this perspective, it is apparent that the imperial connection created discrepancies between expectations and reality that contributed to the instability of colonial politics and to the emotional background of re-

---

[33]Isaac Kramnick, "Reflections on Revolution: Definition and Explanation in Recent Scholarship," *History and Theory* 11 (1972): 31, 34.

[34]Wood, "Rhetoric and Reality," 30.

bellion; that the Revolution itself helped to narrow the gap; and that the increasing correspondence between values and reality played an important part in securing the Revolution's achievements. To contend that the position of the indigenous elite was intimately associated with each of the developments is not to claim that other aspects of the situation were unimportant; nor is it to overlook wide variations in the behavior of individuals who composed the differing local elites. No doubt, too, circumstances in South Carolina represented a unique combination of pride and insecurity. There members of the indigenous elite were both nouveaux and exceptionally riche, and consequently they may have been especially sensitive to questions of status and legitimacy. Furthermore, the extraordinary extent to which British placemen eventually dominated royal offices there made the threat to the native elite unusually tangible and overt. Nevertheless, these considerations do not limit the hypothesis. Ireland seemed to be an ominous portent for all of the American elite. As John Dickinson put it, "Almost all of the *offices* in that poor kingdom . . . now are bestowed upon *strangers.*" In like manner, he continued, "Shall we unquestionably be treated, as soon as the late taxes laid upon us, shall make posts in the 'government' . . . *here,* worth the attention of persons of influence in *Great-Britain.*" Nor were South Carolinians alone in their reaction to British attitudes associated with such policies. Pride was the "bosom passion" of most Americans, an observer remarked in 1783, and any ambassador to them ought to be a "man of rank" who would "stoop to conquer."[35] Finally, it should be noted that nothing in the present argument is meant to imply that frustration, rage, and the ultimate rejection of unattainable values represented unreasonable or childish responses.[36] The analogy be-

---

[35]Bridenbaugh, *Myths and Realities,* 67, 116-17; Martin, *Men in Rebellion,* 50, 109, 115-17; Owen Dudley Edwards, "The American Image of Ireland: A Study of Its Early Phases," *Perspectives in American History* 4 (1970): 199-282; "Letters from a Farmer in Pennsylvania," in *The Political Writings of John Dickinson, 1764-1774,* ed. Paul Leister Ford (New York: DaCapo, 1970) 378, 380; F. Michaelis to Major Beckwith, 4 October 1783, *Report on American Manuscripts in the Royal Institution of Great Britain,* Historical Manuscripts Commission, Fifteenth Report, Appendix 28 (London: His Majesty's Stationery Office, 1909) 4:396.

[36]Loyalists were apt to view the Revolution in such terms. But if Peter Oliver oversimplified matters in attributing the rebellion to the "Pride, Ambition, and Resentment" of its leaders, his point is nevertheless sufficiently relevant to the present hypothesis to raise the question of why a revolutionary elite, whose rebelliousness was associated with doubts about

tween the behavior of adolescents and the founding fathers is little more than a convenient metaphor for illustrating the dilemma that confronts a subcultural elite that seeks to emulate the models of a dominant or established culture.

The analogy has wider applications. If the American Revolution represents the flood tide of a long period of creative provincialism during which Americans—like adolescents developing a contraculture—inverted the traditional values of their parent culture, it is reasonable to suppose that a better understanding of our own origins as a nation can enhance our comprehension of modern protest movements. Conversely, insights from the study of deviant groups may help us to be more perceptive in dealing with the history not only of the Revolution in America, but also of other revolutions elsewhere. There can be no question that the failure of metropolitan authorities to recognize and support local elites provided part of the background for revolt in Roman antiquity, early modern Europe, and Latin America, as well as in the British colonies.[37] Whether these apparently disparate rebellions can be subsumed under a single set of generalizations must await more study. But if we follow Zagorin's suggestion that historians should seek "to clarify the different types of revolution and to develop a model of the causal process of each type," we may discover, without denying the complexities, the ambiguities, and the idealism of the American Revolution—or of any revolution—that with some modifications Carl Becker's famous insight of nearly seventy years ago was on the right track:

---

its legitimacy, could command as much loyalty as it did. One answer implied in this paper is that resisting measures believed to be oppressive, helped to sanction the position of local leaders whose performance presumptively demonstrated concern for the public welfare and a capacity to discharge their responsibilities. See *Peter Oliver's Origin and Progress of the American Rebellion: A Tory View,* ed. Douglass Adair and John A. Schutz (Stanford CA: Stanford University Press, 1961) 145.

[37]Robert Forster and Jack P. Greene, eds., *Preconditions of Revolution in Early Modern Europe* (Baltimore: Johns Hopkins University Press, 1970) 6, 13; Syme, *Colonial Elites,* 38-39; Mark A. Burkholder, "From Creole to Peninsular: The Transformation of the Audiencia of Lima," *Hispanic American Historical Review* 52 (1972): 395-415; Leon G. Campbell, "A Colonial Establishment: Creole Domination of the Audiencia of Lima during the Late Eighteenth Century," ibid., 20.

there is indeed a type of revolution in which the question of who shall rule at home creates anxieties that predispose subcultural elites to raise the question of home rule.[38]

---

[38]Perez Zagorin, "Theories of Revolution in Contemporary Historiography," *Political Science Quarterly* 88 (1973): 52; Carl Lotus Becker, *The History of Political Parties in the Province of New York, 1760-1776* (1909; rpt., Madison: University of Wisconsin Press, 1960) 22.

John Laurens:
Portrait of a Hero _____

If American leaders in general had trouble meeting British standards, John Laurens in particular had difficulty meeting his own imperatives. Nevertheless, his efforts helped to make him an appealing and illuminating figure whose dilemma reveals something about his culture as well as himself. This essay was originally given in 1974 as a lecture sponsored by the Lucy Hampton Bostick Foundation and the Institute for Southern Studies at the University of South Carolina. Revised in the light of comments by the audience, the work was published in American Heritage 27 *(April 1976): 16-19, 86-88, from which it is reprinted with permission.*

How a nation regards its past is itself a fact of considerable historical significance, and it will be interesting to observe the treatment of the founding fathers during the Bicentennial celebration. Indications are that in some quarters at least the military heroes of the Revolution may not fare very well. "They wrote in the old days," Ernest Hemingway noted some years ago, "that it is sweet and fitting to die for one's country. But in modern war there is nothing sweet nor fitting in your dying. You will die like a dog for no good reason." To men who have experienced the agony and frustration of American involvement in Vietnam—in fact, to virtually anyone who seriously considers the possibility of nuclear annihilation—that statement has to make a good deal of sense. Clearly, however, it does not represent the spirit with which some of our predecessors fought the Revolution, least of all John Laurens.

Personally one of the most attractive figures of his generation, John was born in South Carolina in 1754, the son of Henry Laurens, a leading local politician and merchant who eventually became president of the Continental Congress. John received a cosmopolitan education in Charleston, Geneva, and London, where he was enrolled at the Middle Temple. Though impatient to return to America at the outbreak of the Revolution, he remained in England because of his father's desires until January 1777, when he sailed for South Carolina. There he joined the Continental Army, in which he served throughout most of the war. He fought in the Battle of Brandywine, was wounded at Germantown, and spent the winter of 1777-1778 at Valley Forge on Washington's staff. At Monmouth the following summer he escaped unscathed when his horse was shot from under him. A duel followed with General Charles Lee, who had reflected uncharitably upon Washington's fitness to command. Laurens drew praise as well as blood from his antagonist. Meanwhile, during the late summer of 1778, he had served as a liaison officer between the French and American commands during the joint attack on Rhode Island. His linguistic ability made him popular with the French officers and useful to Washington, who spoke no French at all.[1]

Nevertheless, Laurens was able to prevail upon his commander to send him back to South Carolina, where he hoped to raise and lead a regiment of blacks against the British in the South. Although the South Carolina legislature failed to approve his plan, he remained to help defend his native state against British incursions from Georgia. Unsuccessfully attempting to check General Augustine Prevost's forces near the Savannah River, he was again severely wounded. Less than two weeks later, when Prevost's rapid progress brought him to the fortifications of Charleston, Laurens was up and about and was one of the firmest advocates for continued resistance. This time the city held out. Then some four months later, when American and French forces attempted to oust the British from Savannah, Laurens was again present in an important role. Courage, however, proved insufficient to take the city or to defend Charleston against Sir Henry Clinton's massive assault the following year. So John Laurens, along with more than five thousand of his fellow Americans, was captured on 12 May 1780.

---

[1]David D. Wallace, *The Life of Henry Laurens, with a Sketch of the Life of Lieutenant-Colonel John Laurens* (New York: G. P. Putnam's Sons, 1915) 463-64, 471-73; John R. Alden, *General Charles Lee: Traitor or Patriot?* (Baton Rouge: Louisiana State University Press, 1951) 262-64; John C. Miller, *Alexander Hamilton: Portrait in Paradox* (New York: Harper and Row, 1959) 67.

Unlike most of them, though, he was soon exchanged for a British prisoner and was therefore free to accept an assignment from the Continental Congress as special envoy to France. There, in the spring of 1781, his persistence and up-to-date information about the military situation in America helped to pry loose some two million dollars in French aid promised, but not yet delivered, to Benjamin Franklin.[2]

Returning to Boston with the supplies and cash, Laurens rejoined Washington's army in time to take part in the capture of Cornwallis's forces at Yorktown. There he again distinguished himself for heroism in the famous bayonet assault commanded by Alexander Hamilton. Later he also had the satisfaction of conveying Washington's demands for Cornwallis's surrender under terms identical to those that Clinton had imposed upon the garrison of Charleston. Then serving as the officer in charge of prisoners, Laurens doubtlessly discovered a grim pleasure in receiving Lord Cornwallis, who was technically the constable of the Tower of London, where Laurens's own father was still imprisoned after being captured on a diplomatic mission to Holland. Appropriately enough, too, Cornwallis was exchanged for Henry Laurens.[3]

But this was after John had gone back to serve under Nathanael Greene in South Carolina, where, having lived through so much, he met his death in one of the last skirmishes of the war. Although Yorktown had made it clear that the British would end hostilities, neither Greene nor the governor of South Carolina wished to risk prolonging the occupation of Charleston by agreeing to a truce that would have permitted the garrison to draw supplies from the surrounding countryside. In turn, British expeditions sought to gather rice by force. Although the details of the reports differ, it is clear that Laurens was killed in an engagement on 27 August 1782, trying to

---

[2]William Gilmore Simms, "Memoir of John Laurens," in *The Army Correspondence of Col. John Laurens in the Years 1777-8 . . . from Original Letters Addressed to His Father, Henry Laurens, President of Congress,* ed. William Gilmore Simms (New York: Bradford Club, 1867) 25; Wallace, *Life of Henry Laurens,* 450, 477-78, 484-86; Pete Maslowski, "National Policy toward the Use of Black Troops in the Revolution," *South Carolina Historical and Genealogical Magazine* 73 (1972): 12-13; Edward McCrady, *The History of South Carolina in the Revolution, 1775-1780* (New York: Macmillan Co., 1901) 352-53, 362-76; Hamilton to John Laurens, 30 June, 12 September 1780, in *The Papers of Alexander Hamilton,* vol. 2, 1779-1781, ed. Harold C. Syrett (New York: Columbia University Press, 1961) 347, 427.

[3]Miller, *Alexander Hamilton,* 78; Wallace, *Life of Henry Laurens,* 487-88, 494-95.

counter one of these foraging parties. True to form, he appears to have been heroically leading his men against a force that outnumbered them perhaps as much as six to one.[4]

Brave he certainly was, and there is no question that his exploits provide a pretty fair outline of most of the important military actions of the Revolution. Furthermore, he had charm and talent. He was also something of an artist, and he possessed a certain style that drew many men—and perhaps women too—to him. Washington, who was never a particularly demonstrative individual, was fond of him; the more emotional Hamilton loved him. Even when one discounts much of the rhetoric between them as a conscious attempt to imitate Damon and Pythias, it is impossible not to agree with the historian who termed a letter from Hamilton to his friend "one of the most moving" he ever wrote. "You know the opinion I entertain of mankind, and how much it is my desire to preserve myself free from particular attachments" Hamilton remarked to Laurens. Therefore "you should not have taken advantage of my sensibility to steal into my affections without my consent."[5] Unfortunately Laurens's flair perished with him, and its nature must be left largely to our imaginations; luckily his ideals are permanently recorded in his words and his deeds.

Like Washington, he refused to take pay for his military service; when first offered the rank of lieutenant colonel in the Continental Army, he declined it lest he be a source of dissension among those whose promotions came more slowly. That he later accepted the rank—and wished he had done so earlier—perhaps shows that he, too, was human. More important, he carried egalitarianism to a degree most unusual, if not unique, among members of his social class. Receiving the news of a disastrous fire that occurred in Charleston on 15 January 1778, he remarked that he would lament the catastrophe "if it has fallen upon individuals of moderate fortune"; but, he added, "if it affects only a number of rich men, it will contribute to equalizing estates, [and] I shall not regret it." A few months

---

[4]Wallace, *Life of Henry Laurens,* 489; Edward McCrady, *The History of South Carolina in the Revolution, 1780-1783* (New York: Macmillan Co., 1902) 637.

[5]Wallace, *Life of Henry Laurens,* 472; Miller, *Alexander Hamilton,* 22; Gerald Stourzh, *Alexander Hamilton and the Idea of Republican Government* (Stanford CA: Stanford University Press, 1970) 77; Hamilton to John Laurens [April 1779], in Syrett, ed., *Papers of Alexander Hamilton,* 2:35.

later he elaborated these ideas: "I would wish the burthens of society as equally distributed as possible, that there may not be one part of the community appropriating to itself the summit of wealth and grandeur, while another is reduced to extreme indigence in the common cause." He wanted to see "all odious distinctions of jealousy laid aside, for we are all citizens, and have no separate interests. If mediocrity could be established generally, by any means, it would be well; it would ensure us virtue and render our independency permanent. But," he continued, "there never will be virtue in the poor, when there are rich in the same community. By imperceptible and indirect methods, we should labour to establish and maintain equality of fortunes as much as possible, if we would continue to be free."[6] Although these words sound—and probably were—genuinely radical, it could be argued that they represented little more than an expression of the traditional wisdom about the nature of republics. But the same cannot be said about his plans for raising a battalion of black soldiers.

Early in 1778 John Laurens broached the matter to his father, who was then president of the Continental Congress. "I would solicit you to cede me a number of your able bodied men slaves, instead of leaving me a fortune," he wrote. Formed into a unit and trained, they might render important service during the next campaign, he argued. What is amazing about his plan, though, is not merely that he was willing to surrender a large part of his inheritance in order to augment the Continental Army—practically everything he did during the Revolution testifies to his willingness to sacrifice his own private interest in favor of the general welfare. Nor is it even that he was willing to arm slaves—South Carolinians had considered that step during earlier emergencies. Rather, the astonishing aspects of his proposal are its candor, its boldness, and its larger purpose. "We have sunk the African and their descendants below the standard of Humanity," he had earlier remarked, by unjustly depriving them of "the rights of mankind." Service in the revolutionary army would be a stepping-stone to freedom—"a proper gradation between abject slavery and perfect liberty," which would not only prepare a slave to take his place in free so-

---

[6]Wallace, *Life of Henry Laurens,* 473-74, 474 n. 1, 490; George C. Rogers, Jr., *Charleston in the Age of the Pinckneys* (Norman: University of Oklahoma Press, 1969) 28; J. Laurens to H. Laurens, n.d., in Simms, ed., *Army Correspondence of Col. John Laurens,* 130; J. Laurens to H. Laurens, 11 April 1778, ibid., 156-57.

ciety but also establish his claim to it.[7] In short, his was a clever and far-reaching plan for the gradual abolition of slavery. Though his father also favored abolition, he was less than enthusiastic about this particular idea, so John temporarily shelved it.

A year later, after the fall of Savannah, however, the obvious need for additional manpower led Congress to urge the Southern states to enlist three thousand blacks, who would be freed at the end of the war. Fortified with this resolution, Laurens tried to prevail upon the South Carolina legislature to sanction the plan. An overwhelmingly adverse vote produced what his father described as John's first defeat in politics. Although the most important immediate result of these efforts seems to have been a wave of resentment among South Carolinians against the Continental Congress for making such a suggestion, Laurens brought the matter up again in 1782 at the first meeting of the legislature since the British had captured Charleston. This time he did not do much better: his proposal appears to have received about twelve percent of the vote. Although the magnitude of his defeat suggests that he might have been a cold ideologue, completely out of step with his contemporaries, such was not the case. His conduct and the love he inspired among intimates indicate otherwise. In the action at Yorktown he gave quarter when he could, thus setting a humane example followed by others in the assault. In the closing days of the war he was among the minority that favored leniency toward Tories. Not surprising, foes as well as friends lamented his death. The Loyalist editor of the newspaper in Charleston eulogized him by noting that had he not been a rebel, nothing could "tarnish his reputation as a man of honour, or affect his character as a gentleman."[8]

It is therefore easy to sympathize with Henry Laurens, who, a few months after being released from imprisonment, was stunned by news of

---

[7]J. Laurens to H. Laurens, 14 January 1778, in *Army Correspondence of Col. John Laurens,* 108; Peter Wood, *Black Majority: Negroes in Colonial South Carolina from 1670 through the Stono Rebellion* (New York: Alfred A. Knopf, 1974) 127; J. Laurens to H. Laurens, 26 October 1776, in "Letters from John Laurens to His Father, Hon. Henry Laurens, 1774-1776," *South Carolina Historical and Genealogical Magazine* 5 (1904): 206; Wallace, *Life of Henry Laurens,* 475.

[8]Maslowski, "National Policy toward the Use of Black Troops in the Revolution," 8-9, 11-12, 15; Hamilton to Marquis de Lafayette, 15 October 1781, in Syrett, ed., *Papers of Alexander Hamilton,* 2:679-80; Wallace, *Life of Henry Laurens,* 490-91; *Royal Gazette* (Charleston), 7 September 1782.

his son's death. "His philosophy forsook him," reported a fellow American who discovered him at Bath, prostrate with grief. In part because Laurens never really recovered from the pain of his loss, his biographer can still move us with a description of the graves of father and son, marked with simple stones bearing only names, dates, and the Latin inscription on John's: *"Dulce et decorum est / pro patria mori"*—"sweet and proper it is to die for one's country." The head and foot stones, the author notes, "are ten feet two inches apart, giving the impression of the resting place of giants."[9]

Yet it is worth observing that with the exception of a few real intimates, those who knew John Laurens best seem to have mourned him least. Washington's judgment gives a clue to why: "intrepidity bordering on rashness" was his only fault. Greene's report makes the explanation clearer: "Poor Laurens has fallen in a paltry little skirmish. You knew his temper, and I predicted his fate. The love of military glory made him seek it upon occasions unworthy [of] his rank." Such censure of a dead man was unusual for Greene; to understand it we need to recall that he had lost not only an officer but also nearly half of his detachment.[10] Nor was this the first time Laurens had rather foolhardily risked the lives of his troops. At Coosawhatchie, near the Georgia boundary, when he was wounded in 1779, he had disobeyed orders and crossed the river to engage the enemy. Only good luck and the presence of mind of one of his subordinates managed to keep the command from being captured. In short, Laurens was too often ready to back up reckless rhetoric with reckless action. Moreover, his letters were filled with references to death and to his willingness to bleed for his country. Having heard enough of this to make him uneasy, his father asked him what limits he put on his military service. "Glorious death, or the triumph of the cause in which we are engaged" was the response. That John alone—of all of Washington's aides—courted death with sufficient

---

[9]Wallace, *Life of Henry Laurens,* 399, 459; Elkanah Watson, *Men and Times of the Revolution, or Memoirs of Elkanah Watson . . .* , ed. Winslow C. Watson (New York: Dana, 1856) 173.

[10]Wallace, *Life of Henry Laurens,* 489; William Johnson, *Sketches of the Life and Correspondence of Nathanael Greene,* 2 vols. (Charleston SC: A. E. Miller, 1822) 2:342; McCrady, *History of South Carolina in the Revolution, 1780-1783,* 750; Governor John Mathews to Middleton, 25 August 1782, in "Correspondence of Hon. Arthur Middleton, Signer of the Declaration of Independence," ed. Joseph W. Barnwell, *South Carolina Historical and Genealogical Magazine* 27 (1926): 71.

ardor to win it during the war makes it significant that he placed victory second, as if he thereby unconsciously revealed a personal order of priorities.[11]

His background makes this hypothesis plausible. Educated in the classics, he, like many of his contemporaries, grew up the imaginary companion of ancient heroes who died defending liberty. Foremost among them was Cicero, who chose to die at the hand of Mark Antony's men, a martyr to republican ideals. Then, too, there was Cato the Younger, who committed suicide by tearing out his own bowels after being defeated by Caesar. "Conquering causes are dear to the gods," Lucan wrote, "the conquered to Cato." Such men could easily have supplied the models of behavior—fictional or real—that modern psychologists have found to be crucial to the development of personality during adolescence. Thus one of the most frequently quoted lines of Horace, the most popular poet of antiquity among the revolutionary generation, was the one inscribed on Laurens's gravestone.[12] Significantly, it was also the one he had used in requesting his father's permission to return to America. Furthermore, the concept of republicanism itself possessed ethical correlates. Consequently when Americans sought to institutionalize and sanction their revolution by republican forms of government, they endowed their efforts with moral meaning. But in the process they also assumed a heavy burden, for in classical theory and contemporary political thought the stability of republics depended upon the virtue of their people. That is to say, Americans believed that their perilous experiment could succeed only if they proved to be virtuous. One result of such a belief, of course, was to put revolutionary leaders under great pressure to demonstrate that they did in fact measure up. Moreover, for many what has been termed the Puritan ethic augmented the force of the republican imperative. A complex system of values, ideas, and attitudes, this ethic—like Max Weber's concept of the Protestant ethic,

[11]Wallace, *Life of Henry Laurens*, 477; Theodore Thayer, *Nathanael Greene: Strategist of the American Revolution* (New York: Twayne, 1960) 402-403; J. Laurens to H. Laurens, 23 January 1778, in Simms, ed., *The Army Correspondence of Col. John Laurens*, 111; James T. Flexner, *George Washington in the American Revolution* (Boston: Little, Brown, 1968) 539.

[12]Charles F. Mullet, "Classical Influences on the American Revolution," *Classical Journal* 35 (November 1939): 96; Edith Hamilton, *The Roman Way* (New York: W. W. Norton, 1932) 125-26; Carolina Goad, *Horace in the English Literature of the Eighteenth Century* (New Haven: Yale University Press, 1918) 7.

to which it is closely related—involved the notion of a calling. God called a man to a socially useful occupation, and, be it high or low, it was his duty to "labor assiduously at it." Specifically, as Edmund S. Morgan put it in an essay on the Puritan ethic, "he must shun both idleness, or neglect of his calling, and sloth, or slackness in it." In short, it was his duty to strive to be virtuous. Moreover, by the time of the American Revolution this ethic was by no means limited to Puritans, or even to their descendants, though men whose ancestors could be numbered among the Protestant dissenters of the sixteenth and seventeenth centuries may have taken these imperatives most seriously.[13]

That the Laurenses were originally Huguenot refugees, therefore, is a fact of some importance. Henry's letters to his son distill the doctrine. "The Evil of *prodigality* is not confined to the Loss of Money—Loss of time is a greater. . . ." "Loss of Time even at your Age is scarcely redeemable. . . ." "Life is the Gift of God & we are accountable to him not only for, but for the improvement of, it." In particular, John's station in life meant that he was called to leadership. "The Eyes of your friends & of your Country are upon you," his father reminded him, "they are in expectation . . . for your own sake, for theirs & for the sake of posterity disappoint them not by coming up a bundle of Carolina Rushes."[14] Doubtlessly John had received exactly the same kind of counsel from his old tutor, the Reverend B. Henri Himeli, pastor of the Huguenot Church in Charleston, for Himeli considered the minor French novelist Jean François Marmontel to be the wisest author of his age. And to Marmontel, who put the essence of his philosophy in the mouth of one of his characters, the art of governing consisted of "following the suggestions of wisdom and virtue." And finally, as if all this were not enough to influence him, Laurens spent an important part of his formative years in Geneva, that proud remnant of European republicanism in the eighteenth century. It is therefore reasonable to suppose that the imperatives of the age impinged upon him with

[13]Wallace, *Life of Henry Laurens*, 493; Caroline Robbins, "European Republicanism in the Century and a Half before 1776," in *The Development of a Revolutionary Mentality* (Washington: Library of Congress, 1972) 51; Edmund S. Morgan, "The Puritan Ethic and the American Revolution," *William and Mary Quarterly* 3d ser. 24 (1967): 3-43, esp. 4.

[14]Wallace, *Life of Henry Laurens*, 2-5; H. Laurens to J. Laurens, 8 March 1774, in "Letters from Hon. Henry Laurens to His Son John, 1773-1776," *South Carolina Historical and Genealogical Magazine* 3 (1902): 214; H. Laurens to J. Laurens, 6 February 1775, ibid., 4 (1903): 274-76.

special force. Destined to be a leader, he was expected to be a model of republican virtue. For him to have internalized the demands that his surroundings and associates continually reinforced would have been only natural; that he in fact did so seems to be borne out by one of his favorite quotations: ''Where liberty is, there is my country.'' It was the famous motto of Algernon Sidney, the seventeenth-century republican martyr who occupied a high place among the heroes of the revolutionary generation.[15]

Needless to say, living up to these ideals was difficult, and Laurens frequently fell short of them. But again there were special reasons why he should regret his failures more deeply than most. One was his father, who quite simply expected far more than the average parent. Strive to be perfect, he told John. Although Henry admitted that this was impossible for any human being, he frequently acted as though he thought his own offspring was an exception. And, though there is little evidence about John's punishment as a boy, what has survived indicates that his father probably depended a great deal on the threatened deprivation of love. The nature of Henry's ideals as well as the character of his own personality, which made him prone to rigid ethical judgments about persons, would seem to dictate as much. When there was a possibility that John would disobey him by breaking off his education and returning to America before receiving permission, his father remarked that in such an event he would console himself with the thought that he had ''had a son.'' The emphasis was on the past tense; disobedience would bring both material and emotional disinheritance. The important thing about all of this is that empirical findings of the social sciences suggest that this type of punishment may be associated with the development of personalities that direct their aggressions inward rather than outward, against self rather than others.[16]

In addition to his upbringing, two episodes in John Laurens's life indicate that there were tangible reasons for directing aggressions against himself. The first occurred because he was the oldest of three brothers being

---

[15]Wallace, *Life of Henry Laurens*, 463-64, 474-75; John Renwick, ''Belisaire in South Carolina, 1768,'' *Journal of American Studies* 4 (1970): 21, 35; R. R. Palmer, *The Age of Democratic Revolution: The Challenge* (Princeton: Princeton University Press, 1959) 111-39.

[16]H. Laurens to J. Laurens, 22 March 1773, 8 March 1774, in ''Letters from Hon. Henry Laurens to His Son John, 1773-1776,'' *South Carolina Historical and Genealogical Magazine* 3 (1902): 209, 214; Wallace, *Life of Henry Laurens*, 470; Martin Gold, ''Suicide, Homicide, and the Socialization of Aggression,'' *American Journal of Sociology* 63 (1958): 654-55, 660-61.

educated abroad. "You are the Man, the proper Man to be my friend while I live, & the friend of my younger family after my Death; you [are] therefore [the one] on whom, next to God, I rely," his father confided to him. Put in these terms, the care of his younger brothers involved an awesome responsibility, but John accepted it manfully. A bit later he wrote to his father, enclosing letters from "our dear little Jemmy. . . . I promise to take great care of him." This was written about January 1775; within the year John was to write that James, having fractured his skull while playing, was dead at the age of ten. Obviously John was not responsible, but as a later writer observed, his "sensitive nature . . . prompted him to bitter self reproaches."[17] In addition, John was soon to have more justification for feeling guilty: sex. And it was not because he was not forewarned. His father's one-time friend Sir Egerton Leigh had made himself notorious in Charleston by sleeping with Laurens's cousin. On another occasion Henry had used another man as an object lesson for a lecture on the dangers of an imprudent attachment. "There," he wrote, "is a Bar to Fame—to Honest Fame & peace of Mind—the Work & Hopes of Parents—the Labour & Laudable Ambition of all the Years in Youth—tumbled down—by a Baggage of no Value—the Love & friendship of Good Men—of a whole Community—prospect of Glory & future good Days—All—All, sacrificed upon the knees of a little Freckled Faced ordinary Wench—Let other Men Comiserate [sic] his Wretchedness & take Heed." Not too many years later John himself was forced to confess that "Pity" had recently forced him to marry secretly without either parent's permission and that he would soon be a father. Though socially his equal, John's wife was English, and marriage on the eve of his return to America to fight against his wife's native land could hardly be termed prudent. Nor was it necessarily indicative of romance, for Laurens neither took her with him nor waited for the birth of his daughter. And though his wife apparently went to France to meet him in 1781, there seems to be no evidence for the belief that they were presented together at court. In fact, if he saw her at all, it could only have been very

[17]H. Laurens to J. Laurens, 4 January 1775, in "Letters from Hon. Henry Laurens to His Son John, 1773-1776," *South Carolina Historical and Genealogical Magazine* 4 (1903): 269; J. Laurens to H. Laurens [c. 20 January 1775], in "Letters from John Laurens to His Father, Hon. Henry Laurens, 1774-1776," ibid., 5 (1904):201; H. Laurens to J. Laurens, 8 January 1776, ibid., 5 (1904): 135; Simms, ed., "Memoir of John Laurens," in *Army Correspondence of Col. John Laurens*, 20.

briefly. Sometime after he left for America, she died in Flanders.[18] How Laurens felt when he got the news is a fruitful subject for conjecture.

Tragedy was obviously no stranger to him, and it is unlikely that he was ever entirely free from the feeling that he had been inadvertently responsible. Whether he felt the same way about men lost under his command also invites speculation. More certain, though, is the way in which Major John André's fate fascinated both Laurens and Hamilton. In part theirs was no doubt a feeling of "there but for the grace of God go I." André's position as an aide to Sir Henry Clinton was comparable to theirs vis-à-vis Washington. André's negotiations with Benedict Arnold led to his capture and eventual execution; a similar mission with a similar fate was easily within the realm of possibility for either of the two Americans. Hamilton, clearly, was deeply moved by André's courageous death. Laurens's reaction is less well documented, but he could scarcely have shrugged off his friend's observations. After a eulogistic recounting of André's qualities, Hamilton noted in a letter to Laurens: "I am aware that a man of real merit is never seen in so favourable a light, as through the medium of adversity. The clouds that surround him are shades that set off his good qualities. . . . His spectators who enjoy a happier lot are less prone to detract from it, through envy, and are more disposed by compassion to give him the credit he deserves and perhaps even to magnify it."[19] Hamilton and Laurens both knew death to be the only real absolution.

Why Hamilton survived the Revolution and Laurens did not is, therefore, a question worth considering; upon occasion they could be equally foolish. When American forces were in full retreat at Monmouth, Hamilton rushed up to General Lee, brandishing his sword and exclaiming, "I will stay here with you, my dear General, and die with you; let us all die here rather than retreat." Lee considered him to be daft—"much flustered

---

[18]Robert M. Calhoon and Robert M. Weir, "The Scandalous History of Sir Egerton Leigh," *William and Mary Quarterly* 3d ser. 26 (1969): 64; H. Laurens to J. Laurens, 8 October 1773, in "Letters from Hon. Henry Laurens to His Son John, 1773-1776," *South Carolina Historical and Genealogical Magazine* 3 (1902): 90; Wallace, *Life of Henry Laurens,* 465-71, 481; William Manning to John Laurens, 12 July 1777, John Laurens Papers, South Carolina Historical Society, Charleston. First called to my attention by the editors of *The Papers of Henry Laurens,* Manning's letter does not support Wallace's more sympathetic interpretation of John's conduct.

[19]Miller, *Alexander Hamilton,* 70-71; Hamilton to John Laurens, 11 October 1780, in Syrett, ed., *Papers of Alexander Hamilton,* 2:467.

and in a sort of frenzy of valor" was his description of the young colonel. And at Yorktown, Hamilton again rashly exposed himself to death. One reason he outlived Laurens by some twenty years was that he participated in fewer engagements. But had he chosen to, Laurens could have seen much less combat. In 1779, for example, Congress offered him a position as secretary to the American legation in Paris. His command of French would have made him useful there; he had already established his reputation for valor; and his father obviously hoped that he would accept the appointment. Yet John refused.[20] Somehow he could not heed the advice his father had given him after the Battle of Germantown. "No Man can doubt of your bravery, your own good sense will point out the distinction between Courage & temerity nor need I tell you that it [is as] much your duty to preserve your own health & strength as it is to destroy an Enemy." Although one is tempted to conclude that John ignored this admonition because risking his life in battle provided a legitimate way of symbolically rejecting his father's lifelong demands, it is worth noting that Hamilton gave him exactly the same advice: "Adieu my Dear; I am sure you will exert yourself to save your country; but do not unnecessarily risk one of its most valuable sons. Take as much care of yourself as you ought for the public sake and for the sake of Y[ou]r affectionate A. Hamilton."[21]

Interesting as this entire letter is, Hamilton's last point is most significant for present purposes. Antiquity offered the revolutionary generation two related but essentially different models of behavior. The one was the military hero, or republican martyr; the other was the solon, or wise legislator. Hamilton was well aware of the distinction, and except in moments of unusual excitement he subordinated the former to the latter. Laurens either failed to understand the difference or reversed the priorities. Hamilton usually took risks because they served a larger purpose in which his desire to benefit the public and himself were inextricably but consciously intertwined; nowhere is this more clearly apparent than in his death. Though

---

[20]Miller, *Alexander Hamilton,* 31, 77; Wallace, *Life of Henry Laurens,* 478; H. Laurens to J. Laurens, 2 October 1779, in "Correspondence between Hon. Henry Laurens and His Son John, 1777-1780," *South Carolina Historical and Genealogical Magazine* 6 (1905): 157.

[21]H. Laurens to J. Laurens, 8 October 1777, in "Correspondence between Hon. Henry Laurens and His Son John, 1777-1780," ibid., 5; Hamilton to John Laurens, 30 March 1780, in Syrett, ed., *Papers of Alexander Hamilton,* 2:304.

reluctant to accept Aaron Burr's challenge, he felt that he had no choice, because a refusal might compromise his popular reputation to the point where he would be debarred forever from rendering his country further service.[22] In short, despite all his love for glory, Hamilton's military exploits bore a political penumbra; Laurens's political actions, however, carried a military aura.

Hamilton could be manipulative; Laurens could only be demonstrative. It was as if the latter believed the gesture to be more important than the results. When Governor Rutledge apparently tried to stall for time by offering to negotiate with General Prevost while American forces hurried to the defense of Charleston in 1779, Laurens refused to carry his messages, thereby demonstrating both his patriotism and his political naiveté. In France two years later, he was probably not as direct and obtuse as has sometimes been reported, but his impatience with diplomatic niceties could well have wrecked his mission if the French court had not already been favorably disposed. The more subtle Franklin quietly noted after his departure that he had "brusqued the ministers too much, and I found . . . that he had thereby given more offense than I could have imagined."[23] And noble as it was, his attempt to raise a black regiment was cut from the same cloth. His father, who was a wily politician though a man of principles opposed to slavery, cautioned him against ignoring many considerations. "A Work of this importance must be entered upon with Caution & great circumspection." But John replied that "my reputation is at stake. . . . As a Soldier, as a Citizen, as a Man—I am interested to engage in this work." The scheme, he hoped, would not appear to his father to be "the chimera of a young mind, deceived by a false appearance of moral beauty, but a laudable sacrifice of private interest, to justice and the public good." Significantly, these words were remarkably similar to those with which he explained his refusal to take pay for his military service; it was because he wished to give to his country "a pure offering of disinterested services."

---

[22]Douglass Adair, *Fame and the Founding Fathers: Essays,* ed. Trevor Colbourn (New York: W. W. Norton, 1974), particularly the first essay from which the title of the book is taken; Cecelia M. Kenyon, "Alexander Hamilton: Rousseau of the Right," *Political Science Quarterly* 73 (1958): 174.

[23]McCrady, *South Carolina in the Revolution, 1775-1780,* 374; Wallace, *Life of Henry Laurens,* 477; Franklin as quoted in Carl Van Doren, *Benjamin Franklin* (New York: Viking, 1938) 626.

Without deprecating his plan or denigrating his motives, it is possible to suggest that his project was designed not only to save the state from the British and the blacks from slavery but also to demonstrate something about himself. Sincere as he probably was in both of the former aims, it is hard to believe that he could be blind to what every Virginia politician of stature appears to have known at the time: that a frontal attack on slavery—even there, let alone in South Carolina, where planters were more committed to it—would be self-defeating and politically suicidal.[24]

In politics as in war, it seemed, Laurens was willing to destroy himself in order to prove his virtue. Such zeal may make a martyr, but not a politician. Marmontel to the contrary, effective politics demands more than virtue; it also requires the kind of realism about oneself and others that prompted John Rutledge to declare in the Constitutional Convention that the slave trade, which he was then defending, had nothing to do with moral principle; rather it was a matter of economic interest, pure and simple. Given conditions at the time, this was not cynicism on his part, but political horse sense. If the noble imperatives of the classical tradition and the Puritan ethic helped to endow the American Revolution with moral meaning, it was the rational assessment of realities that helped to make it succeed. True to the eighteenth-century ideal, the most creative men of the age were able to maintain something of a balance between the real and the ideal. Laurens, on the other hand, allowed himself to become obsessed by the pursuit of virtue; Hamilton termed him a knight errant.[25]

Ironically, it was precisely this lack of balance that made him attractive to antebellum South Carolinians, for his quest—like theirs—was essentially a romantic and perhaps irrational one. They both protested too much; the continual assertion and eventual suicidal demonstration of their selfless virtue suggests that each found the tension between aspiration and achievement more than could be borne. For only in the heedless disregard

---

[24]H. Laurens to J. Laurens, 22 January 1778; J. Laurens to H. Laurens, 1 June 1778, 10 March 1779 — in "Correspondence between Hon. Henry Laurens and His Son John, 1777-1780," *South Carolina Historical and Genealogical Magazine* 6 (1905): 47, 106, 139; J. Laurens to H. Laurens, 2 February 1778, in Simms, ed., *Army Correspondence of Col. John Laurens,* 116; Robert McColley, *Slavery and Jeffersonian Virginia,* 2d ed. (Urbana: University of Illinois Press, 1973) 131.

[25]Entry of 21 August 1787, *The Records of the Federal Convention of 1787,* ed. Max Farrand, 3 vols. (New Haven: Yale University Press, 1927) 2:364; Hamilton to John Laurens, 22 May 1779, in Syrett, ed., *Papers of Alexander Hamilton,* 2:52.

of personal safety could the cavaliers of the Old South demonstrate that their attachment to slavery was not motivated by self-interest; and only in death could John Laurens prove that he was as virtuous as he sought to be. Thus the kinship of circumstance, as well as of land and blood, helps to explain why Southern politicians and men of letters like Robert Y. Hayne and William Gilmore Simms revered Laurens as "the Bayard of America"—the knight *"without fear,* and *without reproach,"* ready to sacrifice everything in the cause of his country. He was, said Hayne, "the purest and most disinterested of human beings." But that the memory of a man who sought to free the blacks should be invoked to defend their enslavement brings to mind A. E. Housman's lines from "To an Athlete Dying Young": "Smart lad, to slip betimes away / From fields where glory does not stay."[26]

In a sense, Laurens had his day. Bravery such as his was doubtlessly functional in the revolutionary army, where an officer's example often had to substitute for discipline among an amateur soldiery. But the case is not so clear-cut in regard to the common claim that "had it not been for his untimely death," as one historian put it, he might have been "one of the greatest of the younger Founding Fathers." Perhaps. But conditions in the modern world make us more aware that his qualifications as a statesman are somewhat suspect. In short, Laurens exemplified—perhaps more clearly than most of his contemporaries—a dangerous but essential facet of our political tradition. To realize how dangerous it can be we have only to review his own career and that of his nineteenth-century hagiographers; to remember how essential it is too, however, we have only to recall the events of the last few years in which some of our leaders allowed, in the words of Jeb Stuart Magruder, "ambition, loyalty, and partisan passion" to override both judgment and honor.[27] Before we jettison the military heroes of the Revolution, we should recall that this is a mistake few of them, and least of all John Laurens, would have made.

---

[26]Robert M. Weir, "The South Carolinian as Extremist," *South Atlantic Quarterly* 74 (1975): 86-103; Simms, ed., "Memoir of John Laurens," in *Army Correspondence of Col. John Laurens,* 45, 48.

[27]Flexner, *George Washington in the American Revolution,* 539; Jeb Stuart Magruder, quoted in *The State* (Columbia, South Carolina), 26 May 1974.

Rebelliousness:
Personality Development
and the American Revolution
in the Southern Colonies _____

*John Laurens's experiences prompted me to reflect on child-
rearing practices in the Southern colonies; a subsequent invitation to participate in a symposium on the Revolution sponsored by
the North Carolina Bicentennial Committee and other institutions
provided an opportunity to examine some possible relationships
between family life and the character of the Revolution in the area.
Written before the recent explosion of scholarship on Southern
family life, the essay was frankly exploratory, and its conclusions
remain somewhat controversial. I still believe, however, that they
are generally on the right track. The essay was originally published in* The Southern Experience in the American Revolution,
*ed. by Jeffrey J. Crowe and Larry E. Tise. Copyright ©1978 The
University of North Carolina Press, and used with permission of
the publisher.*

About three miles south of the Ashley River shortly after one o'-
clock on the afternoon of 23 December 1765, four young men on horse-
back barred the road to Charleston, South Carolina. Seizing the reins of
the horses drawing several vehicles belonging to the family of Robert Williams, they dragged his stepson from the buggy in which he had been rid-
ing with his fourteen-year-old sister. While the others held the rest of the
party at gunpoint, one of the men leaped into the vehicle, whipped up the
horses, and sped off down the road with the girl. Sometime after the pair
was out of sight, the highwaymen released the rest of the party. Not far

down the road, Williams came upon the vehicle wrecked in a ditch, some of the girl's clothing strewn about in the bushes, and the couple nowhere in sight.[1]

Though we may have our suspicions, we, like Mrs. Williams, want to know exactly what was happening. She posed the question while confronting a cocked pistol; we raise it as a topic of scholarly discussion more than two hundred years later. Whereas she understandably was interested in quick and detailed answers, we can defer them while we seek to put the matter in a wider perspective. In the process, because we know that two of the most active highwaymen later became revolutionary leaders, we, in effect, shall be assessing an observation made by a Loyalist, Johnathan Boucher, who sought partly to explain the Revolution by noting that the "chief Abettors of Violence . . . are young men of Good Parts, but spoil'd by a strange, imperfect, desultory kind of Education." Children, he previously had remarked, were "no longer so respectful and dutiful as they ought to be, and as they used to be."[2] Accordingly this essay will attempt to explore some possible relationships between family life, especially in the plantation colonies, and the nature of the American Revolution.

Admittedly, the limited state of our present knowledge makes the enterprise somewhat speculative, but there are reasons for believing that the attempt might be worthwhile. First, though the Southern family of the late colonial period has yet to be subjected to widespread and intensive scrutiny, social and demographic historians have learned a good deal during the last few years about the situation farther north.[3] Second, though contemporary "studies of family relationships have not yet progressed to the point that . . . well-documented conclusions can be drawn . . . in regard

---

[1]Examination and Deposition of Robert Williams, 14 January 1766, South Carolina Council Journals, 32:688-92, and Pardon of W. Ward Crosthwaite, Barnard Elliott, Benjamin Huger, and John Miles, 3 April 1766, Miscellaneous Records, MM:361, both at South Carolina Department of Archives and History, Columbia (hereafter SCDAH).

[2]Quoted in Edwin G. Burrows and Michael Wallace, "The American Revolution: The Ideology and Psychology of National Liberation," *Perspectives in American History* 6 (1972): 266.

[3]For citations to much of this literature, which clearly reveal its geographic imbalance, see Robert V. Wells, "Family History and Demographic Transition," *Journal of Social History* 8 (1975): 1-19; and Ruby R. Seward, "The Colonial Family in America: Toward a Socio-Historical Restoration of Its Structure," *Journal of Marriage and the Family* 35 (1973): 58-70.

to politically relevant dimensions," as one scholar noted, they tend to indicate that "early learning is an important factor in the developmental psychology of political attitudes." Attempts to correlate specific political beliefs held by parents and children have produced disappointingly negative results, but a number of recent investigations suggest that the "study of the direct transmission of more basic personality orientations might be a fruitful area for future research." Thus, despite considerable criticism since its publication nearly thirty years ago, the central assumption underlying the now-classic study of *The Authoritarian Personality* still appears to be viable.[4] Though Boucher failed to coin neologisms like the "rebellious personality," modern scholarship suggests that he may have been at least partially correct, not only in perceiving the existence of such a phenomenon, but also in accounting for it.

Several recent scholars have attempted to postulate direct or indirect relationships between changes in the colonial family and the coming of the American Revolution. Most of these hypotheses relate to the concept of "modernization." Although its definitions and manifestations appear to be equally innumerable, one of the most important features of the process seems to be a change in the traditional patterns of authority. In North America between the seventeenth and the nineteenth centuries the trend was clearly away from authoritarianism: deference waned; voluntary associations proliferated; and even in the family, children seem to have acquired greater independence at earlier ages. Intimately involved with all of these developments—both as cause and result—was the emergence of a new personality type, the psychologically autonomous individual.[5] To explain the rapid emergence of this new man, especially in the colonies outside of

---

[4]Richard G. Niemi, "Political Socialization," in *Handbook of Political Psychology,* ed. Jeanne N. Knutson (San Francisco: Jossey-Bass, 1973) 129, 136; Nevitt Sanford, "Authoritarian Personality in Contemporary Perspective," ibid., 139-70; R. W. Connell, "Political Socialization in the American Family," *Public Opinion Quarterly* 36 (1972): 330; Stanley A. Renshon, *Psychological Needs and Political Behavior: A Theory of Personality and Political Efficacy* (New York: Free Press, 1974) 240; T. W. Adorno et al., *The Authoritarian Personality* (New York: Harper and Row, 1950).

[5]Richard D. Brown, "Modernization and the Modern Personality in Early America, 1600-1865: A Sketch of a Synthesis," *Journal of Interdisciplinary History* 2 (1971-1972): 201-28, esp. 215-20; Neil J. Smelser, "The Modernization of Social Relations," in *Modernization: The Dynamics of Growth,* ed. Myron Weiner (New York: Basic Books, 1966) 110-21.

New England, Jack Greene has developed a sophisticated version of the Turner thesis in which he argues that the economic opportunities and necessities of the New World placed a premium upon adaptive behavior. Flexibility, in turn, required personal autonomy. But having acquired the requisite personality (presumably over several successive generations), Americans found themselves confronted with British restraints threatening to their ''autonomy as individuals''—an autonomy that had become essential to their self-esteem as well as to their success in colonial society. Thus they responded angrily and rebelliously.[6]

Intrinsically plausible, the argument is also tactically adroit, for it does not depend upon a particular model of the colonial family. Whether the family was authoritarian or permissive, patriarchal or contractual was less important than the character of the father figure a son sought to emulate. All other factors being equal, autonomous fathers, Greene appears to assume, tended to produce even more autonomous sons, and empirical evidence seems to validate this assumption. One investigator found recently that among contemporary families ''with the effects of all of the other variables held constant, the strongest single predictor of our respondents' level of personal control was their parents['] level of personal control.''[7] Thus one of the strong points of Greene's interpretation is its ability to cope with widely differing patterns of authority in American families. Indeed, the chief weakness of his point of view may be merely that he has yet to claim enough for it.

Be that as it may, any attempt to link the Revolution more closely to prior changes in the colonial family must confront the nature of these changes directly. Thus, Philip Greven, whose suppositions were based upon a very detailed knowledge of the situation in Andover, Massachusetts, suggested that by the mid-eighteenth century earlier independence for sons meant that ''their attitudes toward parent-son relations had changed significantly from those of their fathers' and their grandfathers' generations. For Andover's fourth generation, Thomas Paine's call for independence

---

[6]Jack P. Greene, ''Autonomy and Stability: New England and the British Colonial Experience in Early Modern America,'' *Journal of Social History* 7 (1974): 171-94; Greene, ''An Uneasy Connection: An Analysis of the Preconditions of the American Revolution,'' in *Essays on the American Revolution,* ed. Stephen G. Kurtz and James H. Hutson (Chapel Hill: University of North Carolina Press, 1973) 59-61.

[7]Renshon, *Psychological Needs and Political Behavior,* 150.

. . . from the mother-country and from the father-king might have been just what Paine claimed it to be—common sense.'"[8] More recently, Edwin Burrows and Michael Wallace have elaborated this hypothesis in a subtle and suggestive essay. During most of the colonial period, they argue, "Americans accepted British control and authority because the objective disparity between British power and colonial power created in them a deep personal sense of comparative weakness and inferiority." Colonial dependence and weakness in turn produced affection for and imitation of British standards by individual Americans who were "inclined to be acquiescent toward authority and authority figures," in part because of the "structure of both colonial society and the colonial family." But demographic and economic growth of the colonies, along with their increasing military prowess, "transformed the collective image of the colonies from one of weakness and inferiority to one of strength and capability." Furthermore, "the decline of patriarchalism in both colonial society and the colonial family . . . tended to produce less authoritarian and more autonomous personality types," for whom the "arbitrary exercise of imperial authority was likely to be extremely objectionable." Thus British restrictions of the 1760s and 1770s "shattered the personal trust and affection that Americans had had for the English and their King. A widespread feeling of betrayal aroused still more anger against Britain, and may also have released previously repressed resentments at dependency.'"[9]

Undoubtedly, as Bruce Mazlish has put it, Burrows and Wallace basically "have the picture right,"[10] although a few areas may still be a bit out of focus. For example, their contention that the growth of the colonies, in the perception of many Americans, bespoke a "concomitant transformation in the personal identity of significant masses of people" is not entirely convincing. Admittedly, recent studies of the psychology of nationalism appear to substantiate the current existence of such a phenom-

---

[8]Philip J. Greven, Jr., *Four Generations: Population, Land, and Family in Colonial Andover, Massachusetts* (Ithaca: Cornell University Press, 1970) 281.

[9]Burrows and Wallace, "The American Revolution," 167-306. Quotations are from 274, 281, 284, 287-88, and 289.

[10]Bruce Mazlish, "Leadership in the American Revolution: The Psychological Dimension," in *Leadership in the American Revolution* (Washington: Library of Congress, 1974) 122.

enon.[11] But what holds true after the advent of modern nationalism may be more doubtful when applied to historical processes before it. In fact, to assume the existence of such a link between personal and collective capability is to complicate the problem of explaining the Revolution in those Southern colonies whose inhabitants remained acutely conscious of their economic weakness or military impotence. Nor can this objection be answered entirely by assuming that men from such areas identified themselves with America collectively instead of with their local communities. After all, even Patrick Henry's famous statement that he was "not a Virginian, but an American" was uttered during the course of a debate in which he advocated greater voting strength in the Continental Congress for Virginia.[12]

The other major difficulty with Burrows's and Wallace's hypothesis arises from their assumption that changes in the family were as rapid and as great elsewhere in America as in Andover, Massachusetts. Not only does that assumption exceed present knowledge, it is also implausible. Even in regard to New England we might argue—as we could ten years ago—whether the role of the family was expanding or contracting during much of the colonial period. Elsewhere, to paraphrase Edward Saveth, our ignorance remains to this day "almost unmitigated." Perhaps the safest course would be to take a cue from the work of Robert Wells and other demographic historians who have been impressed by the "tremendous complexity and diversity" among families in the New World.[13] That patterns of authority varied as widely as the composition of households ap-

---

[11]Burrows and Wallace, "The American Revolution," 273 n. 13.

[12]Hugh T. Lefler and William S. Powell, *Colonial North Carolina: A History* (New York: Charles Scribner's Sons, 1973) 172, 174; John Shy, "A New Look at Colonial Militia," *William and Mary Quarterly* 3d ser. 20 (1963): 181; Noble Wymberly Jones, Archibald Bulloch, and John Houstoun to president of Continental Congress, 6 April 1775, in *Men of Mark in Georgia,* ed. William T. Northen, 6 vols. (Atlanta: A. B. Caldwell, 1907-1912) 1:214; Merrill Jensen, *The Articles of Confederation* (Madison: University of Wisconsin Press, 1963) 58.

[13]David J. Rothman, "A Note on the Study of the Colonial Family," *William and Mary Quarterly* 3d ser. 23 (1966): 627-34; Bernard Bailyn, *Education in the Forming of American Society: Needs and Opportunities for Study* (1960; rpt. New York: W. W. Norton, 1972) 21-29; Edward N. Saveth, "The Problem of American Family History," *American Quarterly* 21 (1969): 314; Robert V. Wells, "Household Size and Composition in the British Colonies in America, 1675-1775," *Journal of Interdisciplinary History* 4 (1974): 570; Arlene Skolnick, "The Family Revisited: Themes in Recent Social Science Research," ibid., 5 (1975): 712-14, 718.

pears possible, if not probable. Furthermore, even if one accepts the dubious proposition that the decline of patriarchalism was universal, the rate in most places was almost certainly very gradual. In poetry, the "one-hoss shay" may collapse all at once; in history, such processes are apt to be agonizingly slow. One would expect, therefore, to find an extended period of transition, fraught with ambiguity and tension, during which children attempted to assert earlier independence while parents struggled to maintain their authority.

Much evidence indicates that this is precisely what happened in much of the Western world. John Locke, whose *Some Thoughts Concerning Education* made him the Dr. Spock of the eighteenth century, illustrates the nature of the transition. Recognizing that "the time must come" when children "will be past the rod and correction," he noted that the influence of a parent must then be based upon "love and friendship." But until that time, he also believed, "children . . . should look upon their parents as their lords, their absolute governors; and, as such, stand in awe of them."[14] When and where to draw the line between the two conditions was then as now the subject of contention. During the eighteenth century child-rearing manuals began advocating that parents instill independence in their children. Yet as late as the first half of the next century, travelers' accounts reported considerable stress and strain in American families over the subject. And in New England during the late eighteenth century, magazines catering to a middle-class audience (which was doubtless relatively quick to adopt newer trends) expressed values that recently have led a number of sociologists to conclude that "the colonial family was undoubtedly a family in transition, perhaps in some areas in a *more marked transition* than is commonly recognized."[15]

---

[14]The advice of child-rearing manuals was probably not always followed, but some parents at least tried to teach their children "according to Mr. Lock's method (which I have carefully studied." Eliza Lucas Pinckney to Mrs. Bartlett, 20 May 1745, in Harriott Horry Ravenel, *Eliza Pinckney* (1896; rpt., Spartanburg SC: Reprint Company, 1967) 113. John Locke, "Some Thoughts Concerning Education," in *Children and Youth in America: A Documentary History*, ed. Robert H. Bremner, 3 vols. (Cambridge MA: Harvard University Press, 1970) 1 (1600-1865): 133.

[15]Abigail J. Stewart, David G. Winter, and A. David Jones, "Coding Categories for the Study of Child-Rearing from Historical Sources," *Journal of Interdisciplinary History* 5 (1975): 701; Frank J. Furstenberg, Jr., "Industrialization and the American Family," *American Sociological Review* 31 (1966): 326-37; Herman R. Lantz et al., "Pre-Industrial Patterns in the Colonial Family in America: A Content Analysis of Colonial Magazines," *American Sociological Review* 33 (1968): 425.

Nowhere is the nature of that transition more clearly revealed than in the changing pattern of parental control over marriage. As Daniel Scott Smith has observed, up until the early eighteenth century "there existed a stable, parental-run marriage system, in the nineteenth century a stable participant-run system." Intervening was "a period of change and crisis." More recently, Smith and Michael Hindus have further illuminated characteristics of that crisis by their analysis of premarital conception rates. Using a broad sample of American marriages between 1640 and 1971, they discovered the existence of a cyclical trend that reached an all-time high in the last half of the eighteenth century, when approximately one-third of all brides appear to have been pregnant at marriage. Noting that the similarity of economic status between bride and groom indicates that in all probability these courtships remained at least partially constrained by traditional norms, they interpret the high level of premarital conceptions as evidence of conflict within the family. As one contemporary observer put it, these couples "would do the same again, because otherwise they could not obtain their parent's [*sic*] consent to marry." In short, these were shotgun weddings in which the weapon was turned on the older rather than the younger generation. Their frequency, Smith and Hindus persuasively contend, reveals not the "contractual, Lockean and republican nature of the family," but tensions generated by power relationships being challenged.[16]

Though Smith and Hindus draw only a small part of their evidence from the Southern colonies, there are reasons to suspect that such tensions may have been especially characteristic there. On the one hand, as Greene and others have pointed out, personal independence was almost a fetish among the local elites, and the development of personal autonomy appears to have proceeded apace.[17] On the other hand, however, scholars have noted that

---

[16]Daniel Scott Smith, "Parental Power and Marriage Patterns: An Analysis of Historical Trends in Hingham, Massachusetts," *Journal of Marriage and the Family* 35 (1973): 426; Daniel Scott Smith and Michael S. Hindus, "Premarital Pregnancy in America, 1640-1971: An Overview and Interpretation," *Journal of Interdisciplinary History* 5 (1975): 538, 556, 557.

[17]Greene, "An Uneasy Connection," 59-60; Landon Carter, *The Diary of Colonel Landon Carter of Sabine Hall, 1752-1778,* ed. Jack P. Greene, 2 vols. (Charlottesville: University Press of Virginia, 1965) 1:19-20; Robert M. Weir, "The South Carolinian as Extremist," *South Atlantic Quarterly* 74 (1975): 91-92; Greene, "Autonomy and Stability," 189-93.

the antebellum South retained many features of a traditional society—including a high degree of patriarchalism.[18] Thus it appears that geographic dispersal, institutional weaknesses, the exigencies of plantation life, and a number of other factors accentuated contradictory thrusts. The patriarch demanded obedience and subordination; the youth who modeled himself upon the father sought independence and personal control over his own life. For members of the upper classes at least, slavery probably exacerbated conflict. "Boy," that traditional but now dying Southern term for a black man, illustrates why: black slaves and white children shared a similar state of dependency. Quite naturally, therefore, as the diary of Philip Fithian, a tutor in Virginia, clearly shows, planters' children used the slaves as a touchstone by which to determine the appropriateness of their own treatment. Thus attempts to distinguish themselves from those who were in a similarly dependent situation doubtlessly resulted in exaggerated displays of independence. Moreover, parents like Maurice Moore of North Carolina clearly sought to make the same distinction and therefore occasionally may have treated some of these displays with unwonted indulgence.[19] This possibility suggests two explanations for widely varying reports of very lax as well as very strict discipline in Southern households. Undoubtedly, the diversity among families was great, but inconsistencies within single households may have been almost as widespread and frequent.[20] And in-

[18]Eugene D. Genovese, *The World the Slaveholders Made: Two Essays in Interpretation* (New York: Pantheon, 1971) 121-22; Brown, "Modernization and the Modern Personality," 212; Paul Connor, "Patriarchy: Old World and New," *American Quarterly* 17 (1965): 48-62. See also Arthur W. Calhoun, *A Social History of the American Family from Colonial Times to the Present*, 3 vols. (Cleveland: Arthur H. Clark, 1917-1919) 2:69, 334, 337.

[19]Entry of 5 April 1774, Philip Vickers Fithian, *Journal and Letters of Philip Vickers Fithian, 1773-1774: A Plantation Tutor of the Old Dominion,* ed. Hunter Dickinson Farish (Charlottesville: University Press of Virginia, 1957) 92; Philippe Ariès, *Centuries of Childhood: A Social History of Family Life,* trans. Robert Baldick (New York: Alfred A. Knopf, 1962) 26; Maurice Moore, "The Justice of Taxing the American Colonies, in Great-Britain, Considered," in *Some Eighteenth Century Tracts Concerning North America,* ed. William K. Boyd (Raleigh NC: Edwards and Broughton, 1927) 174.

[20]On the one hand, there were parents like Gabriel Manigault who was, as Maurice Crouse has noted, "a stern father, with a short temper and little tolerance for the follies of youth." This description might apply equally well to other South Carolinians like Henry Laurens and his own father, John. The Carters of Nomini Hall, Fithian originally believed,

consistent discipline has ever been a notorious cause of friction between parent and child.

In addition, two other features especially characteristic of life in the Southern colonies probably further increased the prevailing level of conflict. One was the tendency of Southern planters to send their children to England for schooling; the result, undoubtedly, was often a generation gap like that between John Drayton of South Carolina who, according to his grandson, "was a man of indifferent education [and] . . . confined mind" and his son William Henry, whose prose style betrays a clever, polished, and somewhat snobbish prig.[21] The other characteristic feature of the area

also attempted to keep their children "in perfect subjection." On the other hand, even there, he was later to discover, obedience was not always the rule, and travelers like Nicholas Cresswell, the Marquis de Chastellux, and Francisco de Miranda often remarked about undisciplined children. It should be noted, however, that even sympathetic observers frequently revealed biases and assumptions that may have caused them to underestimate the degree of parental control in American families. Maurice A. Crouse, "The Manigault Family of South Carolina, 1688-1783" (Ph.D. dissertation, Northwestern University, 1964) 120; David D. Wallace, *The Life of Henry Laurens* (New York: G. P. Putnam's Sons, 1915) 470; Fithian to Rev. Enoch Green, 1 December 1773, and entries of 11 February and 6 June 1774, Farish, ed., *Journal and Letters of Fithian,* 26, 64, 116; entry of 19 July 1777, *The Journal of Nicholas Cresswell, 1774-1777* (New York: Dial, 1924) 270; entry of 31 December 1780, *Travels in North America in the Years 1780, 1781 and 1782 by the Marquis de Chastellux,* ed. Howard C. Rice, Jr., 2 vols. (Chapel Hill: University of North Carolina Press, 1963) 1:221; entry of August 1783, *The New Democracy in America: Travels of Francisco de Miranda in the United States, 1783-1784,* ed. John S. Ezell (Norman: University of Oklahoma Press, 1963) 23-24; Calhoun, *A Social History of the American Family,* 2:64.

For evidence suggesting that inconsistencies in discipline may sometimes have resulted from conflicting lines of authority within the family, see "Extracts from the Diary and Letters of John Harrower, Indentured Servant, 1773-1776," in *A Documentary History of Education in the South before 1860,* ed. Edgar W. Knight, 5 vols. (Chapel Hill: University of North Carolina Press, 1949-1953) 1:646; and John Davis, *Travels of Four Years and a Half in the United States of America during 1798 . . . 1802,* ed. A. J. Morrison (New York: Henry Holt, 1909) 97.

For further discussions of ambiguity, ambivalence, and variety in parent-child relationships, see Edmund S. Morgan, *Virginians at Home: Family Life in the Eighteenth Century* (Charlottesville: University Press of Virginia, 1952) 8; and John Walzer, "A Period of Ambivalence: Eighteenth-Century American Childhood," in *The History of Childhood,* ed. Lloyd de Mause (New York: Psychohistory, 1974) 351, 362-63.

[21]Carl Bridenbaugh, *Myths and Realities: Societies of the Colonial South* (New York: Atheneum, 1963) 35, 101; John Drayton, *The Carolinian Florist of Governor John Drayton of South Carolina, 1766-1822,* ed. Margaret B. Meriwether (Columbia: University of South Carolina Press, 1943) xxv; and William Henry Drayton, ed., *The Letters of Freeman, etc.* (London, 1771).

appears to have been an unusually high rate of early mortality among parents. The South Carolina lowcountry was undoubtedly exactly what it was reputed to be—a most unhealthy place. Even among Virginians an astonishing number of future revolutionary leaders—including Washington, Jefferson, George Mason, Edmund Pendleton, and Peyton Randolph—lost fathers at an early age.[22] Thus in all probability a disproportionately high percentage of youths grew up under forms of tutelage that could be perceived as less legitimate than that of their natural parents. That fact, of course, by no means signifies that they all experienced difficulty with surrogate father figures. Undoubtedly, many were like Edward Rutledge, who is reputed to have been known for his "filial affection and obedience," though he grew up under the care of his older brother John. Nevertheless, the parental death rate almost certainly increased the potential for conflict during childhood and youth, for even in the eighteenth century the stepchild relationship was a byword for contention.[23] Thus conditions widespread in the Southern colonies make it reasonable to suppose that many revolutionary leaders matured in homes where the boundaries of the permissible occasionally were vague, the situation ambivalent, and relationships with authority figures not infrequently strained.

Much scattered evidence appears to support these suppositions. Boucher, as we have seen, believed children to be increasingly disobedient. If one prefers Whig to Tory testimony, one can turn to Landon Carter whose mature son Robert Wormley, "Wild Bob," delighted in vexing

---

[22]Bridenbaugh, *Myths and Realities,* 69. Without attempting to be exhaustive, one might add to this list; Benjamin Harrison and George Wythe (Virginia); John Penn (North Carolina); Christopher Gadsden, Ralph Izard, Rawlins Lowndes, Andrew Pickens, Edward, Hugh, and John Rutledge, Thomas Sumter (South Carolina); Lachlan McIntosh and George Walton (Georgia). Relatively early loss of a mother would add many more, including Henry Laurens, and his son John, Thomas Lynch, Jr. (South Carolina); Abraham Baldwin, Jonathan Bryan, and the Habersham brothers, John and Joseph (Georgia). Unfortunately most research on the effects of a parent's death upon a child has tended to neglect the historical context and is therefore of limited value for present purposes, but see Elizabeth Herzog and Cecelia E. Sudia, "Fatherless Homes: A Review of Research," *Children* 15 (1968): 177-82; and Carmi Schooler, "Childhood Family Structure and Adult Characteristics," *Sociometry* 35 (1972): 255-69.

[23]Quoted in Dorothy C. Smith, "The Revolutionary Service of Edward Rutledge" (M.A. thesis, University of South Carolina, 1947) 2. For the spectrum of relationships between mothers and stepchildren, see Julia Cherry Spruill, *Women's Life and Work in the Southern Colonies,* intro. Ann Firor Scott (New York: W. W. Norton, 1972) 62-63.

him—or at least so the old man thought. Schoolmasters' reports from Virginia and North Carolina both before and after the Revolution contain frequent accounts of difficulty in managing rebellious youths. Among prominent individuals, John Drayton appears to have had an especially hard time with his sons. "Very wild and ungovernable" was the report on one of the younger, Glen, who was studying in Britain, while his older brothers prompted their father to write: "I am so unhappy and made so miserable in two of my Sons . . . [who take] no Council from me nor yet pay no obedience." They in turn apparently considered him a "Tyrant."[24] Only a great deal of further research will permit us to evaluate these examples with much certainty, but such friction may have been common, though perhaps the Draytons' was unusually intense. If this was indeed the case, during childhood and adolescence members of the local elites in the Southern colonies acquired a large and explosive emotional baggage.

This probability suggests that Smith and Hindus may have been especially perceptive when they observed that the "very ambiguity of the relationship between parents and children heightened the salience of the familial analogy for the parallel struggle that was developing between the colonies and the mother country." Ambiguity and conflict in each case obviously facilitated the conscious perception of the one as an analogue of the other. So, too, did the traditional propensity—despite Locke's work—to conflate patriarchal and royal authority.[25] But significant as such conscious perceptions were, the subconscious transfer of emotions from the one context to the other was doubtlessly even more important. For as Benjamin Rush—who was both a pioneer psychiatrist and a revolutionary leader—noted, emotional reactions "may be induced by causes that are

---

[24]Carter, *Diary*, 1:52-54; Walker Maury to Theodorick Bland, 14 September 1786, in Jane Carson, *James Innes and His Brothers of the F. H. C.* (Charlottesville: University Press of Virginia, 1965) 50; entry of 6 June 1774, Farish, ed., *Journal and Letters of Fithian*, 116; James Reed on the school at Newbern, 15 February 1772, in Knight, ed., *Documentary History of Education in the South*, 1:95; John Drayton to James Glen, 24 December 1769, 14 March 1770, James Glen Papers, 1738-1777, South Caroliniana Library, University of South Carolina, Columbia; John Drayton, *The Carolinian Florist*, xxv.

[25]Smith and Hindus, "Premarital Pregnancy in America," 557; Gordon J. Schochet, "The Family and the Origins of the State in Locke's Political Philosophy," in *John Locke, Problems and Perspectives: A Collection of New Essays*, ed. John W. Yolton (London: Cambridge University Press, 1969) 81-98; Winthrop D. Jordan, "Familial Politics: Thomas Paine and the Killing of the King, 1776," *Journal of American History* 60 (1973): 299-301.

forgotten; or by the presence of objects which revive the sensation of distress with which at one time it was associated, but without reviving the cause of it in the memory."[26] Accordingly, the figures of speech employed by revolutionary leaders help to account for the intensity of their reaction to British measures. The "epithets of parent and child have been so long applied to Great Britain and her colonies," George Mason fumed, "that . . . we rarely see anything from your side of the water free from the authoritative style of a master to a schoolboy. . . . Is not this a little ridiculous?" Equally revealing is the tendency of Americans to refer to Britain not only as an "illiberal stepdame" but also as a "vile imposter—an old abandoned prostitute." The old prostitute is perhaps more significant than the stepdame, for the latter could be—and no doubt was in part—used in a conscious attempt to sanction resistance by stigmatizing British authority as illegitimate. But cursing Britain as an old imposter went beyond conscious utility. Rather, it recapitulated a pattern of behavior frequently observed among adolescents who attempt to assuage guilt over their increasing estrangement from their parents by imagining that these ugly old people are not really their parents but imposters.[27]

Why, one should ask at this point, is it worth knowing that the Revolution called forth and drew upon emotions that had been conditioned by the childhood experiences of revolutionaries? Was it not primarily a political revolution, understandable in conventional political terms, without the necessity of recourse to what at first glance appear to be only marginally relevant considerations? Certainly, at least on one level, the Revolution is largely comprehensible in purely political terms. But some aspects remain puzzling from most conventional perspectives. As Pauline Maier observed in reviewing Robert Calhoon's fine book about the Loyalists,

[26]Quoted in Erik H. Erikson, *Dimensions of a New Identity: The 1973 Jefferson Lectures in the Humanities* (New York: W. W. Norton, 1974) 101. For a more technical discussion of some varieties of this phenomenon, see Fred Weinstein and Gerald M. Platt, *The Wish to Be Free: Society, Psyche, and Value Change* (Berkeley and Los Angeles: University of California Press, 1969) 148.

[27]George Mason to the Committee of London Merchants, 6 June 1766, in *Prologue to Revolution: Sources and Documents on the Stamp Act Crisis, 1764-1766,* ed. Edmund S. Morgan (Chapel Hill: University of North Carolina Press, 1959) 158-59; David Ramsay, *History of the American Revolution,* and *New York Journal,* 25 May 1775, both in Burrows and Wallace, "The American Revolution," 192, 202; Lea Barinbaum, "Identity Crisis in Adolescence: The Problem of an Adopted Girl," *Adolescence* 9 (1974): 547.

"after 500 pages, the reader may well conclude that the Loyalists were not much different from other Americans." Many of them remain enigmas; and thus Burrows and Wallace have postulated the existence of a "distinctive Loyalist 'personality' " that remained "psychologically dependent on England. The prospect of living without a system of external supports and restraints filled them with anxiety."[28] Doubtlessly, this is an accurate characterization of some Loyalists, but it scarcely fits others. Among the others, some—but not all—may perhaps be more readily understood from the perspective outlined here. William Bull II and Alexander Garden may be good examples. Bull was lieutenant governor of South Carolina; Garden was the most distinguished contemporary physician in Charleston. There appears to be little evidence—other than their Loyalism—for considering either a dependent personality; to each, the influence of an oath—for one, the royal oath of office, for the other, the Hippocratic—may have been decisive. Each, however, especially disliked and avoided contention. Bull was "so very obliging that he never obliged," according to one very contentious Whig, Christopher Gadsden. Garden refused to serve in the revolutionary army, even as a doctor, because he wished to remain "a peaceable Person to follow his Profession."[29] In short, Loyalism or vacillation may have been associated with a personality type that was less dependent than fearful of contention. Although there is insufficient evidence to be certain about Bull and Garden, some youths may have found conflict with their parents so threatening that they could not bear to go through a similar experience again—which is not to say that they were dependent personalities.

The phenomenon of lingering allegiance may also be easier to understand when the Revolution is approached as a drama that evoked childhood emotions. Richard Henry Lee voiced a commonly accepted axiom when he remarked that "nothing can be more certain than that allegiance & protection are reciprocal duties." Thus allegiance made little intellectual sense

---

[28]Jack P. Greene, "The Social Origins of the American Revolution: An Evaluation and an Interpretation," *Political Science Quarterly* 88 (1973): 20; *New York Times Book Review,* 3 February 1974, 33; Burrows and Wallace, "The American Revolution," 295-99.

[29]For Bull, see *Dictionary of American Biography,* s.v. Bull, William, Jr.; for Garden, see Edmund B. Berkeley and Dorothy Smith Berkeley, *Dr. Alexander Garden of Charles Town* (Chapel Hill: University of North Carolina Press, 1969) 269, passim. Christopher Gadsden, *The Writings of Christopher Gadsden, 1746-1805,* ed. Richard Walsh (Columbia: University of South Carolina Press, 1966) 71.

after August 1775 when Americans were proclaimed to be in rebellion and thereby formally denied the protection of the Crown. Indeed, it can be argued, allegiance to a king always makes the most sense when seen as the culturally sanctioned projection of attitudes and emotions that first have been developed and conditioned in the family setting. Accordingly, several scholars have come close to suggesting that in abandoning the nurturing and protective role, British authorities unleashed upon George III all of the repressed hostilities of Americans toward their own fathers. The flood of hostility was in some ways remarkable, and perhaps no other perspective will account fully for the popularity of the assault upon the king in Thomas Paine's *Common Sense*.[30] Less commonly observed is that "anger at an unnatural 'parental' betrayal" did not, as has been claimed, sweep "away once and for all that affection for England." That affection remained resilient in the lower South, even among such leading revolutionary figures as John Rutledge, Henry Laurens, and Rawlins Lowndes, who retained strong vestiges of their former loyalty—at least until the British occupation of 1780–1782.[31] In fact, the evocation of this undertone of lingering affection is part of what gives the Declaration of Independence its somber dignity. Doubtlessly one of the main reasons the document still can move men who have had no experience with rebellion on a national scale is that they have had such experience on a personal level; it is also equally probable that the Declaration and the movement it epitomized took the form they did partly because revolutionary leaders were sons before they be-

---

[30]Richard Henry Lee to Patrick Henry, 8 September 1777, in *The Letters of Richard Henry Lee*, ed. James C. Ballagh, 2 vols. (New York: Macmillan Co., 1911-1914) 1 (1762-1778): 320-21; Merrill Jensen, ed., *English Historical Documents*, vol. 9 of *American Colonial Documents to 1776* (New York: Oxford University Press, 1969) 850-51. Winthrop Jordan hints at such an interpretation, especially in regard to Thomas Paine. Greene, as well as Burrows and Wallace, approaches the matter somewhat more varily. Jordan, "Familial Politics," 296, 301-304; Greene, "An Uneasy Connection," 63-64, 79-80; Burrows and Wallace, "The American Revolution," 270, 304.

[31]Burrows and Wallace, "The American Revolution," 291; Wallace, *Life of Henry Laurens*, 377-78; Rawlins Lowndes to James Simpson, 20 May 1780, Clinton Papers, William L. Clements Library, University of Michigan, Ann Arbor; Edward McCrady, *The History of South Carolina in the Revolution, 1780-1783* (New York: Macmillan Co., 1902) 587; idem, *The History of South Carolina in the Revolution, 1775-1780* (New York: Macmillan Co., 1901) 238. See also Fred M. MacFadden, Jr., "Popular Arts and the Revolt against Patriarchalism in Colonial America," *Journal of Popular Culture* 8 (1974): 286-94.

came revolutionaries, and their emotions were equally ambivalent in both cases.

All of which is to say that there was a significant irrational component to the American Revolution. Without an understanding of this element the movement may be inexplicable, at least in Georgia and South Carolina. In the populous colonies to the north resistance may have appeared to have a reasonable chance of success. Thus William Lee could report from London that "the ministers attend much to the motions in Virginia, for they think *you will fight."* But in the two southernmost of the thirteen colonies, Whigs and Loyalists alike were acutely aware not only of their prosperity under imperial control but also of their extreme vulnerability without the concomitant British protection. With slaves in their midst and Indians on their borders, sparsely scattered South Carolinians and Georgians believed they needed outside assistance against even relatively weak foes. From any rational point of view, challenging Britain was virtually tantamount to suicide. Knowing this, British observers like Richard Oswald, a slave merchant with close ties to the area, assumed that Southerners were only bluffing, that they would never dare to revolt. In short, British authorities expected them to act rationally, and the expectation proved wrong. There were, of course, many reasons why men were willing to run the awesome risks that rebellion entailed, but one of the most important was emotion. For if, as Edmund Morgan has remarked, self-interest can strengthen one's commitment to principles,[32] it also can undermine the commitment. And in this case something had to supplement self-interest. Without anger, it is therefore doubtful that there would have been a Revolution in this area. And without the tensions that appear to have characterized families in the Southern colonies, whether there would have been enough anger is a question about which one can only speculate.

[32]William Lee to Rodham Kenner, 15 May 1775, *Letters of William Lee, 1766-1783,* ed. Worthington C. Ford, 3 vols. (1891; rpt., New York: Burt Franklin, 1968) 1:157; M. Eugene Sirmans, *Colonial South Carolina: A Political History, 1663-1763* (Chapel Hill: University of North Carolina Press, 1966) 334-42; McCrady, *South Carolina in the Revolution, 1775-1780,* 314; William W. Abbot, *The Royal Governors of Georgia, 1754-1775* (Chapel Hill: University of North Carolina Press, 1959) 159; Richard Oswald to Lord Dartmouth, 21 February 1775, Dartmouth Papers, 3, 13, Staffordshire County Record Office, Stafford, England; Edmund S. Morgan, *The Birth of the Republic* (Chicago: University of Chicago Press, 1956) 52-53.

Ultimately, of course, that question can never be answered with certainty. Yet the hypothesis that prompts it can be tested in various ways. Among these, one of the more interesting may be to extend its application. If conflict and tension at home during youth accentuated emotions that fueled the Revolution, it should be possible to establish plausible links between this putative family background and the goals of revolutionary leaders. Fawn Brodie and Erik Erikson recently have sought to make precisely such connections concerning Thomas Jefferson. As the latter notes, Jefferson, who had struggled to discharge the responsibilities of an eldest son while still lacking full control of his own property, was as "a lawgiver . . . forever preoccupied with matters of the generations." High on the list of all the tyrannies over the mind of man that he opposed were those, like entail, that might be called the tyranny of the older generation. No doubt the effect of his own experience contributed to his belief that constitutions should terminate every two decades.[33] The idea, to be sure, represented an attempt to combine the safeguards of a written constitution with the flexibility of British practice. That the life span of constitutions was to be identical to the minority of each new generation is most suggestive.

If Jefferson's career appears to provide grounds for suspecting that the ends as well as the means of the Revolution can be correlated to its leaders' earlier struggles for personal independence, the relationship also raises a more important and complex question. Why were the results in each case—of youthful rebellion and of colonial revolt—so creative and successful? The scope of the question and of the present paper obviously preclude anything but a most tentative answer. But I can suggest, once again, that the revolutionary crisis and its outcome recapitulated the earlier adolescent crisis—that the successful resolution of the one prepared the way for the successful outcome of the other. In one form or another, this argument has been applied to other revolutionary situations by other scholars. In particular, Erikson has suggested that Luther and Gandhi resolved their own identity crises in ways that uniquely fitted them for the role of charismatic leaders in their respective societies. And Bruce Mazlish, who rejects the notion that American revolutionary leadership was predominantly charis-

---

[33]Fawn M. Brodie, *Thomas Jefferson, An Intimate History* (Toronto: Bantam Books, 1975) 26-27, 48-49, 79, 316, 432; Erikson, *Dimensions of a New Identity*, 72; Merrill D. Peterson, *Thomas Jefferson and the New Nation: A Biography* (New York: Oxford University Press, 1970) 113-17.

matic, has modified Erikson's interpretation to fit Washington.[34] Thus—
to reverse an old biological metaphor—there is little that is new in the general belief that phylogeny recapitulates ontogeny, or that the developing
revolutionary situation recalls the previous psychological evolution of the
individuals involved. What may be novel in the American situation, however, is the scale of the phenomenon. The relative absence of charismatic
leaders suggests that they were superfluous—or, perhaps, ubiquitous.
Having sought and achieved personal autonomy during youth, most American leaders doubtlessly felt little need to subordinate themselves to a charismatic figure, for they were he.

If so, a closer look at the conditions that promoted the successful quest
for personal autonomy in America may be worthwhile. If our suspicions
about the situation in the Southern colonies are correct, that quest appears
to have been both unusually successful and unusually contentious. How to
account for the apparently unlikely conjunction of these two characteristics therefore becomes the question. One explanation may be that the harmonious family is a vestige of the Garden of Eden, perhaps equally
mythical. Increasingly, students of the family are beginning to suspect that
not harmony but a considerable degree of conflict may have been the rule.
In addition, they are beginning to discover that such conflict may have been
far less damaging than they once believed. As some notably candid re-
searchers, who followed a group of men and women from birth to adult-
hood only to find that many of their early predictions proved to be wrong,
observed, "we had not appreciated the maturing utility of many painful
. . . experiences which in time, if lived through, brought sharpened
awareness, more complex integrations, better skills in problem solving,
clarified goals, and increasing stability."[35] Less immediately apparent,
however, is what enabled Americans to overcome the guilt necessarily entailed by rebellion against a previously accepted authority figure.

------

[34]Erik H. Erikson, *Young Man Luther: A Study in Psychoanalysis and History* (New
York: W. W. Norton, 1962) 15, 22, 206; Erik H. Erikson, *Gandhi's Truth: On the Origins
of Militant Nonviolence* (New York: W. W. Norton, 1969) 407; Mazlish, "Leadership in
the American Revolution," 116, 117, 127-31. For the view that Washington was a charismatic leader, see Seymour M. Lipset, *The First New Nation: The United States in Historical and Comparative Perspective* (Garden City: Anchor Books, 1967) 19-26, 362-63;
and Marcus Cunliffe, *George Washington: Man and Monument* (New York: New American Library, 1958) 166-67, passim.

[35]Skolnick, "The Family Revisited," 710, 714-15, 718.

In particular, if there was an intimate connection between family life in the Southern colonies and the nature of the American Revolution, the mechanisms by which individuals justified rebellion in each case must have been closely related. The explanation offered by Greene, who observed that British authorities forfeited their mantle of authority by violating what colonials perceived as the moral order, covers the political but not the familial rebellion. The interpretation advanced by Lewis Feuer subsumes both kinds of revolts, but even he would not argue for its particular relevance to the American Revolution. In other cases, however, he notes that rebels frequently have sought to cope with their guilt feelings by seeking " 'back to the people' identification." A "would-be parricide," the rebel "can conquer his guilt only with the demonstration that he is selfless and by winning the comforting maternal love of the oppressed." Among American revolutionaries, Thomas Burke of North Carolina is one of the very few who might fit this model. Having quarreled with his Irish uncle who raised him, Burke came to America where he soon became identified with the revolutionary movement. "My zeal," he later wrote, "was a passion for the liberty of mankind. I could not stand aloof from the struggle."[36] Even allowing for words written in retrospect under the influence of Enlightenment rhetoric, Burke sounds atypical enough to make one suspect that the psychological mechanisms by which he assuaged guilt were not the same as those of most of his fellow Southerners. The question therefore remains: how did young men nerve themselves to revolt against their fathers; how did American revolutionaries sanction their rebelliousness? In the final analysis, we must return to the notion that maturation of the individual, in the one case, and colonial growth, in the other, appeared to render illegitimate the authority that hitherto had been perceived as legitimate.

Why? Because in colonial society the son sought to emulate the father, to behave as he would have under similar circumstances. That is, sons internalized parental standards and values. A most illuminating symbolic representation of the process occurs in the nether world of myth and Freudian fantasy where men killed and ate the tribal patriarch. Such cannibalism

---

[36]Greene, "An Uneasy Connection," 77-78; Lewis S. Feuer, *The Conflict of Generations: The Character and Significance of Student Movements* (New York: Basic Books, 1969) 529-30; Elisha P. Douglass, "Thomas Burke, Disillusioned Democrat," *North Carolina Historical Review* 26 (1949): 151, quotation from 153.

presumably conferred the father's extraordinary power upon his successors, who sought to ingest its magical sources with the father. Amid the restraints of civilization and the conscious mind, the model takes the place of the flesh, while values substitute for magic. In each case, parricide is carried on in the name of the father, and the system of beliefs that sanctioned his authority legitimizes the revolt of the sons. Thus it is not really surprising to find that in the American Revolution men who called themselves Sons of Liberty resisted a king whose crown and lineage had symbolized British freedom. Nor is it even surprising to find, as Winthrop Jordan has done, that Americans figuratively and in some ways quite literally consumed the Crown. Indeed, it seems entirely natural that they did so in the firm belief that their forefathers would have been proud of them.[37]

Ultimately, therefore, to understand both the American Revolution and the men who led it, one must know what qualities parents esteemed in their sons. One was independence, but independence was generally considered to be a manly virtue; obedience a boyish one. Indeed, independence in manhood depended upon obedience in childhood, for only the discipline of the one made possible the freedom of the other. As Locke noted, "Every man must some time or other be trusted to himself, and his own conduct; and he that is a good, a virtuous, and able man, must be made so within." The man who had not learned regular habits and self-control in childhood was a threat as well as a "burthen to Society and himself," as Eliza Lucas Pinckney observed. Industry was most prized for its utility in maintaining a well-regulated life. "The greatest conquest is a Victory over your own irregular passions," she reminded her brother in urging him to "lay down betimes a plan" for his "conduct in life." Some forty years later, Jefferson revealed that he shared the same belief when he wrote to his daughters that work was the way to avoid hysteria.[38] So, too, did a less prominent revolutionary leader from South Carolina, Thomas Ferguson, who directed the executors of his will to be especially careful in keeping his sons

---

[37]Jordan, "Familial Politics," 294-308; Advertisement for a History of Carolina from 1663-1721, *South Carolina Gazette and Country Journal* (Charleston), 18 February 1766; Letter of 25 April 1770, *South Carolina Gazette* (Charleston), 17 May 1770; Brodie, *Thomas Jefferson,* 28.

[38]John Locke, "Some Thoughts Concerning Education," 1:133; Eliza Pinckney to [Daniel Horry, Jr.], 16 April 1782, in "Letters of Eliza Lucas Pinckney, 1768-1782," ed. Elise Pinckney, *South Carolina Historical Magazine* 76 (1975): 167; Eliza Lucas Pinckney to George Lucas, Jr., 1745, in Ravenel, *Eliza Pinckney,* 64-65; Bernard Bailyn, "Boyd's Jefferson: Notes for a Sketch," *New England Quarterly* 33 (1960): 390.

busy until they were twenty-one, "so as to give a true Relish for Industry, being well convinced that the Habit of Idleness is productive of the most fatal Consequences to Youth." However anachronistic it would be to apply Michael Walzer's recent insight to these men and women, they frequently acted as if they understood that only the discipline of the Puritan saints made possible the liberalism of Locke.[39]

In the socialization of their children, as in virtually every area of life from architecture to zoology, they exhibited a rage for order and regularity. Nothing could be farther from the truth in most cases, one suspects, than Henry Adams's comment that the "life of boyhood in Virginia was not well fitted for teaching self-control or mental discipline."[40] In fact, the frequency of injunctions like those quoted above, as well as the surprising depth of commitment to what Edmund Morgan has termed the Puritan Ethic on the part of wealthy Anglicans in the Southern colonies, suggests that local circumstances may have given these virtues special and continued relevance. Relatively weak institutional support made self-discipline socially and psychologically more important. So, too, undoubtedly, did the presence of slaves. Certainly, if Fithian's impression was accurate, planters like Robert Carter of Nomini Hall strove to make their plantations, like their minds, islands of good order and regularity in a potentially chaotic world.[41] Furthermore, the flux and tension within the family itself may have

---

[39]Will of Thomas Ferguson, proved 20 May 1786, Charleston County Wills, 22 (1786-1793): 18, Works Progress Administration Transcripts, SCDAH. Ferguson was a member of the First and Second Provincial Congresses, 1775-1776; the General Assembly, 1776-1778; the Legislative Council, 1776; the House of Representatives, 1778-1780; and the Privy Council, 1776-1782. Michael Walzer, *The Revolution of the Saints: A Study in the Origins of Radical Politics* (New York: Atheneum, 1968) 302-303.

[40]Although Winthrop Jordan termed it a "penchant for order," it may have been more what eighteenth-century men would have called a "ruling passion." Jordan, *White over Black: American Attitudes toward the Negro, 1550-1812* (Chapel Hill: University of North Carolina Press, 1968) 482. Henry Adams, *John Randolph* (Boston: Houghton Mifflin, 1898) 6. The interest shown by early biographers in Patrick Henry's boyhood "indolence" suggests that they may have realized such a background would have been unusual among his contemporaries as well as surprising for a man of his later accomplishments. See, for example, Moses Coit Tyler, *Patrick Henry* (Boston: Houghton Mifflin, 1898) 5. That this picture is distorted even in Henry's case is suggested by Richard R. Beeman, *Patrick Henry: A Biography* (New York: McGraw-Hill, 1974) 4.

[41]Edmund S. Morgan, "The Puritan Ethic and the American Revolution," *William and Mary Quarterly* 3d ser. 24 (1967):1-43, esp. 7; entry of 15 December 1773, Farish, ed., *Journal and Letters of Fithian*, 31-32. See also Abraham Baldwin's comments on education quoted in Northen, ed., *Men of Mark in Georgia*, 1:8-9.

heightened the commitment of many among both fathers and sons to stability and order.

At any rate, personal order and regularity clearly were among the most
pervasive, earliest, and persistently inculcated of all cultural imperatives,
and the inculcation depended at least in part upon the threatened deprivation of love. As Richard Henry Lee wrote to his sons, Thomas and Ludwell, "whilst you continue to behave as well as you have done, my tenderest
affection shall always be placed on you," and the same sentiment was expressed by many other parents—including Jefferson and Henry Laurens.[42]
However cruel the technique may appear to be, and whatever its hidden
costs, it seems to have been effective. Certainly the revolutionary generation contained some of the most rigorously self-disciplined individuals one
would want to meet—like Jefferson—whose lives were, insofar as the
contingencies of life and the vagaries of the human heart permit, models
of good order and regularity.[43] If ever men were schooled to be masters of
their own lives, these were they.

Just as surely, however, if ever men were reared to resist external authority, these also were they. For to threaten the withdrawal of love for the
failure to live up to certain standards was to say, in the plainest possible
manner, that some values were greater than love—greater even than the
nurturing love of a parent upon which, to a young child, life itself seemed

---

[42]10 May 1777, in Ballagh, ed., *The Letters of Richard Henry Lee*, 1:288; Brodie,
Thomas Jefferson, 45; Wallace, *Life of Henry Laurens*, 470.

[43]Wallace, *Life of Henry Laurens*, 46, passim; Eliza Lucas Pinckney, *The Letterbook
of Eliza Lucas Pinckney, 1739-1762*, ed. Elise Pinckney and Marvin Zahniser (Chapel Hill:
University of North Carolina Press, 1972) 34-35; Brodie, *Thomas Jefferson*, 1-3. Although
Brodie termed Jefferson the most "orderly" and "Most controlled" of our "great presi-
dents," Jordan could still observe that she probably underrated "the power of the eighteenth-century cultural atmosphere. This is to say, that in any other age" a man of Jefferson's
emotions "would have devoted himself to quarreling, wenching, boozing, and generally
messing up his historical reputation." Obviously, the cultural atmosphere was British as
well as American and the young Englishman who would later become a leader of the Revolution in North Carolina, James Iredell, had been in the colonies less than two years when
he began a journal on 22 August 1770 by observing, "As I spend too much time in an idle,
unprofitable manner, I have thought of an expedient, which may perhaps correct my conduct a little. I am determined to set down the history of every day, . . . so that, by this
method, I shall review the conduct of my time." Perhaps, however, it is significant that
this resolution came to him in Edenton, North Carolina. See Jordan's review of Brodie's
Thomas Jefferson in *William and Mary Quarterly*, 3d ser. 32 (1975): 510-11; Griffith J.
McRee, ed., *James Iredell* (1857-1858 rpt., New York: Peter Smith, 1949) 1, 29, 65.

to depend. Implicit here was the notion that some values were great enough to sanction resistance against even the most legitimate of authorities. And among these imperatives one of the most important was self-control—the imposition of order and regularity upon one's own life. A trivial incident from John Rutledge's childhood, therefore, becomes illuminating. The first recorded episode of his rebelliousness, at age eleven, involved a refusal to study "literature and the arts" because, he claimed to believe, such pursuits were corrupting and conducive to idleness. Naturally, as an individual developed greater control of himself, external controls became increasingly irksome, superfluous, and—most important—potentially disruptive of the internally imposed patterns of order. The process of maturation therefore dictated that self-control ultimately meant both control of self and independence from the control of others. Of necessity, the two were inseparable. Thus the revolutionary generation was being taught that the dependent and disordered life was not worth living. This form of tutelage was not apt to produce boys or men who, because of fear or guilt, would be incapable of challenging authority. Rather, it was a form of schooling that tended to make self-evident Mason's observation that there was "a passion natural to the mind of man, especially a free man, which renders him impatient of restraint." Finally, however, it was a form of education that produced men who justified their impatience by their restraint. Not all were moderate revolutionaries, though most were, but they were men for whom order was the ultimate sanction of rebelliousness and revolution.[44]

Herein may lie some of the most important links between the family background of the Southern elite and the nature of the Revolution. Youthful experience taught that rebellion need not lead to chaos, that in fact it might be a prerequisite for order, and that the risk was worth taking. Thus Americans could resist, on a piecemeal basis, imperial restraints that threatened to limit de facto colonial autonomy; and when less drastic measures proved ineffective, they could pledge their lives, their fortunes, and

---

[44]Richard Barry, *Mr. Rutledge of South Carolina* (New York: Duell, Sloan, and Pearce, 1942) 12. Although Barry's work is neither documented nor very reliable, this episode is plausible. Mason to Committee of London Merchants, 6 June 1766, in Morgan, ed., *Prologue to Revolution,* 162. Cf. Greene, "Autonomy and Stability," 192. For a suggestive discussion of the ways in which this impulse could lead to attempts to impose order on others, see Charles G. Sellers, Jr., "Making a Revolution: The North Carolina Whigs, 1765-1775," in *Studies in Southern History,* ed. J. Carlyle Sitterson (Chapel Hill: University of North Carolina Press, 1957) 23-46.

their sacred honor in defense of independence. Significantly, they increasingly justified their rebelliousness in the name of order. According to Henry Laurens, British measures threatened to produce "dire confusion," while William Henry Drayton believed that Britain had created a situation "pregnant with horrible uproar and wild confusion." Over and over again, these charges were repeated until Jefferson immortalized them in the Declaration of Independence.[45] For the gist of the indictment against George III was not merely that he failed to protect colonial liberty—or even that he had actively infringed upon it—but that in doing both he had created disorder and confusion. In the final analysis the perception of this fact may have been a large part of what helped to make the Declaration acceptable to many Americans. It is therefore not surprising that, as many scholars have observed, the culmination and most characteristic expression of the American Revolution was to be found in the constitutions it produced.[46] Because "domestic Tranquillity" and the "Blessings of Liberty" seemed to be one and inseparable at some of the deepest levels of consciousness, as well as of political prudence, these constitutions became the ultimate sanction of rebellion.

Thus we have some fascinating paradoxes: violence undertaken in the name of order, and a revolution that drew energy and direction from the irrational and yet remained among the most rational of revolutions on record—one that was, despite its substratum of emotion, "infused," as one

---

[45]Henry Laurens to John Laurens, 8 February 1774, in "Letters from Hon. Henry Laurens to His Son John, 1773-1776," *South Carolina Historical and Genealogical Magazine* 3 (1902): 140; [William Henry Drayton], "A Letter from 'Freeman' of South Carolina to the Deputies of North America, Assembled in the High Court of Congress at Philadelphia," 10 August 1774, in *Documentary History of the American Revolution*, ed. R. W. Gibbes, 3 vols. (1853-1857; rpt., Spartanburg SC: Reprint Company, 1972) 1:27; Thomas Jefferson, "A Summary View of the Rights of British Americans," in *The Portable Thomas Jefferson*, ed. Merrill D. Peterson (New York: Viking, 1975) 10, 14-16; "Declaration of the Causes and Necessity for Taking Up Arms," 6 July 1775, in Jensen, ed., *American Colonial Documents to 1776*, 846-47; South Carolina "Association," adopted 3 June 1775; in *Extracts from the Journals of the Provincial Congresses of South Carolina, 1775-1776*, ed. William E. Hemphill and Wylma A. Wates (Columbia: South Carolina Archives Department, 1960) 36.

[46]Hannah Arendt, *On Revolution* (New York: Viking, 1965) 139-41; R. R. Palmer, *The Age of the Democratic Revolution: A Political History of Europe and America, 1760-1800* (Princeton: Princeton University Press, 1959) 214-35.

commentator has observed, "by *mind* to a degree never approximated since and perhaps never approximated before."[47]

To quote this apt description is to put the present interpretation in perspective. My attempt here has not been to reject more conventional interpretations, nor even to supplant some of the more unconventional ones, but to supplement them. Briefly and starkly stated, the thesis of this essay has been that family life and child-rearing practices in the Southern colonies contributed to a particular kind of rebelliousness that revealed itself on the grand as well as lesser scales. Hitherto we have sought to demonstrate this proposition by an abstract discussion of developments in the larger sphere. But if the point of view is valid, it should be equally useful in helping us to understand concrete events at the domestic level. Let us therefore return to the earthy plane upon which we began to see if the present perspective helps to make the sequel of our opening drama more understandable—indeed, perhaps almost predictable.

Williams and his stepson, you will recall, had found the vehicle wrecked in a ditch, clothes strewn about, and the young couple, William Ward Crosthwaite and Sarah Hartley, gone. Obviously acquainted with the highwaymen and apparently suspecting collusion on Sarah's part, the two men sought to convince all the ministers in the area not to marry the pair, though it was lamentably clear that Crosthwaite had had Sarah "a Considerable time in the woods by himself." But the efforts of the two men proved to be in vain, for within hours of the kidnapping the couple, who lacked a marriage license, took their vows before the rector of the local parish. To justify his participation the minister posed the crucial question: "Suppose Mr. Crosthwaite shou'd debauch or has debauched your Sister?" To which her brother could only reply that he "would rather have her an honest Woman than a Whore."[48]

This was one of those times, it seems, when even the literal shotgun could be effectively turned against the restraints imposed by familial authority and when one might engage with impunity in flagrant acts of re-

---

[47]Irving Kristol, "The Most Successful Revolution," *American Heritage* 25 (April 1974): 37.

[48]Examination and Deposition of Robert Williams, and Information and Deposition of Thomas Hartley, 14 January 1766, South Carolina Council Journals, 32:692, 697, SCDAH.

belliousness. In response to Mrs. Williams's demand to know what was going on, one of the highwaymen, Barnard Elliott, replied, "God damn you[,] Madam[,] Crosthwaite is my friend[.] I dont care if it should cost me £10,000 & all the money'd Men in the Province will approve our Conduct & stand by us." He was correct. Though arrested and indicted for a felony, the kidnappers had no difficulty in finding sureties for their bonds, nor in being quickly pardoned after the girl testified that she had gone willingly. Indeed, the minister claimed that Crosthwaite had acted like "a Man of Courage & an officer."[49] Regularization of the couple's relationship by marriage and the ensuing community approval suggest that the episode was a peculiarly eighteenth-century act of American rebelliousness—a minirevolution in which the end was not liberation from restraints but the "foundation of freedom."[50] Thus it is not surprising to find that at the time of her kidnapping, Sarah Hartley "was legally intitled unto a Considerable Substance in Lands and Goods." Nor is it anticlimactic to learn that her second marriage, after Crosthwaite's premature death, was to a widower merchant. Finally, it appears somehow fitting that one of the gunmen, Benjamin Huger, died while fighting the British in 1779; while another,

---

[49]Williams's Deposition, Petition of Robert Williams and Thomas Hartley, and Hartley's Deposition, 14 January 1766, ibid., 690, 686-87, 698; Pardon of W. Ward Crosthwaite, Barnard Elliott, Benjamin Huger, and John Miles, 3 April 1766, Miscellaneous Records, MM:361-62, SCDAH. For Crosthwaite, see "Officers of the South Carolina Regiment in the Cherokee War, 1760-1761," *South Carolina Historical and Genealogical Magazine* 3 (1902): 205.

[50]The distinction between revolution and mere rebellion is Hannah Arendt's. If the point is valid in this context, one might expect to find that among the middle and upper classes, at least, the incident of illegitimacy remained low even though the rate of premarital conceptions skyrocketed during the late eighteenth century. Although isolating the operative values might prove to be a monumental task, statistically parallel trends in illegitimacy and premarital pregnancy probably mask significant variations in the behavior of different classes. It should, therefore, be noted that this paper has focused upon values and behavior doubtlessly characterizing individuals of relatively high socioeconomic status. Arendt, *On Revolution,* 140; Smith and Hindus, "Premarital Pregnancy in America," 539; Edward Shorter, "Illegitimacy, Sexual Revolution, and Social Change in Modern Europe," in *The Family in History: Interdisciplinary Essays,* ed. Theodore K. Rabb and Robert I. Rotberg (New York: Harper and Row, 1971) 67-70.

Barnard Elliott, became the orator who read the Declaration of Independence at the ceremonies in Charleston celebrating its adoption.[51]

[51]Williams's Deposition, 14 January 1766, South Carolina Council Journals, 32:692. For Crosthwaite's death, see *South Carolina Gazette,* 2 November 1769. For Sarah's second marriage, see Robert G. Stewart, *Henry Benbridge, American Portrait Painter* (Washington: Smithsonian, 1971) 40; and "Records Kept by Colonel Isaac Hayne," *South Carolina Historical and Genealogical Magazine* 10 (1909): 167. McCrady, *South Carolina in the Revolution, 1775-1780,* 179, 358.

"The Violent Spirit," the Reestablishment of Order, and the Continuity of Leadership in Postrevolutionary South Carolina ⎯⎯⎯⎯⎯⎯⎯⎯⎯⎯⎯⎯

How order emerged from the disorder of the American Revolution is an important and still insufficiently studied question. Order as a goal is a general theme of the preceding essay; one of the mechanisms for establishing it is the subject of the following article. It was originally given in 1982 at a symposium sponsored by the United States Capitol Historical Society and the Institute of Early American History and Culture in cooperation with the United States Congress. All papers presented at this conference appear in An Uncivil War: The Southern Backcountry during the American Revolution *ed. by Ronald Hoffman, Peter J. Albert, and Thad W. Tate (Charlottesville: University Press of Virginia, 1985) from which this essay is reprinted with permission.*

Among the many intriguing questions concerning the American Revolution one of the most puzzling, to quote historian John Shy, is "how a national polity so successful, and a society so relatively peaceful, could emerge from a war so full of bad behavior, including perhaps a fifth of the population actively treasonous (that is, loyal to Crown)." What makes the question difficult, of course, is that common sense suggests a direct correlation between the amount of disorder and violence, on the one hand, and postwar social and political instability, on the other. And if the aftermath of the Revolution in the other parts of the nation appears puzzling, the situation in South Carolina seems to be almost inexplicable. For that state, in the words of one scholar, had "seethed in the early 1780's with the irregular campaigns" of partisan leaders, but then soon returned "to stability and internal unity almost unparalleled even among the relatively tranquil histories of the states of the American Union." Indeed, it was perhaps the prime example of an area in which, to use the words of another historian, Ronald Hoffman, "a rather unpopular Whig elite managed to emerge from a near anarchic revolutionary situation with much of its authority still intact."[1] South Carolina in this period thus seems to have been a historical paradox. Although present knowledge is still too limited to permit an accurate assessment of the uniqueness of South Carolina's experience, the degree to which it contradicts conventional assumptions about revolutionary wars and their aftermath gives general significance to an understanding of how local authorities reestablished public order and their own legitimacy.

Perhaps the most expeditious way of approaching the problem is to begin by questioning the putative correlation between social disruption and change, which in a sense was Shy's strategy in noting that "the character of the war itself" made Americans aware of "their own political peril" and channeled their energies into combating the specter of anarchy.[2] But precisely how Americans went about this has perhaps never been adequately spelled out, certainly not for South Carolina. Some of their efforts are, of course, obvious or have been described; others, if pursued, would extend far beyond the confines of what is feasible here. Accordingly, this essay will focus on some of the most misunderstood and consequently neglected aspects of the process.

As many historians have recognized, South Carolina was the scene of some of the most vicious fighting in the war. "The lower South," historian Don Higginbotham has noted, "was ravaged by the war as no other section of the country. Its governmental processes had collapsed, and its

<hr/>

[1] John Shy, *A People Numerous and Armed: Reflections on the Military Struggle for American Independence* (London: Oxford University Press, 1976) 15; Russell F. Weigley, *The Partisan War: The South Carolina Campaign of 1780-1782* (Columbia: University of South Carolina Press, 1970) 73; Ronald Hoffman, "The 'Disaffected' in the Revolutionary South," in *The American Revolution: Explorations in the History of American Radicalism*, ed. Alfred F. Young (DeKalb: Northern Illinois University Press, 1976) 293.

[2] Shy, *A People Numerous and Armed*, 17.

society had disintegrated to the point that it approached John Locke's savage state of nature." As Hoffman observed, "No more chaotic a situation can be imagined than that of the lower South in the years from 1780 to 1783." It is all too easy to find evidence for their generalizations. The earliest American historians perpetuated many accounts of British atrocities so their wartime outrages are consequently well known. One of the most notorious incidents occurred shortly after the British captured Charleston in the spring of 1780, when Banastre Tarleton's Legion overtook a fleeing unit of Virginians near the border of the two Carolinas. Exactly what happened cannot be learned from the contradictory reports, but it seems that Tarleton's men slaughtered the Americans while they tried to surrender. "This barbarous massacre," according to David Ramsay, who wrote about the fighting in South Carolina shortly after it ended, "gave a more sanguinary turn to the war," as Americans soon retaliated with cries of "Tarleton's Quarter."[3] Bloody enough already, the struggle reached some sort of a climax, at least in local legend, when a Tory later known as Bloody Bill Cunningham led a raid through the western part of the state during the autumn of 1781. At Cloud's Creek he and his men surprised thirty Whigs and hacked twenty-eight of them to death after they capitulated; across the Saluda River at Hayes's Station the Tory raiders dispatched eight more men in similar fashion.[4]

Whig atrocities have been less well publicized, but even regular army officers such as Light Horse Harry Lee sometimes let violence get out of hand, as when he sanctioned the summary execution of prisoners captured at Fort Motte in the spring of 1781. Francis Marion put an end to those executions, but despite his popularity Marion had trouble restraining his men who, it was reported, whipped prisoners "almost to death." In fact, some Tories who fell into Whig hands fared even worse. A John Stilwell was thrown from his horse in one engagement and, according to his com-

[3]Don Higginbotham, *The War of American Independence: Military Attitudes, Policies, and Practice, 1763-1789* (New York: Macmillan Co., 1971) 361, 375; Hoffman, "The 'Disaffected' in the Revolutionary South," 292; David Ramsay, *The History of the Revolution of South Carolina, from a British Province to an Independent State,* 2 vols. (Trenton NJ: Isaac Collins, 1785) 2:110. For a graphic account of one such massacre of prisoners by Americans, see John C. Dann, ed., *The Revolution Remembered: Eyewitness Accounts of the War for Independence* (Chicago: University of Chicago Press, 1980) 202.

[4]Richard Maxwell Brown, *Strain of Violence: Historical Studies of American Violence and Vigilantism* (New York: Oxford University Press, 1975) 81.

manding officer, was then "desired to surrender, which he did; he was asked for his pistol, he delivered it up and was instantly shot through the body with it; he complained of this behaviour," and, the account continued, "he was abused and ordered to deliver his sword, he did and was cut through the skull in five or six places with his own sword, and when a [British] party brought him home . . . his brains, that is part of them, were two inches issued from his head. He preserved his senses perfect for two days, and told regularly the same story, then died."[5] Not without reason, a British officer reported that the enemy "uniformly murdered in cold blood, all our Militia whom they have been able to get at." Late in the war some of the survivors compiled a list of more than three hundred of their fellows who, they claimed, had been "massacred" in South Carolina. Some of these alleged murders involved court proceedings, and others, like the hangings that were supposed to have occurred in Charleston immediately after the British evacuation, may have been figments of the Loyalists' imagination. Nevertheless, the compilers of the list claimed to have had specific information about the enumerated men, such as Robert Love and another individual who were "killed asleep." They were certain that "at least thrice the number have been Butchered" in similar manner.[6] Americans later implicitly corroborated many of these charges when they acknowledged that an order to send a prisoner "to Halifax" (North Carolina) or to grant him a "Georgia parole" was the equivalent of a "thrust with the bayonet." There is no better capsule description of the society in which such practices flourished than the incident related by a British major, George Hanger, who had become convinced that the backcountrymen of the Carolinas were "more Savage than the Indians." According to Hanger, one of "this distinguished race of men" tracked an enemy for two

[5]Charles Royster, *Light-Horse Harry Lee and the Legacy of the American Revolution* (New York: Alfred A. Knopf, 1981) 37; Levi Smith's account, *Royal Gazette,* 17 April 1782, in *The Price of Loyalty: Tory Writings from the Revolutionary Era,* ed. Catherine S. Crary (New York: McGraw-Hill, 1973) 290; Colonel John Watson to Francis Marion, 15 March 1781, in *Documentary History of the American Revolution,* ed. R. W. Gibbes, 3 vols. (1853-1857; rpt., Spartanburg SC: Reprint Company, 1972) 3:39.

[6]Nisbet Balfour to Lord Cornwallis, 21 May 1781, Cornwallis Papers, PRO 30/11/6, folio 97, and Thomas Fletchall and Others to the King, 19 April 1782, CO5/82, folios 296-99, British Public Record Office, London, microfilms available at South Carolina Department of Archives and History, Columbia (hereafter referred to as SCDAH).

hundred miles through the woods, shot him down before his own door, and rode away to boast of the exploit.[7]

Whether the killer in this case was Whig or Tory is immaterial; he could have been either. Both sides were guilty of atrocities, especially during 1781 when neither could really control the countryside; so sorting out the various charges and countercharges in an attempt to assign blame is therefore neither feasible nor useful. Nevertheless, a pattern does emerge from the last three years of the war. At first, Sir Henry Clinton and other British commanders were interested in conciliating as much of the populace as possible. Mindful of the counterproductive looting and burning on General Augustine Prevost's march through lower South Carolina in 1779, Clinton reminded subordinates the following year, "For God's sake no irregularities." But the approach of Horatio Gates's army toward Camden in August 1780 "seemed," as one Loyalist observed, "to be a signal for a general revolt in the disaffected parts of the back Country," and British officers soon adopted a policy of calculated severity. Thus, for example, Major James Wemyss burned some fifty houses in a swath more than seventy miles long through the northeastern part of the state. Further experience with a war in which, according to one Loyalist, "every man is a soldier" and distinguishing friend from foe was often impossible, tended to make the British less restrained and less discriminating in their use of violence.[8]

As the conflict swung in their favor, American authorities, on the other hand, became increasingly aware of the need to curb irregularities as a means of restoring order. Thus in August 1781 Governor John Rutledge issued a proclamation against plundering, and the commander of the Southern army, Nathanael Greene, threatened to impose the death penalty

---

[7]Joseph Johnson, *Traditions and Reminiscences Chiefly of the American Revolution in the South* (1851; rpt., Spartanburg SC: Reprint Company, 1972) 567; Ramsay, *The History of the Revolution in South Carolina,* 2:365; George Hanger, *The Life, Adventures, and Opinions of Colonel George Hanger [Baron Coleraine] Written by Himself,* 2 vols. (London: J. Debrett, 1801) 2:404-405.

[8]Clinton to Alexander Innes, 19 February 1780, in Historical Manuscripts Commission, *Report on American Manuscripts in the Royal Institution of Great Britain,* 4 vols. (London: His Majesty's Stationery Office, 1904-1909) 2:93; "Colonel Robert Gray's Observations on the War in Carolina," *South Carolina Historical and Genealogical Magazine* 11 (1910): 141, 157; George C. Rogers, Jr., *The History of Georgetown County, South Carolina* (Columbia: University of South Carolina Press, 1970) 129; Jerome J. Nadelhaft, *The Disorders of War: The Revolution in South Carolina* (Orono: University of Maine at Orono Press, 1981) 57.

on men caught marauding.[9] But partisan operations almost inevitably encouraged the kind of thing Rutledge and Greene were trying to control, and before the war was over the legislature was forced to sanction legalized plunder to support troops.

As many men realized, condoning such behavior was risky. In 1776 Charles Lee, a Whig general who understood the utility of partisan operations, sought to mount an expedition against the British in St. Augustine by recruiting men with the promise of plunder. This idea disturbed Arthur Middleton, who was then one of the South Carolinian delegates to the Continental Congress. Believing Lee to be "an odd fish," Middleton was shocked at "the predatory intention" of his plan. "Instead of that noble Spirit which should animate the Soldiers of a free State," Middleton cautioned, "let us beware of encouraging a Spirit of a different kind & of converting them into a Band of Robbers egg'd on by avaricious Views; when that is the Case, adieu to all Liberty, peace & happiness." Others shared Middleton's fears. Greene, too, later became alarmed that the vicious civil war would undermine the stability of postwar institutions. There was good reason to believe that these forebodings would prove accurate. Judge Aedanus Burke, for example, was certain at the end of the war that South Carolinians had become so habituated to killing the British that they had "reconciled their minds to the killing of each other." Another politician, Pierce Butler, remarked at the outbreak of the French Revolution that had the French "felt as much of the Miseries of Civil War" as he and other Carolinians, "They would enter on the business with Caution. When Once the Dogs of Civil War are let loose it is no easy matter to Call them back."[10]

---

[9]William Moultrie, *Memoirs of the American Revolution, So Far as It Related to the States of North and South Carolina and Georgia,* 2 vols. (1802; rpt., 2 vols. in 1, New York: New York Times and Arno, 1968) 2:407-409; Clyde R. Ferguson, "Carolina and Georgia Patriot and Loyalist Militia in Action, 1778-1783," in *The Southern Experience in the American Revolution,* ed. Jeffrey J. Crow and Larry E. Tise (Chapel Hill: University of North Carolina Press, 1978) 192.

[10]Middleton to William Henry Drayton, 14 September 1776, in "Correspondence of Arthur Middleton, Signer of the Declaration of Independence," ed. Joseph W. Barnwell, *South Carolina Historical and Genealogical Magazine* 27 (1926): 143-44; Higginbotham, *The War of American Independence,* 375; Burke to the Grand Jury of Charleston, 9 June 1783, in John Almon, *American Remembrancer* 16 (1783): 286-87, quoted in Jerome J. Nadelhaft, "The Revolutionary Era in South Carolina, 1775-1788" (Ph.D. dissertation, University of Wisconsin, 1965) 151; Pierce Butler to Reverend [Weeden] Butler, 15 March 1789, The Letters of Pierce Butler, 1784-1799, Add. Ms. 16603, folio 57, The British Library, London.

Evidence of physical destruction and social disruption had been all around Butler. Considering the relatively limited technology available to eighteenth-century armies, one is amazed at the damage to the countryside that an army could inflict. Free to rejoin the American army after an exchange of prisoners, General William Moultrie, accompanied by a small guard, made the ride of about a hundred miles from the Georgetown area to Greene's camp southwest of the Ashley River in 1782. It was, he recalled, the "most dull, melancholy, dreary ride that any one could possibly take." A countryside that had once been filled with "live-stock and wild fowl of every kind, was now destitute of all. It had been so completely checquered by the different parties, that not one part of it had been left unexplored; consequently, not the vestiges of horses, cattle, hogs, or deer, &c. was to be found. The squirrels and birds of every kind were totally destroyed." The dragoons with him told him that "on their scouts, no living creature was to be seen, except now and then a few camp scavengers [vultures], picking the bones of some unfortunate fellows, who had been shot or cut down, and left in the woods above ground." Whigs and Tories, in the words of one of the latter, "dared not sleep in their Houses, but concealed themselves in swamps," for fear of being murdered. Indeed, shortly after hostilities had ostensibly ended, a Scottish minister who had left the area around Beaufort and later returned found that "all was desolation. . . . Every field, every plantation, showed marks of ruin and devastation. Not a person was to be met with in the roads. All was gloomy." All society, he continued, "seems to be at an end. Every person keeps close on his own plantation. Robberies and murders are often committed on the public roads. The people that remain have been peeled, pillaged, and plundered. Poverty, want, and hardship appear in almost every countenance. A dark melancholy gloom appears everywhere, and the morals of the people are almost entirely extirpated."[11]

Given what Governor Benjamin Guerard termed this "uncommonly Cruel War," the bitterness of South Carolinians toward the British and the Tories is understandable. Even generally merciful Whigs who advocated leniency toward most former Loyalists revealed a barely controlled rage.

---

[11]Moultrie, *Memoirs of the American Revolution,* 2:352-55; "Gray's Observations on the War in Carolina," 154; Account of Reverend Archibald Simpson, 1783-1784, in *Port Royal under Six Flags,* ed. Katherine M. Jones (Indianapolis: Bobbs-Merrill, 1960) 138-39.

"I detest the British Army, and despise from my Soul the mass of unfeeling men which compose its Officers," Aedanus Burke remarked after the British surrender at Yorktown. Later, looking back on the British occupation of South Carolina, he observed that "Their treatment was so extravagantly outrageous, that no description will ever give a just idea of it; and to myself who was a witness and a sufferer, it appears like a dream, and almost incredible to me."[12] Christopher Gadsden, a member of the legislature who had been imprisoned at St. Augustine by the British, would later prove to be remarkably fair to Loyalists. Yet in December 1781, soon after his return to South Carolina, he encountered two Carolinians who had congratulated the British commanders after their victories at Charleston and Camden. They extended their hands in greeting, whereupon Gadsden told them that he did not shake hands with "Rascals." As a bystander later described the incident, one of the Loyalists then asked, "What do you think will be done to us? Done to you says G; why hang'd to be sure." Six months later Edward Rutledge declared that he "would as soon have an Alliance with a Band of Robbers as with the People of Great Britain." Even Francis Kinloch, who remained on affectionate terms with the man who had been his guardian and a governor of South Carolina, informed his old friend that "such scenes have been perpetrated by Officers whom I could Name, & whose families are amongst the first in Great Britain, as would make you, and every worthy Englishman blush for the degeneracy of the Nation. The consequences of such bad policy, & of such conduct has been that South Carolina is again in the hands of the Americans." Kinloch added that "The lower sort of People, who were in many parts, particularly in South Carolina, originally attached to the British Government, have suffered so severely, & been so frequently deceived, that Great Britain has now a hundred enemies, where it had one before."[13]

---

[12]Theodora J. Thompson and Rosa S. Lumpkin, eds., *Journals of the House of Representatives, 1783-1784* (Columbia: University of South Carolina Press, 1977) 317; Burke to Arthur Middleton, 16 October 1781, in "Correspondence of Arthur Middleton," ed. Barnwell, *South Carolina Historical and Genealogical Magazine* 26 (1925): 187; Aedanus Burke, *An Address to the Freemen of the State of South-Carolina . . . by Cassius* (Charleston, 1783) 27.

[13]Edward Rutledge to Arthur Middleton, 12 December 1781, 26 February, 23 June 1782, in "Correspondence of Arthur Middleton," ed. Barnwell, 208; 27 (1926):8-9, 17-18; Francis Kinloch to Thomas Boone, 1 October 1782, in "Letters of Francis Kinloch to Thomas Boone, 1782-1788," ed. Felix Gilbert, *Journal of Southern History* 8 (1942):91-92.

Accordingly, when the first legislature to meet since the British had overrun the state in the spring of 1780 assembled at the small town of Jacksonborough in January 1782 (because the enemy still occupied Charleston), "passions," in the words of one contemporary, ran "very high." The governor's opening speech appeared to reflect the general feeling. In the last two years, John Rutledge reminded the legislators, "The good People of this state have not only felt the Common Calamities of War, but from the Wanton and Savage manner in which it has been prosecuted they have experienced such severities as are unpractised and will Scarcely be Credited by Civilized Nations." There followed a catalog of horrors including prison ships, the exile of families "without the means of support," and the treatment of prisoners of war—some murdered in "Cold Blood" and others "delivered up to Savages and put to tortures under which they expired." In fact, the British used "Indians, Slaves, and desperate Banditti of the most profligate characters" to accomplish "their infamous purposes." Rutledge maintained that "neither the Tears of Mothers, nor the Cries of Infants could excite in their Breasts, pity or Compassion, not only the peaceful Habitations of the Widow, the aged and infirm, but the Holy Temples of the most high were consumed in flames kindled by their Sacreligious hands." He then observed that the state had been lenient with the Loyalists but that it was time for the legislature "to determine, whether the forfeiture and appropriation of their Property should not take place."[14] Given such antagonism, most Tories might have considered themselves lucky to be left anything at all.

Considering what might have happened, the Loyalists came off rather well. The Jacksonborough Assembly passed a series of acts disfranchising all who had not met specific conditions, amercing—or imposing a capital tax on the estates of—a number of individuals, and, most important, banishing approximately 375 men whose property was to be confiscated. In 1783 the next legislature followed up these measures with another act confiscating the estates of all Loyalists who had left the state with the British. Ultimately, the militia commanders of the various districts returned the

---

[14]Edward Rutledge to Arthur Middleton, 2 Feb. 1782, in Barnwell, "Correspondence of Arthur Middleton," 27 (1926): 3; A. S. Salley, Jr., ed., *Journal of the House of Representatives of South Carolina, January 8, 1782 to February 26, 1782* (Columbia: State Company, 1916) 9, 10, 13.

names of nearly 700 individuals who belonged in this category.[15] But at the same time as the legislature added this later act vastly increasing the number of men penalized, it began considering petitions from those named in the first acts and, in many cases, lessening or entirely remitting their penalties.

There are several ways of accounting for these measures. The simplest perhaps is Moultrie's explanation. "When it comes to be considered," he observed, that "the very men who composed that legislature were yet in the field, and many of them had been fighting during the whole war; and some of them perhaps with their wounds still bleeding; and others just returned from captivity and banishment, it is not to be wondered at, that they should be in an ill humour, and displeased with their countrymen" who had been Tories. Yet, he continued, "when they had got possession of their country again, and peace was restored, they were softened with pity, and had compassion for their fellow citizens." Moultrie himself was a member of the 1783 legislature and therefore in a position to know. As far as his analysis went he was undoubtedly correct. Some members of the Jacksonborough legislature, like the one who had killed "his fourteen" or his colleague who had twenty-five notches on the barrel of his pistol, probably intended to make politics a continuation of war. "Twould make you laugh were you to attend this Committee" (which reported the confiscation acts), Burke observed to Arthur Middleton, "tho' the Subject is a melancholy one. Every one gives in a List of his own and the State's enemies." And at one time, if Burke's figures are accurate, nearly a thousand names were on tentative but official lists.[16] Similar assumptions about the essential nature of the punitive legislation account for much contemporary criticism of the acts. According to a perhaps apocryphal story, when the measures were being discussed, one proponent noted "that there was a voice in his ears crying, 'slay, slay, utterly slay the Amalekites' "—at which another member observed that he too heard "a voice in his ears, but it was like unto

---

[15]Thomas Cooper and David J. McCord, eds., *The Statutes at Large of South Carolina*, 10 vols. (Columbia: A. S. Johnston, 1836-1841) 4:510-11, 516-23, 523-25, 568-70; Nadelhaft, *The Disorders of War*, 83; Robert W. Barnwell, Jr., "Report on Loyalist Exiles from South Carolina, 1783," South Carolina Historical Association, *Proceedings* (1937) 43-46.

[16]Moultrie, *Memoirs of the American Revolution*, 2:325-26; Burke to Arthur Middleton, 25 January 1782, in Barnwell, "Correspondence of Arthur Middleton," 26 (1925): 192-93.

the voice of a long eared animal." In similar fashion Kinloch condemned "the violent spirit of injustice which prevails in councils," comparing it to "the same cruel joy" that "animates a child to torment some helpless insect." For a while he refused to take part in politics partly because of it.[17]

One cannot ignore the emotional element behind this legislation, but it would be myopic to see nothing more. Many of the men at Jacksonborough were experienced politicians and, as such, were subject to imperatives that should have constrained their behavior. "Private men," Gadsden observed, "are thrown frequently into passions and extravagences . . . but the representatives of a State, when met on a public duty, are supposed to be without passion." That such an astute politician as John Rutledge needed to be reminded that intelligent politics involved more than emotional reflexes is inconceivable. If that had been the case, however, he could scarcely have escaped repeated reminders, since he worked closely with Greene, who espoused leniency and cautioned Southern governors that "legislatures should follow policy not their own private resentments. A man in his Legislative capacity is not at liberty to consult his own private feelings in determining upon measures, but how they will affect the interests of his Country."[18] Furthermore, Rutledge was scarcely a demagogue but was rather one of the most consistently conservative local Whigs, a man who had long been reluctant to sever the British connection. His inflammatory call for confiscation, therefore, demands explanation.

One answer is that he was applying the stick while offering a carrot to the Loyalists. About three months earlier, on 27 September 1781, Rutledge had issued a proclamation offering pardon to most Tories who would surrender themselves within thirty days and agree to serve six months in the Whig militia. Continuing the same policy, the Jacksonborough legislature passed an act confirming and extending the terms of the governor's amnesty. Although the proclamation and the act applied only to men who

---

[17]John Belton O'Neall, *Biographical Sketches of the Bench and Bar of South Carolina*, 2 vols. (1859; rpt., Spartanburg SC: Reprint Company, 1975) 1:24; Kinloch to Thomas Boone, 27 June, 1 September 1783, in Gilbert, "Letters of Francis Kinloch to Thomas Boone," 95, 96, 97.

[18]Gadsden to Major General Francis Marion, 17 November 1782, in *The Writings of Christopher Gadsden*, ed. Richard Walsh (Columbia: University of South Carolina Press, 1966) 196-97; Greene to Governor John Martin, 12 March 1782, Greene Papers, Library of Congress, Washington, D.C.

had given themselves up before the meeting of the legislature, such concessions conveyed a message of "better late than never" to tardy Loyalists. Moreover, it scarcely seems coincidental that the chairman of the house committee that enumerated those to be penalized, John Laurens, supervised much of the intelligence-gathering operation for Greene.[19] The pressure was effective. Doubtless some of the leaks about the proceedings at Jacksonborough were deliberate. Certainly the Loyalists still with the enemy in Charleston were well aware of what was going on, and, as one observer noted, the prospect of confiscation made them frantic. Many deserted to the Americans. While the legislature was still in session, Burke reported that "above one hundred of their adherents (the inhabts. of Chas. Town & the Country) have deserted over to us, and more are daily coming over their Lines." Some six months later "the Crowds of repenting, & returning Sinners" were large enough to make Edward Rutledge suspect that the British were about to evacuate the city.[20] Many of the repentant found their penance appropriately reduced. Even the man who has come down in history as the "Benedict Arnold of the South," Andrew Williamson, supplied information to the Americans, and General Greene in turn later interceded with the legislature in his behalf. As a result, his estate was amerced rather than confiscated.[21]

In addition, Rutledge and others hoped that confiscated property could be used to help finance the war. For all that anyone knew at the time, it might be necessary to lay siege to Charleston to dislodge the British, and the Continental Congress had called upon South Carolina to provide more troops. Paying them presented a problem, however, for it was neither politically expedient nor feasible to levy taxes in 1782. The obvious solution lay in the use of confiscated property. Congress had recommended that course to the states as early as 1777, and most of them had already taken

[19]Gibbes, *Documentary History of the American Revolution,* 3:175-78; Cooper and McCord, eds., *Statutes at Large of South Carolina,* 4:526-28; Salley, ed., *Journal of the House of Representatives,* 21, 22; Greene to John Mathews, 22 December 1782, Greene Papers, William L. Clements Library, Ann Arbor, Michigan.

[20]Raymond G. Starr, "The Conservative Revolution: South Carolina Public Affairs, 1775-1790" (Ph.D. dissertation, University of Texas, 1964) 127; Burke to Arthur Middleton, 25 January 1782, Edward Rutledge to Arthur Middleton, August 1782, in Barnwell, ed., "Correspondence of Arthur Middleton," 26 (1925): 191; 27 (1926): 21.

[21]Johnson, *Traditions and Reminiscences,* 148; Thompson and Lumpkin, eds., *Journals of the House of Representatives, 1783-1784,* 32, 33, 42, 205, 553, 569.

it. Burke noted that deliberations in the committee considering the subject frequently concerned less what a man had done than "what Estate he has." When a rich man became the topic, it was said that a cry went up, "a fat sheep; a fat sheep—prick him! prick him!"[22] Accordingly, the legislature decided to pay troops with confiscated slaves. Perhaps another reason for supporting the legislation was that a number of prominent politicians—including Edward Rutledge and Benjamin Guerard—eventually purchased confiscated property. Certainly the Tories professed to see sordid motives at work, and one, writing in the *Royal Gazette,* claimed that confiscation was designed at least partly "to gratify the Back-countrymen with a share of the plunder, and keep them in good humour."[23]

Yet a closer look at the proceedings suggests that if private plunder and public revenue were the primary objects of the punitive acts, the matter was conducted very strangely indeed. In the first place, remission of the penalties began well before the state had made much if any progress toward reducing its debt. Second, the original confiscation and amercement acts were not designed to maximize the proceeds. In fact, as Edward Rutledge observed, almost everyone in whose behalf something could be said escaped confiscation and, like others, Rutledge worked hard to keep friends and relatives off the list. Obviously, the whole business was, as he repeatedly stated, extremely "painful" to him. Thus his intention was to compile a list of prominent individuals (not, as he said, "insignificant Characters") and to do it as quickly as possible.[24] Given these criteria, it is scarcely surprising that many of those whose property was confiscated had signed the addresses congratulating Sir Henry Clinton and Lord Corn-

---

[22]Burke to Arthur Middleton, 25 January 1782, Edward Rutledge to Arthur Middleton, 28 January 1782, in Barnwell, ed., "Correspondence of Arthur Middleton," 26 (1925): 193, 212; James W. Thompson, "Anti-Loyalist Legislation during the Revolution," *Illinois Law Review* 3 (1908): 81-90, 147-71; Alexander Garden, *Anecdotes of the Revolutionary War in America, with Sketches of Character of Persons* . . . (Charleston: A. E. Miller, 1822) 196.

[23]Cooper and McCord, eds., *Statutes at Large of South Carolina,* 4:520; Walter B. Edgar and Louise N. Bailey, eds., *Biographical Directory of the South Carolina House of Representatives: The Commons House of Assembly, 1692-1775* (Columbia: University of South Carolina Press, 1977) 573; "Sales at Jacksonborough the 15th of August 1782. . . . " Commissioners of Forfeited Estates Account of Sales Book, 1782-1783, SCDAH, *Royal Gazette* (Charleston), 16 February 1782.

[24]Edward Rutledge to Arthur Middleton, 2, 14 February 1782, in Barnwell, ed., "Correspondence of Arthur Middleton," 27 (1926): 3, 5, 8-9.

wallis on their victories in South Carolina; published in Loyalist newspapers, these addresses provided convenient lists of conspicuous offenders.
Nowhere, it should be added, did Rutledge sound like a man who was enjoying his revenge or reveling in the prospect of large returns. Nevertheless, he not only supported the principle of confiscation but drafted the basic
act.[25] That he was courting popularity by bowing to the pressure to punish
Tories, as some of his political opponents implied, is a possibility, but one
should not hastily conclude that this was the case without carefully examining the opposition to these acts.

The most vocal critics of the punitive legislation were Christopher
Gadsden and Aedanus Burke. Before the Jacksonborough legislature met,
Gadsden hoped that Carolinians would "pursue every prudent, reasonable, humble and truly political step, devoid of passions and vindictive
resolutions." Revenge, he believed, was "below a brave man; vengence
belongeth to the Almighty; He has claimed it expressly as His right, wisely
foreseeing the shocking havoc man would make with such a weapon left
to his discretion." While the bill was under consideration, Gadsden "fought
it through," he later observed, "inch by inch, as unjust, impolitic, cruel,
premature," and unfair to innocent families and men who had acted under
duress. Believing that it might stiffen the enemy's resistance, he tried to
have passage of the act postponed until Charleston was recovered from the
British, reminding his fellow members of the legislature "of the proverb
not to sell the bear-skin before they had catched the bear." During the last
part of the debate, he even held up his hands and declared that "before I
would give my vote for such a Bill I would suffer them to [be] cut off."
But, as he conceded, his efforts were "all to no purpose." For his part,
Burke posed "one political Question. Can Property be secure under a numerous democratic Assembly which undertakes to dispose of the property
of the Citizen? The men of property in our house join heartily in this measure, but they do not reflect the time may come when the Precedent will
be execrated by their posterity." Burke, however, went further than most
opponents of confiscation in also condemning the amercement acts, which
he feared would permanently stigmatize Loyalists. Taking his argument to

---

[25]Robert W. Barnwell, Jr., "Addressers of Clinton and Arbuthnot," South Carolina
Historical Association, *Proceedings* (1939): 44; Ella Pettit Levett, "Loyalism in Charleston, 1761-1784," ibid., (1936): 6-9; Edward Rutledge to Arthur Middleton, 26 February
1782, in Barnwell, ed., "Correspondence of Arthur Middleton," 27 (1926): 7.

the public in the form of a pamphlet addressed "To the Freemen of the State of South-Carolina," written under the pen name of Cassius, he argued that "the experience of all countries has shewn, that where a community splits into a faction, and has recourse to arms, and one finally gets the better; a law to bury in *oblivion* past transactions is absolutely necessary to restore tranquility." In short, he added, "My idea of managing internal enemies, or seditious revolters, is this, either to drive them out of the State altogether; at least the leaders of them, or make them our Friends by Pardoning."[26]

Without doubt, a number of men agreed with him and objected to the confiscation acts as written, but to conclude that most of them opposed all punishment of Tories is to overlook their own statements. Middleton wanted banishment of the individuals in question and lifetime deprivation of the use of their property. Gadsden admitted that "a just retaliation, upon an abandoned and cruel enemy, may be sometime absolutely necessary and unavoidable," and Burke wanted "an act of amnesty and oblivion, with as few exceptions as possible" who would be entitled to a hearing.[27] Advocates of the punitive acts such as Edward Rutledge, who wished to keep them limited, repeatedly made similar statements. At least among articulate members of the old lowcountry elite, considerable agreement existed that there should be some confiscation and punishment of Tories; the disagreement arose over the question of how much. At this point one has to ask, Why bother with confiscation at all if many who favored it wished to keep it as minimal as possible? Aside from pressuring Loyalists to jump the British ship, there is one obvious answer, and Burke himself gave it. He expected a measure "calculated to make people friends, and reconcile to each other men whose fate it was to live together," and he assumed it would take the form of a general amnesty,"with some exceptions to satisfy publick justice" as, in his words, "You would throw a Tub to a whale

---

[26]Gadsden to Morton Wilkinson, September [1781], Gadsden to Major General Francis Marion, 17 November 1782, in *Writings of Christopher Gadsden,* 174, 195; Burke to Arthur Middleton, 25 January, 14 May 1782, in Barnwell, ed., "Correspondence of Arthur Middleton," 26 (1925): 193, 200; Burke, *An Address to the Freemen,* 42, 48.

[27]Arthur Middleton to Burke, 7 April 1782, in Barnwell, ed., "Correspondence of Arthur Middleton," 27 (1926): 29; Gadsden to Morton Wilkinson, September [1781], in *The Writings of Christopher Gadsden,* 174; Burke, *An Address to the Freemen,* 54.

to satisfy the vengeance of those who had suffered. This,'' he admitted, ''was necessary, I believe.''[28]

Few public figures who had any acquaintance with the recent history of the state would have disagreed with him. Deference to established leaders may have been the rule under normal conditions, but crises involving crucial issues and powerful emotions might make common men very assertive, especially when the credentials of their leaders were open to question. Take, for example, the unusually revealing incident that occurred after the first battle of Ninety-Six in November 1775 when Loyalist and Whig officers negotiated a truce permitting the besieged Whigs to keep their small cannon—whereupon, the Whig commander later reported, ''Their people to the number of between three and four hundred surrounded the house where we were and swore if the swivels were not given up they would abide by no articles.'' As a result, ''The gentlemen of the opposite party declared upon their honor that if we'' agreed in writing to surrender the guns, ''they would return them, which they have done.''[29] Memories of the Regulator movement nearly a decade earlier probably helped the leaders on both sides see the utility of a charade designed at least in part to maintain their authority. Certainly that upheaval had provided object lessons in popular initiative and the perils of insensitive leadership.

More specifically, the Regulator movement appeared to establish an axiom that was to be repeatedly demonstrated during the revolutionary period: nothing was so apt to render established leaders irrelevant as their failure to punish those whom the populace considered to be wrongdoers. In 1766 a rash of crime in the backcountry led to the arrest and conviction of a number of outlaws. When the governor pardoned them, backcountrymen organized themselves and administered vigilante justice. In 1778, when the president of the state, Rawlins Lowndes, sought to postpone the deadline for taking an oath of allegiance prescribed by the legislature, those who objected to such apparent leniency toward Tories almost rioted, and Lowndes found himself in danger of being impeached. Not wishing to make the same mistake again, the local leadership later executed two Loyalists

---

[28]Edward Rutledge to Arthur Middleton, 28 January 1782, Burke to Arthur Middleton, 14 May 1782, in Barnwell, ed., ''Correspondence of Arthur Middleton,'' 26 (1925): 212, 200.

[29]Andrew Williamson to William Henry Drayton, 25 November 1775, in Gibbes, *Documentary History of the American Revolutionary,* 1:218.

who were suspected of arson, largely, as Moultrie admitted, "to appease the people." Marion worked harder to protect his prisoners but his ability to command obedience was limited. One Loyalist militia officer who sought his protection discovered that "his life was threatened even if found in the Generals Tent"; Marion himself had to spirit another man away to save him.[30]

British commanders had similar difficulties. As one official observed after the fall of Charleston, the Loyalists, "elated with their present Triumph, and resentful for their past Injuries, . . . are clamourous for retributive Justice, and affirm that the Province will never be settled in Peace until those People whose persecuting spirit hath caused such calamities to their fellow subjects shall receive the punishment their Iniquities deserve. Indeed, I am convinced there are some who are deservedly so obnoxious that whatever measures may be adopted by Government, it will be impossible for them to escape the Effects of private Resentment." He was correct, and once again treatment that seemed excessively lenient produced popular disturbances. Thus, a Tory mob broke windows in the house of a local merchant who sought and received permission to go to England rather than serve in the British militia.[31]

The meaning was clear to contemporaries. Being too soft on offenders—whether criminal, Whig, or Tory—invited the populace to take care of the matter in its own way and risked a popular challenge to duly constituted authorities. Where, in the words of a contemporary, "the lower and rougher class . . . breathed nothing but the bitterness of vengeance" while the older elite was struggling to maintain its political footing in a ravaged land full of hatred, it would have been both futile and foolhardy for a revolutionary government, which was attempting to establish order and its own legitimacy, to have ignored the popular demand for retributive

---

[30]Richard M. Brown, *The South Carolina Regulators* (Cambridge MA: Belknap Press of Harvard University Press, 1963); Robert M. Weir, *Colonial South Carolina—A History* (Millwood NY: KTO, 1983) 212-13, 275; Carl Vipperman, *The Rise of Rawlins Lowndes, 1721-1800* (Columbia: University of South Carolina Press, 1978) 211-13; Moultrie, *Memoirs of the American Revolution,* 1:331; Thompson and Lumpkin, eds., *Journals of the House of Representatives, 1783-1784,* 17; Jerome J. Nadelhaft, "The 'Havoc of War' and Its Aftermath in Revolutionary South Carolina," *Histoire Sociale* 12 (1979): 108.

[31]"James Simpson Reports to Sir Henry Clinton on the Disposition of the Charleston Inhabitants toward the Crown," 15 May 1780, in *The Price of Loyalty,* 277; Thompson and Lumpkin, eds., *Journals of the House of Representatives, 1783-1784,* 149.

justice. Controlling popular disturbances by force was scarcely feasible, especially in the backcountry where the militia was often as much a part of the problem as a solution. Scarcely six months before the Jacksonborough legislature met, for example, a party of Colonel LeRoy Hammond's unit had been engaged, according to reports Greene received, in plundering "without mercy" and murdering "the defenseless people just as private peak prejudice or personal resentments shall dictate." Given such realities, Lieutenant Governor William Bull's assessment of the situation during the Regulator movement of the 1760s still applied: repression was impossible and flexibility on the part of the authorities was the "surest and only method of quieting the minds" of the populace. Furthermore, joining their constituents in punishing Tories enabled local leaders to distance themselves from the enemy and thereby demonstrate their patriotism. Thus, throwing "a Tub to a whale" in the closing days of the war was not merely a matter of bowing to political pressure in the ordinary sense of the word. As Governor Benjamin Guerard told members of the legislature in 1784, "Our political life and death" were at stake.[32]

In short, one of the most useful perspectives from which to view the confiscation acts is provided by Pauline Maier's observation about the prerevolutionary period, namely, that "revolutionary institutions . . . curtailed the recourse to violence; embryonic popular government and mob pressure remained alternative expressions of community convictions and hostilities." Appropriately modified to suit the altered context, that insight applies equally well to the postwar period. That the legislature clearly understood the situation is revealed by the confiscation acts themselves, which stated that the laws were enacted in part because "the peace and safety of this State require that proper examples should be made of such atrocious offenders." That the observation was accurate is demonstrated by Burke's difficulties in attempting to hold court. "Several members [of the legislature] & others of the Back Country warned me," he observed, "ag[ains]t admitting Lawyers to plead for the Tories, and as to myself, that

[32]Johann David Schoepf, *Travels in the Confederation,* trans. and ed. Alfred J. Morrison (1788; rpt., New York: Bergmann, 1968) 204; Greene to Andrew Pickens, 5 June 1781, quoted in Ferguson, "Carolina and Georgia Patriot and Loyalist Militia in Action," in Crow and Tise, eds., *The Southern Experience in the American Revolution,* 192; William Bull to Lord Hillsborough, 10 September 1768, Transcripts of Records Relating to South Carolina in the British Public Record Office, 32:40, SCDAH; Thompson and Lumpkin, eds., *Journals of the House of Representatives, 1783-1784,* 405-406.

I should be cautious how I adjudged any point in their favor." Fearing that legal proceedings in this atmosphere would make him "a tool to gratify the fierce revenge of the people, " Burke reluctantly set out on the circuit, and the results confirmed his judgment.[33] American dragoons impressed his horses and the enemy overtook one of his colleagues on the bench, Henry Pendleton. Repeatedly searching the house in which the judge was hiding, the British unit eventually found Pendleton rolled up in a rug. As a result of such harassment, most courts failed to meet during the spring of 1782. Burke was relieved, though somewhat prematurely, for on a later circuit he discovered how limited his own authority remained. The crucial test came at Ninety-Six, where Matthew Love was on trial for participating in Cunningham's massacres. Burke ordered him discharged on the grounds that killing in war could not be considered murder. Whereupon, after a decorous delay during which the judge left the courtroom, a number of local men took the prisoner out and hanged him.[34]

This episode suggests that the benefits of punitive legislation were greater than most members of the legislature initially envisaged. Men like Edward Rutledge wished to be as merciful as possible toward Loyalists, yet they also wanted to open the courts immediately, apparently because they regarded these institutions as alternatives to mob violence and symbols of reestablished governmental authority. Burke, who had more experience on the circuit than most of the lowcountry gentry, realized that the results were apt to be quite different—that the courts would either become the instruments of mob violence or provoke a serious challenge to a government that could ill afford it. What neither supporters nor opponents of the acts seem to have recognized at first is that punitive legislation rep-

---

[33]Pauline Maier, "The Charleston Mob and the Evolution of Popular Politics in Revolutionary South Carolina, 1765-1784," *Perspectives in American History* 4 (1970): 185; Cooper and McCord, eds., *Statutes at Large of South Carolina,* 4:519; Burke to Arthur Middleton, 14 May, 6 July 1782, in Barnwell, ed., "Correspondence of Arthur Middleton," 26 (1925): 201, 202, 205.

[34]Charles Cotesworth Pinckney to Arthur Middleton, 24 April 1782, in Barnwell, ed., "Correspondence of Arthur Middleton," 27 (1926): 62; Burke to Arthur Middleton, 14 May 1782, ibid., 26 (1925): 202; JoAnne McCormick, "Civil Procedure in the Camden Circuit Court, 1772-1790," in *South Carolina Legal History,* ed. Herbert A. Johnson (Columbia: University of South Carolina Press, 1980) 252; William L. McDowell, Jr., "Colonial and Early State Court Records in the South Carolina Archives," ibid., 272; Burke to Benjamin Guerard, 14 December 1784, enclosed in Guerard to House of Representatives, 24 January 1785, Governors' Messages, Records of the General Assembly, SCDAH.

resented a temporary alternative to court action that could provide a reasonably satisfactory solution to these problems. Partly because many believed that the legislature had done its duty in punishing the Loyalists and thereby obviated the need for private initiative in the matter, the governor could inform the house in February 1784 that "the utmost decorum and tranquility" prevailed. No state, he continued, had exceeded South Carolina "in moderation, quiet, good order and prudence since the recovery of our Country." Unfortunately, he exaggerated; scattered popular responses to official attempts at mercy throughout 1783 and 1784 gave an indication of what, in the absence of the confiscation acts, would probably have occurred on a much wider scale. In Charleston, rioters warned some recipients of legislative clemency to leave the state; near Camden a group of Whigs apparently led by Thomas Sumter attempted to intimidate a William Reese with a beating that resembled Regulator rituals; and on Fishing Creek neighbors may have killed eight Tories who failed to leave.[35] And this, it should be noted, was after the government had more than two years in which to reestablish its authority and restore order.

Despite the scattered violence, by 1783 and 1784 the legislature was in a better position to run the risks associated with showing mercy to the Loyalists, and there were good reasons for doing so. In the first place, the punitive legislation had created numerous problems. In 1783 alone the House of Representatives received more than 250 petitions dealing with the confiscation and amercement acts. In some instances, Whigs claimed they had purchased slaves and other property from Tories only to find that the seller could not convey title because his property had been confiscated; in other cases, it turned out that ardent Whigs were the heirs of Loyalists whose entire estates were declared forfeit; in still other instances, individuals maintained that they had mistakenly been put on the confiscation lists. Most common, however, were petitions from women like Florence Cook, the wife of a carpenter, who noted that the confiscation of her husband's property "deprived [her] of her rights of dower, and her daughter (whome

---

[35]Thompson and Lumpkin, eds., *Journals of the House of Representatives, 1783-1784*, 403; Adele S. Edwards, ed., *Journals of the Privy Council, 1783-1789* (Columbia: University of South Carolina Press, 1971) 117; "To the Public," *Gazette of the State of South Carolina*, 6 May 1784, in Walsh, ed., *The Writings of Christopher Gadsden*, 201-202; Anne K. Gregorie, *Thomas Sumter* (Columbia: R. L. Bryan, 1931) 207-209. For the possibility that reports of the incident on Fishing Creek involved some calculated exaggeration intended to intimidate Tories, see Nadelhaft, "The 'Havoc of War,' " 120.

she has always endeavourd to inculcate in the love of the Liberty of this her Native Country) [of] the future Claim of the Inheritance of her Father.'' Minty Musgrove, the widow of John, did ''not attempt to Excuse her late husbands conduct but as he is now no more,'' she sought relief. A legatee of Jeremiah Savage, whose estate had been confiscated, succinctly observed that the Loyalist in question was ''politically dead'' and prayed to be allowed the inheritance.[36]

A host of cases alleged to involve extenuating circumstances of one kind or another presented more difficult questions. David Bruce, a printer who had ''resided 24 Years in Charles Town, and . . . maintained an honest Character,'' claimed that he had ''never taken up Arms, or Acted in any Post'' against the Whigs, but that he had ''been much distressed Since the Fall of Charles Town, for printing in favour of America.'' Other petitioners maintained that they had taken protection from the British to avoid being sent to prison ships, or to protect their families, and some militia officers claimed that they had taken commissions to prevent them from falling into the hands of individuals less acceptable to their neighbors. One man even noted that because his health was bad he had been given the option of becoming a militia officer so that he would be exempt from duty as a sentinel, which suggests something about the condition of the British militia. Indeed, if all of these petitions were truthful, one might wonder about some of the other British adherents. Elizabeth Mitchell, for example, observed that ''for many Years preceeding his death'' her husband was ''a man of very distracted Mind and if he has been Guilty of any Acts to Occasion the displeasure of the Legislature, Such misconduct must have been the result of insanity only.'' And Eleanor, the wife of a cooper, James Mackey, believed ''that if he incautiously made himself in any degree conspicuous for an adherence and attachment to the British Government it was because his simplicity and timidity made him a miserable Dupe to the Suggestions & persuasions of more artfull designing and malignant Men.'' In exile and having been ''pursued by a series of unlucky Accidents, and now sinking under the pressure of accumulated misfortunes,'' he could hope for no relief, she observed, but ''from the humane & forgiving temper of this honorable house.''[37] And so the petitions went, seemingly without end.

---

[36]Thompson and Lumpkin, eds., *Journals of the House of Representatives, 1783-1784,* ix, 22, 47, 54, 65-66, 95, 134, 171.

[37]Ibid., 12, 23, 25-26, 66, 113-14, 144, 387, 409.

As Edward Rutledge had noted earlier, "The Difficulty of knowing what is best to be done" in such cases was sufficient to be "a very considerable Drawback" to his joy at the British evacuation of Charleston. Other members of the legislature took their responsibilities in dealing with the petitioners equally seriously. At first, committees of both the house and senate, usually composed of individuals from the areas in which the petitioners resided, considered pleas for relief. Soon, however, the number of petitions prompted the appointment of a large joint committee including members from each parish and district. Frequently meeting at night, the committee members held hearings at which the petitioners and members of the public could present evidence.[38] As early as February 1783 the committees were recommending leniency in some cases. Joseph Seabrook, the committee discovered, "bore a British Commission of Captain of Militia on Edisto Island, yet it was not of his own seeking but by the unanimous choice of the Inhabitants for the purpose of preserving Order & preventing of Plunder, & that in the execution of his Office he did not oppress the people in other respects." Accordingly, the committee recommended that his estate be amerced twelve percent rather than confiscated and that he be permitted to remain in the state. Mitchell, the committee found, "was generally thought to be a man not in his perfect senses for some time past"; the committee recommended that his estate be restored to Elizabeth and their children. John Walter Gibbes, the committee felt, appeared "to be a Character beneath the attention or Resentment of this House; his turn for Buffoonery seems to have been a principal inducement for his being taken notice of by the British Officers to whom he was attached no longer than whilst they remained Masters of the Town." Believing "that he would not be a dangerous Person, to the Government, if suffered to reside among us," the committee recommended that his estate be amerced rather than confiscated. David Bruce, "having formerly been active in promoting the Interest of America, particularly by printing the Pamphlet entitled *Common Sense* rendered him self very obnoxious to the British, and hoping to avoid

---

[38]Rutledge to Arthur Middleton, August 1782, in Barnwell, ed., "Correspondence of Arthur Middleton," 27 (1926): 21; Thompson and Lumpkin, eds., *Journals of the House of Representatives, 1783-1784,* 18, 27, 407, 410; Journals of the Senate, 6 January to 17 March 1783, 10, 11; Journals of the Senate, 6 January to 26 March 1784, 28, 29, SCDAH; Edwards, ed., *Journals of the Privy Council, 1783-1789,* 4; Legislative Committee Minutes: Committee on the Confiscation Act, 1783-1784, Examination of Persons on the Confiscation Bill, 1783, SCDAH.

persecution was prevailed upon by his fears & the insinuations of Artful Persons to sign the [Loyalist] Address. But your Committee are of opinion, that if permitted to reside among us he will in [the] future demean him self as a good citizen & endeavour to make amends for past misconduct."[39]

Attempting to deal with such cases on their own merits alone would have imposed a heavy workload, but the legislature did not operate in a vacuum, and the remission of penalties, like their original imposition, inevitably became an exercise in statecraft. On 4 February 1783, for example, the "inhabitants of the upper part of Prince George's Parish," being "greatly allarmed from a report which Prevails through the Country . . . that petitions are makeing out for Pardoning the most atrotious offenders against the State," ardently prayed that the legislature would "never be Induced to Pass any Resolve, act, or Law, so as to rank the worthy Cytizens of this, or any other of the united States, with such a set of Miscriants as those their adhereants & abetters, who have Joined their Enemy to Massacree" Americans. Three days later another petition, signed by about 150 inhabitants of Prince Frederick's Parish protested—in terms similar enough to suggest collaboration with the petitioners from Prince George—against the "almost or Genl. Amnesty" which, it was rumored, "is to take place this Sessions. May God forbid such an Unanimity [*sic*]." Clearly, to pass a general act of amnesty was to risk real trouble. On the other hand, withholding mercy also had its pitfalls. To do so often seemed unfair and, as Arthur Middleton observed about the confiscation act itself, "abhorrent to the dignified Spirit of pure & genuine republicanism." Recent history had also demonstrated that such behavior on the part of the British had undermined their authority. Finally, the text of the preliminary treaty of peace with Great Britain was made public by the end of April 1783. As Kinloch noted, it required "that Congress should recommend restitution to the different States, but," he also observed, "the recommendations of Congress are more like the pastoral Letters of a Bishop, than anything else I can think of" and had little chance of being obeyed.[40] Whatever might be the case

---

[39]Thompson and Lumpkin, eds., *Journals of the House of Representatives, 1783-1784*, 131, 210, 219, 220.

[40]Ibid., 92, 103-104; Arthur Middleton to Burke, 7 April 1782, in Barnwell, ed., "Correspondence of Arthur Middleton," 27 (1926): 29; Edwards, *Journals of the Privy Council, 1783-1789*, 32; Kinloch to Thomas Boone, 27 June 1783, in Gilbert, ed., "Letters of Francis Kinloch to Thomas Boone," 95.

with some Americans, however, South Carolinians were still too dependent on British trade and credit to ignore these provisions of the treaty.

Thus, it is scarcely surprising to find that the legislature considered the possibility of a general amnesty, even before the text of the peace treaty arrived. Interestingly enough, Colonel John Baxter, a representative from Prince Frederick's Parish who had served with Marion, made the motion; Gadsden seconded it, and the house promptly voted it down. The legislators continued to reject the measure as late as 1787. In the interim, however, they rescinded or lessened the penalties individually for most of those who petitioned. No doubt a majority of the legislature was reluctant to have undeserving Loyalists escape punishment; many members, with good cause, feared the popular reaction to a general amnesty. At least one historian has argued that the act of 1783 confiscating the property of those who left the state with the British—most of whom were from the backcountry—appeased western representatives and thereby divided the opposition to individual acts of clemency. The lack of a comparable concession in 1787, he implies, helps to account for the relatively solid vote of backcountry representatives against a general repeal.[41] Perhaps, but it is also worth noting that the issues were really somewhat different.

To have passed a general act of amnesty would have removed the legislature from the center of the stage. Had the punitive legislation done nothing else, it served an immensely useful role in making the legislature the focal point of the debate over one of the key issues of public policy during the postwar period. The acts moved the question indoors, from the streets and countryside to the legislative chambers. Even those who petitioned against leniency in effect accepted the idea that the legislature was the proper forum for deciding such questions. Accordingly, the time-consuming process of considering each case individually helped to legitimate the authority of the revolutionary legislature, much in the same way that Lance Banning has suggested that the party battles of the 1790s helped to legitimate the United States Constitution. The document and the political

---

[41]Thompson and Lumpkin, *Journals of the House of Representatives, 1783-1784,* 218; Nadelhaft, "The Revolutionary Era in South Carolina," 123-25. It should be noted that this interpretation has been modified in the author's more recent book. See Nadelhaft, *The Disorders of War,* 79, 97.

body became—each in its own way—the fixed point of reference to which appeal was made.[42]

Furthermore, a blanket repeal of the punitive legislation would have forfeited another benefit accruing from the piecemeal method. It can be glimpsed in the petition of Jacob Valk, who addressed the house in the hope that "your Honours will think him an object worthy of your Clemency and take off the Proscription, whereby His Children a son and daughter American Born may one day or other remember with gratitude Your act of Benevolence." If the acts themselves demonstrated that the state could wield the instruments of vengeance and thereby strike terror, their repeal showed that the representatives of the people could also be merciful and thereby prompt gratitude. The process was not unlike that by which a "bloody penal code" and liberal use of the pardoning power supported the ruling classes in Britain during the eighteenth century. There, Douglas Hay has recently argued, the courts schooled a people "in the lessons of Justice, Terror and Mercy."[43] In South Carolina the legislature and the confiscation acts schooled former Loyalists in the power of the new state and the benevolence of its leaders. No blanket repeal of the punitive acts could convey these lessons with the force of an individual hearing and the equivalent of a personal reprieve.

On the one hand, the notion that the end justifies the means is an abhorrent doctrine; yet, on the other, it is apparent that, at least in South Carolina, "the violent spirit" in the legislature not only operated to moderate the violent spirit out of doors but also helped in a number of ways to generate popular support for the new government and its leaders on the part of both former Loyalists and Whigs. Obviously, the whole process did not work perfectly; the initial harsh laws did not completely preempt private vengeance, and subsequent leniency prompted some resentment against the legislature itself. Moreover, Burke and the other opponents of the confiscation acts were right; bills of attainder were odious and risky, and to assure themselves—as well as their British trading partners—that they would

---

[42]Lance Banning, "Republican Ideology and the Triumph of the Constitution, 1789-1793," *William and Mary Quarterly* 3d ser. 31 (1974): 167-88.

[43]Thompson and Lumpkin, eds., *Journals of the House of Representatives, 1783-1784*, 46; Douglas Hay, "Property, Authority and the Criminal Law," in Douglas Hay et al., *Albion's Fatal Tree: Crime and Society in Eighteenth-Century England* (New York: Pantheon, 1975) 63.

not have recourse to such measures again, the founding fathers made them unconstitutional. No doubt the resulting stigma is one reason that so many historians have been quick to condemn the punitive legislation as arbitrary and "impolitic." One also has to admire and sympathize with a man like Burke who was deeply "shocked at the very idea of trying & condemning to death after so singular, so complicated & so suspicious a Revolution."[44] But given the kind of revolution he so accurately described, as well as a concomitantly weak and embryonic state, one has to ask what was going to substitute for lynch law or the bloody assizes, and how were men whose fate it was to have to live together to be reconciled. Despite Burke's fears and reasonable reservations, it is highly doubtful that his contemporaries had any other options that would have worked better than the ones ultimately adopted. Whether the same was true in other states is for other historians to decide. But if it was, we are confronted with a paradox in which one answer to the question of "how a national polity so successful, and a society so relatively peaceful, could emerge from a war so full of bad behavior" seems to be, in part, more ostensibly bad behavior.

---

[44]Edward McCrady, *The History of South Carolina in the Revolution, 1780-1783* (New York: Macmillan Co., 1902) 583; Burke to Arthur Middleton, 6 July 1782, in Barnwell, ed., "Correspondence of Arthur Middleton," 26 (1925): 205.

The Role
of the Newspaper Press
in the Southern Colonies
on the Eve of the Revolution:
An Interpretation* ────────────────

Commenting upon one of the leading men in South Carolina after the Revolution, a contemporary noted that he had been "highly mounted" before the war. The same could have been said about many other postwar leaders throughout the Southern states.† *As the preceding essay argues, a combination of luck and political wisdom led to the adoption of specific measures that helped to keep the elite in the saddle, but as this essay attempts to demonstrate, the seat itself had some built-in props. One of these, modern communication theory would suggest, was a strategic position in the flow of information. Written at the invitation of the American Antiquarian Society for its volume commemorating the bicentennial of the Revolution, this essay first appeared in* The Press and the American Revolution, *ed. Bernard Bailyn and John B. Hench (Worcester MA: American Antiquarian Society, 1980), where it*

───────────────

*The author would like to thank friends and colleagues for many helpful suggestions. In particular, Professors Calhoun Winton and Stephen Meats called attention to illustrative material about Robert Wells and William Gilmore Simms, while Carol and Suzanne Weir supplied the item from "Peanuts." Generous support from the Southern Studies Program and the Department of History of the University of South Carolina enabled Lacy Ford, JoAnne McCormick, James Scafidel, and George Terry to provide valuable assistance in collecting numerical data.

†William Pierce, "Character Sketches of Delegates to the Federal Convention," in *Records of the Federal Convention of 1787,* ed. Max Farrand (New Haven: Yale University Press, 1927) 3:96.

benefited much from the editors' criticisms. It is reprinted here by permission of the American Antiquarian Society.

As David Ramsay noted nearly 200 years ago, "the pen and the press" presumably "had merit equal to that of the sword" in achieving American independence, and with few exceptions his intellectual successors in the historical profession as well as contemporary participants on both sides of the revolutionary controversy have agreed with this assessment. Even Ambrose Serle, who observed the Revolution at close range from British headquarters in New York, claimed that the influence of the newspapers was second only to that of the ministers in raising "the present Commotion." Later students of the subject have overwhelmingly concurred, as one of the most distinguished phrased it, in believing that the "movement [toward independence] could hardly have succeeded without an ever alert and dedicated press." Historians have also generally proposed that such services in behalf of American freedom not only instilled "a newspaper-reading habit which has characterized all succeeding generations," but also firmly established "the opinion-making function of the press" and thereby contributed substantially to the democratization of American politics.[1] So pervasive has this interpretation become that it now permeates general accounts of the Revolution as well as histories of the communications media in America.[2]

The present popularity of this point of view results from several factors. One of the most important, certainly, is a belief inherited from the

---

[1]David Ramsay, *The History of the American Revolution*, 2 vols. (1789; rpt., New York: Russell and Russell, 1968) 2:319; Arthur M. Schlesinger, *Prelude to Independence: The Newspaper War on Britain, 1764-1776* (New York: Alfred A. Knopf & Random House, Vintage Books, 1957) 284 (Serle quote), 285, 296. See also Philip Davidson, *Propaganda and the American Revolution, 1763-1783* (Chapel Hill: University of North Carolina Press, 1941) 225-45.

[2]John C. Miller, *Origins of the American Revolution*, rev. ed. (Stanford: Stanford University Press, 1959) 288-93; Merrill Jensen, *The Founding of a Nation: A History of the American Revolution, 1763-1776* (New York: Oxford University Press, 1968) 128; Frank Luther Mott, *American Journalism: A History, 1690-1960,* 3d ed. (New York: Macmillan Co., 1962) 107-108; John Tebbel, *The Media in America* (New York: Thomas Y. Crowell, 1974) 34-50.

eighteenth century that an enlightened and informed populace will behave wisely in the long run. British authorities such as Serle, who established a Tory paper in New York to promulgate the truth, were therefore virtually compelled to assume that the American people had been misled by the Whig press. Conversely, in seeking aid from the court of France, Silas Deane sought to justify the Revolution by claiming that every American had "some Education," and even "the very poorest" furnished themselves "with Gazettes & political publications, which they read, observe upon and debate in a Circle of their Neighbors." Thus, he argued, "They are not an ignorant unprincipled rabble, heated and led on to the present measures by the artful & ambitious few." More alert to—or perhaps more willing to discuss—the machinations of the artful few, but believing them in this case to have been generally on the side of the angels, the Progressive historians of the early twentieth century could encompass both the Whig and Tory points of view within an ambivalent frame of reference that permitted them to recognize the prerevolutionary newspapers as perhaps "the finest instance of the propagandists' activity" in educating the American public.[3] Although the ease with which this interpretation conforms to our patriotic assumptions and intellectual proclivities should perhaps make us wary of accepting it uncritically, its ability to subsume both Tory and Whig testimony suggests a more valid reason for its continued vitality. In short, despite recent scholarship which indicates that American polemicists were often less interested in "propagandizing" their audience than in explaining their own positions, the Progressive view of the revolutionary press was based upon too much evidence to be hastily discarded.

Most of this evidence, however, has been derived from the study of the northern and middle colonies. Close examinations of the situation in the South are scarce, and the contemporary observers so frequently quoted usually had Northern ties. Even Ramsay, who wrote in South Carolina, spent most of the prerevolutionary period in Pennsylvania and New Jersey. Further, the recent work of scholars seems to indicate that the press

---

[3]Schlesinger, *Prelude to Independence*, 292: Silas Deane, "Memoire," 24 September 1776, in *Facsimiles of Manuscripts in European Archives Relating to America, 1773-1783*, ed. Benjamin F. Stevens, 25 vols. (1889-1895; rpt., Wilmington: Mellifont, 1970) 6: document 585, folios 225-26; Davidson, *Propaganda and the American Revolution*, 225; Bernard Bailyn, ed., *Pamphlets of the American Revolution, 1750-1776* (Cambridge MA: Belknap Press of Harvard University Press, 1965) 8, 17.

in the eighteenth century was generally more elitist than most historians
had hitherto realized, and though no one has yet worked them out in detail,
the implications of this scholarship would appear to have special relevance
to the role of the newspapers in the Southern colonies.[4] For Deane's idyllic
description of an America in which "Schools and Colleges are more Numerous . . . than perhaps in any other Country" and where the "Voice of
the poorest is equall to that of the richest" in public debate, though doubtlessly exaggerated, was probably a good deal more descriptive of his native Connecticut than of South Carolina, where public schools were rare
and a local college only an abortive dream until the nineteenth century. Although the testimony of a British merchant with economic interests in the
area is presumably as suspect as that of an American minister with a cause
to plead, Richard Oswald may have been more accurate than Deane in
characterizing the Southern provinces when he noted that in the three most
important "a Sort of Aristocracy prevails" by which "these [leading]
Families have a great weight in all the affairs of the Country." Indeed, their
weight was sufficient, a tutor to one of them cautioned an old acquaintance
from New Jersey, to make the society so different from what he had been
accustomed to that he would "find the tables turned the moment" he entered Virginia.[5]

That such differences in social structure did not differentiate the press
in the two areas seems highly unlikely in the light of one of the axioms of
modern communications research, which holds that "the structure of social communication reflects the structure and development of society."
Proceeding on the assumption that newspapers are but one aspect of social
communication, this paper attempts a preliminary reassessment of their role

---

[4]Gordon S. Wood, "The Democratization of Mind in the American Revolution," in
Leadership in the American Revolution (Washington: Library of Congress, 1974) 65, 67-
70; Richard D. Brown, "Knowledge is Power: Communications and the Structure of Authority in the Early National Period, 1780-1840" (Paper delivered at the annual meeting
of the American Historical Association, 28 December 1974).

[5]Deane, "Memoire," 24 September 1776, 6; document 585, folio 225; Richard Oswald, "Plan Submitted for Breaking up the American Confederacy by Detaching One of
the Southern Provinces," enclosed in Oswald to Lord Dartmouth, 9 February 1775, Facsimiles, 24: document 2032, 2; Philip Fithian to John Peck, 12 August 1774, in *Journal
and Letters of Philip Vickers Fithian, 1773-1774: A Plantation Tutor of the Old Dominion,*
ed. Hunter Farish (Charlottesville: University Press of Virginia, Dominion Books, 1968)
161.

in the Southern colonies on the eve of the Revolution. For the sake of clarity, the ensuing discussion will be organized along Harold Lasswell's classic paradigm for the study of communications: who says what to whom with what effect?[6]

I

To ask "who says" is to wonder who controls the press. Although the immediate answer would seem to be the printers who compiled the newspapers, the question is complicated by pressures upon the men who decided what and what not to print. At times, especially in the earlier colonial period, material might be sufficiently scarce to preclude much choice, and printers printed virtually everything available. But increased trade, better communications, and the intensifying prerevolutionary debate permitted—in fact, demanded—greater selectivity and by the 1760s printers were regularly postponing or excluding items on the basis of length, character, or political priorities.[7] Ironically, the increased freedom of choice involving sensitive materials imposed constraints of its own. Like Linus in the comic strip "Peanuts," many printers learned that "life is full of choices, but you never get any." Referring to himself in the third person, Andrew Steuart, who published the *North-Carolina Gazette* at Wilmington, expressed the essence of the resulting dilemma when he asked, "What Part is he now to act? . . . Continue to keep his Press open and free and be in Danger of Corporal Punishment, or block it up, and run the risque of having his Brains knocked out? Sad Alternative." Not always quite so unacceptable, the alternatives—such as they were—nevertheless often dictated such a narrow course that Adam Boyd preferred to operate the *Cape-Fear Mercury* alone. "The Times are very critical," he explained to a would-

---

[6]William Schramm, "Communication Development and the Development Process," in *Communications and Political Development,* ed. Lucian W. Pye (Princeton: Princeton University Press, 1963) 34. Sidney Kobre, whose *Development of the Colonial Newspaper* (Pittsburgh: Colonial, 1944) was a pioneering attempt to treat the subject in its social context, limited his coverage to Baltimore northward after 1750. For a recent attempt to evaluate and elaborate Lasswell's format, see Daniel Lerner, "Notes on Communication and the Nation State," *Public Opinion Quarterly* 37 (1973-1974): 546-47.

[7]Mott, *American Journalism,* 55-56; Alexander A. Lawrence, *James Johnston, Georgia's First Printer* (Savannah: Pigeonhole, 1956) 9-10; Ronald Hoffman, *A Spirit of Dissension: Economics, Politics, and the Revolution in Maryland* (Baltimore: Johns Hopkins University Press, 1973) 56.

be partner, "& at all Times the Director of a printing office is liable to Censure & . . . you would like as little to bear Censure for Me as I would for you."[8]

Ironically, once again, navigating the tricky political waters between Scylla and Charybdis was usually most difficult for men whose monopoly of local printing would superficially appear to have placed them in a strong position. In actuality, however, their rare skills could subject them to especially intense pressure. Thus, in Georgia, where a parliamentary subsidy assisted an unusually effective governor in contesting the power of the lower house of the legislature, the relative equilibrium dictated neutrality. "I have endeavoured," James Johnston could therefore honestly say in 1775, "to conduct myself, in the Publication of my Paper, as impartially as I co[ul]d," and his paper continued to contain polemics reflecting both sides of the controversy until it ceased publication early in 1776. Undoubtedly, Johnston then fled because the pressure had become too great for him after the local Council of Safety searched his print shop for anything "that might endanger the public safety." Contrary to what has sometimes been implied, though, Georgia patriots did not close Johnston's press—in fact, they even promised to guarantee his safety if he would continue to operate it.[9]

Lacking an effective guarantee of his safety, Robert Wells would probably have been unable to maintain his paper had he not been in Charleston where special circumstances permitted greater latitude than most printers enjoyed. Coming to South Carolina from Scotland in 1752, Wells discovered a prosperous urban market that enabled him to establish a lucrative trade in books and stationery well before the prerevolutionary controversy erupted; and by the end of the colonial period his "Great Stationery and Book-Store on the Bay"—which supplied customers from North Carolina to the Floridas—appears to have been the largest establishment of its kind south of Philadelphia. Further, Wells enjoyed the patronage of royal officials. Accordingly, in 1766 his shop printed the regimental order book for the Ninth British Regiment, while he served as marshal of the local vice-

[8]Steuart quoted in Charles C. Crittenden, "North Carolina Newspapers before 1790," *James Sprunt Studies in History and Political Science* 20:1 (1928): 37; Boyd quoted in Douglas C. McMurtrie, *A History of Printing in the United States*, vol. 2, *Middle and South Atlantic States* (New York: R. R. Bowker, 1936) 350.

[9]Lawrence, *James Johnston*, 9-18.

admiralty court and as public auctioneer. In addition, Wells was a close friend and business agent of John Stuart, the superintendent of Indian affairs for the southern district of North America.[10] What his exact relationship with the royal governors was is not so clear, but it may have been more than coincidental that his first newspaper, the *South-Carolina Weekly Gazette*, commenced publication not long after William Henry Lyttelton and the local Commons House quarreled over the quartering of British troops. Certainly its successor, the *South-Carolina and American General Gazette*, was unusual in praising British regulars for their good order, sobriety, and piety! Be that as it may, Wells was equally singular among local printers for his approval of the Stamp Act, which imposed a substantial tax on American newspapers. Perhaps he could afford it; later he was to estimate his combined income at well over £2,285 sterling per year.[11] In short, royal patronage and a dominant position in the book trade enabled Wells to continue publishing the *Gazette* despite the "great deal of ill will" that, a royal official testified, he thereby incurred. Nevertheless, in the May of 1775 when rumor proclaimed that his friend Stuart was attempting to organize the Cherokee Indians for an attack upon local Whigs, both men sought safety in flight. Robert's son John, who took over the *Gazette*, then not only sought to make it more pleasing to patriot leaders, but also sold cartridge supplies and military training manuals. Although John pursued

---

[10]Evidence by Robert Wells, 25 March 1784 and 24 November 1787, Examinations in London: Memorials, Schedules of Losses, and Evidence, South Carolina Claimants, American Loyalists, Audit Office Transcripts, 56:539, 542, Manuscript Division, New York Public Library, New York; hereinafter cited as Loyalists' Trans. Calhoun Winton, "The Colonial South Carolina Book Trade," *Proof: The Yearbook of American Bibliographical and Textual Studies* 2 (1972): 81-82; Winton, "English Books and American Readers in Early Florida," in *Eighteenth-Century Florida and the Revolutionary South*, ed. Samuel Proctor (Gainesville: University Presses of Florida, 1978) 110-21; 17 August 1771, South Carolina Council Journals, 36:170, South Carolina Department of Archives and History, Columbia (hereafter cited as SCDAH). For further indications of Wells's early book trade on Elliott Street prior to establishment of the *American General Gazette*, see his ad in the *South Carolina Gazette*, 1 July 1756, and Christopher Gould, "Robert Wells, Colonial Charleston Printer," *South Carolina Historical Magazine* 79 (1978): 23-49.

[11]Clarence S. Brigham, *History and Bibliography of American Newspapers, 1690-1820*, 2 vols. (Worcester MA: American Antiquarian Society, 1947) 2:1041; M. Eugene Sirmans, *Colonial South Carolina: A Political History, 1663-1763* (Chapel Hill: University of North Carolina Press, 1966) 320-24; *South Carolina and American General Gazette*, 9 January 1769; Robert Wells to [?], 13 August 1765, South Carolina Miscellaneous, Box 1, New York Public Library; Wells, Loyalists' Trans., 56:539.

an equivocal course that included service in the American militia as well
as later publication of the *Royal Gazette,* he eventually became a Loyalist.[12] Like James Johnston, he may have been as much buffeted by circumstance as guided by principle. Robert Wells, on the other hand, was clearly
unwilling to equivocate, and his readiness to incur substantial economic
loss as a Loyalist appears to testify to his political commitment.

The situation of the Whig printers, who backed the winning cause and
hence had no need to explain the pressures of circumstance, was less clear
cut. The case of Peter Timothy, perhaps the most famous of Southern
printers, was especially ambiguous. In South Carolina "the Opposition to
Tyranny was raised by a single inconsiderable Man here, under all the Dis-
couragements imaginable, even [Christopher] Gadsden doubting whether
it could be attempted," Timothy boasted in recounting his exploits: "I was
both a Member of and Secretary to the Congresses, General Committee,
Charles-Town Committee; Chairman (and did all the Business) of the
Committee of Observation and Inspection . . . and also Secretary to the
Councils of Safety." These activities may have been the result of a rea-
soned commitment to the patriot cause, and they most certainly were not
crude attempts to advance his economic position. Indeed, they usurped most
of the time that he had hitherto given to the printing business, and he abandoned the *South-Carolina Gazette* late in 1775.[13] Nevertheless, Timothy
kept his options open for quite a while, and his choice clearly reveals his
awareness of political realities.

The son of its founder, Timothy had been printing the *South-Carolina
Gazette* for twenty-five years by 1764 when he temporarily suspended
publication to reorganize finances. Upon resuming the newspaper later the

[12]Wells, Loyalists' Trans., 56:542, 553; John R. Alden, *John Stuart and the Southern
Colonial Frontier* (1944; rpt., New York: Gordian, 1966) 170; Henry Laurens to John Laurens, 26 September 1775, in "Letters from Hon. Henry Laurens to His Son John, 1773-
1776," *South Carolina Historical and Genealogical Magazine* 5 (1904): 75; *South Carolina and American General Gazette,* 4 August, 8 September 1775; Isaiah Thomas, *The
History of Printing in America, with a Biography of Printers,* 2d ed., 2 vols. (1874; rpt.,
New York: Burt Franklin, n.d.) 1:344, 351.

[13]Timothy to Benjamin Franklin, 12 June 1777, in Douglas C. McMurtrie, "The Correspondence of Peter Timothy, Printer of Charlestown, with Benjamin Franklin," *South
Carolina Historical and Genealogical Magazine* 35 (1934): 128-29; Edward C. Lathem,
comp., *Chronological Tables of American Newspapers, 1690-1820* (Barre MA: American
Antiquarian Society and Barre Publishers, 1972) 13.

same year, he turned it into what Lieutenant Governor William Bull, Jr. later would call the "conduit Pipe" for "principles . . . imbibed & propagated from Boston & Rhode Island." On the day before the Stamp Act was to go into effect, Timothy issued an oversized number, its columns bordered in funereal black, and announced that because his subscribers refused to purchase newspapers printed on stamped paper, he was suspending publication. His own words best describe the sequel: "By taking upon me a Place in the Post. [sic] Office at the Time of the Stamp Act, discontinuing Printing, while its Operation was in Suspense; and declining to directly support and engage in the most violent Opposition" he was transformed "from the most *popular* . . . [in]to the most *unpopular* Man in the Province." His actions, he later believed, "so exasperated every Body" that they took "every Step to injure, and set up Crouch (a worthless Fellow) against me, whom they support with their utmost Zeal and Interest." Thereafter, though one ostensible correspondent claimed that he did not deserve the "*coolness which you unfortunately labour under,*" Timothy was convinced that he would remain suspect until he had another opportunity to "distinguish" himself "in the Cause of America."[14] During the controversy over the Townshend Duties, he attempted to do so with only partial success. In 1772, having resolved to retire from the printing business, he turned active management of the *Gazette* over to two new partners, while he sought a Crown appointment as naval officer in the port of Charleston. But he failed to obtain the position; one of his partners died, and the other, Thomas Powell, ran afoul of the placemen in the royal council by printing some of its proceedings without official authorization. Jailed for contempt, Powell eventually dropped out of sight after being released on a writ of habeas corpus issued by two justices of the peace who, like most of their colleagues in the lower house, claimed that the council was not an upper house of the legislature and therefore lacked the power of commitment. Benefiting from a simultaneous resolution of the Commons, Timothy then resumed publication of the *South-Carolina Gazette* under the

---

[14]*South Carolina Gazette,* 10 March 1764, 31 October 1765, 3 October 1768; Bull to Lord Dartmouth, 10 March 1774, and to Board of Trade, 3 November 1765, Transcripts of Records Relating to South Carolina in the British Public Record Office, 34:18 and 30:281-82, SCDAH (hereafter cited as Trans., S. C., SCDAH); Timothy to Benjamin Franklin, 3 September 1768, in "Four Letters from Peter Timothy, 1755, 1768, 1771," ed. Hennig Cohen, *South Carolina Historical Magazine* 55 (1954): 162.

proud banner "*Printed by* PETER TIMOTHY, *Printer to the Honourable the* COMMONS HOUSE *of* ASSEMBLY."[15] Evidently, he had at last found the cause in which he could distinguish himself, and the cloud of suspicion departed.

"Crouch," however, did not. Charles was his first name, and he had once been Timothy's apprentice. Though a competent individual, he appears to have had a fondness for gambling, strong drink, and other diversions, so Timothy discharged him in 1754. His subsequent obscurity, his willingness to defy the Stamp Act (a trait that a Whig who knew him implied was most characteristic of printers who had little to risk), and Timothy's statement that he was "set up" all suggest that Crouch found men who were willing to invest in a new enterprise. Precisely who they were remains unknown, but members of the Commons House were probably among them.[16] At least there is every reason to believe that Crouch's paper, the *South-Carolina Gazette and Country Journal,* was initially designed to be the voice of the House. Thus the first issue, which appeared on 17 December 1765, carried the resolves against the Stamp Act that the Commons had ordered published so "that a just Sense of Liberty, and a firm Sentiments [*sic*] of the Loyalty, of the Representatives of the People of this Province, may be known to their Constituents, and transmitted to Posterity." Although he failed to retain a monopoly of the public business, Crouch continued his newspaper, which appears to have been a financial success, almost until his death in 1775.[17]

---

[15]Hennig Cohen, *The South Carolina Gazette, 1732-1775* (Columbia: University of South Carolina Press, 1953) 4; Timothy to Franklin, 24 August 1772, in *Letters of Peter Timothy, Printer of Charleston, South Carolina, to Benjamin Franklin,* ed. Douglas C. McMurtrie (Chicago: Black Cat, 1935) 15; Jack P. Greene, ed., *The Nature of Colony Constitutions: Two Pamphlets on the Wilkes Fund Controversy in South Carolina by Sir Egerton Leigh and Arthur Lee* (Columbia: University of South Carolina Press, 1970) 31-33; *South Carolina Gazette,* 8 November 1773.

[16]Timothy to Franklin, 14 June 1754, in McMurtie, ed., *Letters of Peter Timothy to Benjamin Franklin,* 13; Thomas, *History of Printing in America,* 2:10. That Crouch borrowed money from John Paul Grimke one year to the day after the appearance of his first issue does not necessarily indicate the termination of an earlier loan, but that Peter Manigault (speaker of the Commons, 1765-1772) later loaned money to Thomas Powell of the *South Carolina Gazette* is certain. Court of Common Pleas, Judgment Rolls, 002, 076B, 0080A (1768), SCDAH; Inventory of Peter Manigault's Estate, & (1772-1776) 413, SCDAH. For an interesting physical description of Crouch at about eighteen years of age, see Timothy's ad for his runaway apprentice, *South Carolina Gazette,* 5 February 1753.

[17]29 November 1765, South Carolina Commons Journal, 37:31, SCDAH; McMurtrie, *History of Printing in the U.S.,* 331; Thomas, *History of Printing in America,* 1:345. The first two issues of Crouch's paper were entitled the *South Carolina Gazeteer and Country Journal.*

Meanwhile, in North Carolina the lower house also clarified its relationship with the local printer. Both houses of the legislature and the governor joined in appropriating a salary for a public printer in 1751. James Davis accepted the appointment and established a newspaper at New Bern that appeared rather irregularly under different names until 1778. Early in the 1760s, however, doubts that he had fulfilled the terms of his contract, questions about the proper location of the public printer, and rivalry among public authorities complicated the picture. At this time Andrew Steuart, an Irishman recruited in Pennsylvania by a committee from North Carolina, established a press at Wilmington. There, backed by the governor and council, he printed another *North-Carolina Gazette* while Davis, supported by a majority of the lower house, continued as public printer at New Bern. Whereupon the governor, Arthur Dobbs (another Irishman), appointed Steuart "printer to his Majesty in this Province." Deeming the appointment to be "of a new and unusual nature, truly unknown either to our Laws or constitution," the lower house refused to sanction it, and for the next two years both printers claimed to be the public printer. In 1766, however, Steuart lost his commission from the governor for printing material against the Stamp Act and discontinued the paper. Thus his types appear to have been idle until 1769 when he, like both Crouch and Timothy at later dates, drowned. Although such a fate could hardly be considered an occupational hazard, nonpayment was; and the lower house successfully asserted its authority over the public printer by denying Steuart all but token compensation while persuading the council to approve full payment to Davis. After Steuart's death, Adam Boyd, a local figure without training as a printer, took over his equipment and established the *Cape-Fear Mercury,* which he published intermittently through most of 1775. During the last year of its existence, this paper was supported by the revolutionary Wilmington Committee of Safety.[18]

Ties between government and the press were equally close in Virginia where the *Virginia Gazette,* established thirty years earlier, was the only paper published in Williamsburg as late as 1766. Within the next decade, however, political exigencies combined with intricate family relationships among printers to more than triple the number of newspapers. Late in 1765

---

[18]McMurtrie, *History of Printing in the U.S.,* 338-44, 349, 351; Jack P. Greene, *The Quest for Power: The Lower Houses of Assembly in the Southern Royal Colonies, 1689-1776* (Chapel Hill: University of North Carolina Press, 1963) 292-94; Thomas, *History of Printing in America,* 1:339.

Joseph Royle transferred active management of the *Gazette* to Alexander Purdie, who suspended it for several months during the Stamp Act crisis. Soon after resuming publication, Purdie joined John Dixon (who had recently married Royle's widow) in a partnership that lasted until 1775 when the former established his own *Virginia Gazette,* while the latter took William Hunter, Jr. as his partner. Hunter, who eventually became a Loyalist, had inherited his interest from his father, who had managed the *Gazette* in the 1750s. Meanwhile, a third *Gazette* also entered the field in May 1766. Its printer, William Rind, had come to Williamsburg at the invitation of Thomas Jefferson and some other leading local men. Perhaps Rind attracted their attention by his willingness to print the resolutions of the House of Burgesses against the Stamp Act in the *Maryland Gazette.* At the time of this event, Rind was the junior partner of Jonas Green. At any rate, Rind soon became the public printer in Virginia. After his death in 1773, his widow, Clementina, succeeded to the post and continued the newspaper for another year until she followed her husband to the grave and John Pinkney took over. Not long thereafter, however, a leading revolutionary patriot from North Carolina, Willie Jones, helped to bring Pinkney southward to replace Davis as the public printer at Halifax, but Jones's loan proved to be a bad investment when Pinkney died in 1777.[19]

In Maryland, as in Virginia, there was only one paper during much of the period under consideration. Benefiting from governmental largess, Green in 1745 established the *Maryland Gazette,* which he continued to publish until his death twenty-two years later. Thereafter, it was printed first by his widow, Anne Catherine (until 1775), and then by their son Frederick. A wit as well as a Whig, Jonas Green suspended publication of the *Gazette* in response to the Stamp Act, but on 10 December issued a sheet called "AN APPARITION of the *MARYLAND GAZETTE,* Which is not Dead, but only Sleepeth." Using a skull and crossbones to depict the revenue stamps, Green also lamented that "the Times" were "Dismal, Doleful, Dolorous, Dollar-less." In 1773, however, a man less noted for his sense of humor established a competitor to the *Maryland Gazette.* He was the publisher of the *Pennsylvania Chronicle,* William Goddard, who soon turned management of the *Maryland Journal and Baltimore Advertiser* over

---

[19]McMurtrie, *History of Printing in the U.S.,* 284, 288, 290-91, 344, 457; Edmund S. Morgan and Helen M. Morgan, *The Stamp Act Crisis: Prologue to Revolution,* rev. ed. (New York: Crowell-Collier, Collier Books, 1963) 128; Greene, *Quest for Power,* 290.

to his sister while he sought to set up a continental postal system. Two years later, John Dunlap, who also printed a paper in Philadelphia, the *Pennsylvania Packet*, established the *Maryland Gazette; or the Baltimore General Advertiser* under the management of James Hayes, Jr.[20]

Even more than the short-lived *Virginia Gazette or, Norfolk Intelligencer* (June 1774 to September 1775), which was silenced when Lord Dunmore seized its press, the *Baltimore Advertiser* presaged a new era of journalism that would prove to be less characteristic of the South than of other areas. "Advertisers," not "gazettes," these newspapers, like those of similar name founded after the war, were designed to facilitate commerce more than government.[21] In the case of the other papers under consideration, the situation was reversed. Nothing illustrates the role that even the printers themselves expected to play more clearly than a brief report carried by Timothy's *Gazette* in 1765: "We hear that a patent for a council and assembly, for the government of . . . Nova Scotia, is ordered to be made out and registered, and their meeting appointed to be held at Halifax, where types and other implements for printing will soon be sent." Like the *London Gazette*, which for a hundred years had been the official organ of government, these Southern weeklies remained adjuncts of the state. Almost all were founded by printers who enjoyed public subsidies, and most of them continued to benefit from government support in one way or another. In fact, Timothy received more than £5,000 sterling in 1764 from public printing, and the owners of the *Virginia Gazette* seem to have been only slightly less dependent on the government.[22]

---

[20]McMurtrie, *History of Printing in the U.S.*, 23, 115-17, 120, 125; Thomas, *History of Printing in America*, 2:156; Aubrey C. Land, *The Dulanys of Maryland* (Baltimore: Johns Hopkins University Press, 1968) 268; *Maryland Gazette*, 19 September, 10 October 1765.

[21]McMurtrie, *History of Printing in the U.S.*, 292; Allan R. Pred, *Urban Growth and the Circulation of Information: The United States System of Cities, 1790-1840* (Cambridge MA: Harvard University Press, 1973) 20-26.

[22]*South Carolina Gazette*, 6 April 1765; Solomon Lutnick, *The American Revolution and the British Press, 1775-1783* (Columbia: University of Missouri Press, 1967) appendix; Thomas Cooper and David McCord, eds., *The Statutes at Large of South Carolina*, 10 vols. (Columbia SC: A. S. Johnston, 1836-1841) 4:199; Stephen Botein " 'Meer Mechanics' and an Open Press: The Business and Political Strategies of Colonial American Printers," *Perspectives in American History* 9 (1975): 143. Richard Beale Davis, *Intellectual Life in the Colonial South, 1585-1763*, 3 vols. (Knoxville: University of Tennessee Press, 1978) 2:595.

That many of these newspapers could have survived without subsidies is doubtful. In rural areas personal contact provided the fabric of local economic life, and none of the papers published outside of Charleston carried a great deal of advertising. Most of the advertising in the *North-Carolina Gazette* promoted the printer's own wares, while the provincial government supplied nearly one-fifth of the advertisements in the *Georgia Gazette*.[23] Only in Charleston, which was the busiest seaport south of Philadelphia, could ads generate a substantial amount of revenue. There in the 1760s the *South-Carolina Gazette,* for example, averaged approximately eighty-eight items per issue. If each advertiser paid the customary rate of £1 (South Carolina currency) for three insertions, advertisements would have brought in slightly more than £29 per week. Converting currency to sterling and assuming that the *Gazette* appeared weekly, one finds that annual income from advertisements was probably close to £215.[24]

How this sum compared to the revenue derived from subscriptions is more difficult to estimate. Ads generated only about one-third of the amount derived from sales of the *Pennsylvania Gazette.* But the figures are less

[23]Estimates based on a numerical count of advertisements in one randomly selected issue per year—cross-checked against column inches in three other similarly chosen issues—indicate that the *Maryland Gazette* carried approximately forty-two advertisements per issue between 1763 and 1775; the *Virginia Gazette* (Royle, Purdie and Dixon, Dixon and Hunter), fifty-five; the *Virginia Gazette* (Rind and, later, Pinkney), forty-two (computed on an adjusted basis, 1766-1775); and the *Georgia Gazette,* thirty-two. The comparable figure for all North Carolina newspapers—calculated from Wesley H. Wallace, "Advertising in Early North Carolina Newspapers, 1751-1778" (M.A. thesis, University of North Carolina, 1954) 20, 26—was seven. Next to the *Georgia Gazette* in which approximately seventeen percent of the advertisements were government notices, the *South Carolina and American General Gazette* carried the highest proportion of administrative notices (roughly eight percent). See also Ronald Hoffman, "The Press in Mercantile Maryland: a Question of Utility," *Journalism Quarterly* 46 (1969): 536-44.

[24]During 1767-1768, fairly "normal" years in South Carolina, the *Country Journal* carried approximately ninety-seven ads per issue, and the *American General Gazette* seventy-six. Jacob M. Price, "Economic Function and the Growth of American Port Towns in the Eighteenth Century," *Perspectives in American History* 8 (1974): 157, 162-63; Cohen, *South Carolina Gazette, 1732-1775,* 9. Normally, after 1725, the rate of exchange between South Carolina currency and sterling was approximately seven to one. Henry Laurens to John Knight, 24 August 1764, in *The Papers of Henry Laurens,* vol. 4, 1 September 1763—31 August 1765, ed. George C. Rogers, Jr. (Columbia: University of South Carolina Press, 1974) 380; and John J. McCusker, *Money and Exchange in Europe and America, 1600-1775: A Handbook* (Chapel Hill: University of North Carolina Press, 1978) 223-24. It should also be noted that the *Gazette* often failed to appear as scheduled.

certain for other newspapers. In most cases comparable records are lacking, and Timothy's claim that the circulation of his *Gazette* was "as extensive . . . as any in America" suggests that printers may have deliberately concealed low circulation rates. Furthermore, there was probably a good deal of promotionalism hidden in notices like the one demanding payment from more than 1,000 subscribers to the *Virginia Gazette*.[25] Thus even such explicit statements need to be treated with caution. In theory, however, they might be checked by indirect methods. For example, one could compute the total output by knowing when an issue went to press, the maximum capacity of the press per hour, and the time when the paper appeared. The average output of a colonial press was between 80 and 120 copies an hour; Timothy wanted ads submitted before noon Saturday; and his paper was supposed to appear on Monday. But the attempt to calculate the maximum press run possible under these conditions fails because the amount of type set before the deadline remains unknown and some colonial papers—including the *South-Carolina Gazette*—seldom appeared on the day they were dated.[26] Consequently, convincing estimates of circulation figures are rare. Few English provincial papers printed many more than 1,000 copies before 1760; and the *Virginia Gazette* may have had only 800 subscribers as late as 1765. Carl Bridenbaugh's average of 1,550 is therefore probably too high for most Southern colonial newspapers. Yet if he is correct for the *South-Carolina Gazette*, subscriptions at £3 currency per year would have yielded £664 sterling,[27] and Timothy—like Franklin—would have found the newspaper itself nearly three times as remunerative as the sale of advertising space.

Yet neither of these items appears to have been the major source of a printer's income. Only newspapers that operated on a shoestring, such as the *North-Carolina Gazette*, required quarterly payment. Others fre-

[25]Botein, " 'Meer Mechanics' and an Open Press," 148; *South Carolina Gazette*, 25 August 1764; Schlesinger, *Prelude to Independence*, 304.

[26]Lawrence C. Wroth, *The Colonial Printer* (1938; rpt., Charlottesville: University Press of Virginia, 1964) 80, 234; Kobre, *Development of the Colonial Newspaper*, 27; *South Carolina Gazette*, 25 August 1764; Thomas, *History of Printing in America*, 2:170.

[27]G. A. Cranfield, *The Development of the Provincial Newspaper, 1700-1760* (London: Oxford University Press, 1962) 176; Botein, " 'Meer Mechanics' and an Open Press," 150 n. 47; Carl Bridenbaugh, *Cities in Revolt: Urban Life in America, 1743-1776* (London: Oxford University Press, 1971) 388; Cohen, *South Carolina Gazette, 1732-1775*, 7. See also Schlesinger, *Prelude to Independence*, 303-304.

quently contained notices demanding remittances from tardy subscribers who may have continued to receive their papers for as long as eight years without payment. However reluctant printers may have been to alienate customers, few would have been so lax in collecting had they not possessed more important sources of revenue from the sale of books, stationery, and other goods. Such sales provided at least fifty percent of the income received by the printers of the *Virginia Gazette* in 1764, and Wells's bookstore obviously accounted for most of his business.[28]

Not government printing alone but a combination of activities—which often involved retail trade, publishing a newspaper, and job printing—provided the key to economic success. Significantly, however, the combination usually depended on a single set of customers, for, by and large, those who sought a printer's skills, news, or goods were men of property. Where books and stationery were expensive, where the discretionary income of most individuals was limited, and where a year's subscription to a newspaper might cost more than a week's wages for a laborer, the paying customers at least usually came from the upper levels of society.[29] Only where a printer's competitive position was exceptionally strong or local leaders unusually divided could he afford to alienate a substantial portion of them.

Moreover, few printers felt compelled to do so. As Franklin's well-known career should remind us, most printers sought to be—and some actually were—men of wealth and influence. By almost any standard, Jonas Green was one of the first citizens of Annapolis. Not long after founding the *Maryland Gazette,* he joined the Tuesday Club, which included local clergymen, professionals, officials, and members of the assembly. Green himself eventually became an alderman of the city, a local vestryman, postmaster, clerk of the races, and secretary of the masonic society. James Davis was postmaster of New Bern, sheriff of Craven County, and a member of the local assembly. Timothy's offices, in addition to those enumer-

[28]*North Carolina Gazette,* 15 November 1751; Cohen, *South Carolina Gazette, 1732-1775,* 8; Botein, " 'Meer Mechanics' and an Open Press," 143.

[29]Governor Arthur Dobbs to Board of Trade, 4 January 1775, in *A Documentary History of Education in the South before 1860,* vol. 1 of *European Inheritances,* ed. Edgar W. Knight (Chapel Hill: University of North Carolina Press, 1949) 706; Crittenden, "N.C. Newspapers before 1790," 17, 21.

ated above, included a seat in the Commons House. Without belaboring the point, one finds evidence in these examples that the printers frequently rose to be at least marginal members of the local establishment. Like many such upwardly mobile men, or those who aspire to become upwardly mobile, they usually subscribed to the values of the group from which they sought acceptance.[30] Furthermore, being immigrants, many found it especially important to demonstrate that they did in fact share these values.

Although such considerations alone would undoubtedly have predisposed printers to become zealous champions of the local leadership, other circumstances helped to insure that most in fact became spokesmen of the lower houses of assembly. In the first place, men of property dominated these bodies, and Alexander Purdie's ambiguous reference to *"the Publick, for whose Favour I am a Candidate"*—by which he could have meant the legislature as well as the public at large—neatly reflects the economic and political realities of a society in which most of the Burgesses were members of that "great tangled cousinry" constituting the Virginia gentry. In the second place, with the possible exception of Georgia, the lower houses were the most powerful branch of local government by the 1760s. Thus, as we have so clearly seen in the case of North Carolina, they were in a crucial position to control public patronage. Moreover, they possessed the most effective legal restraint on the press. To be sure, printers could be charged with libel, and most sought to minimize the risk by refusing to print a polemic unless they knew the author's identity. More cautious yet, Anne Green even asked some of her more vehement correspondents to post bond to indemnify her in the event of a suit. Nevertheless, such suits were rare by the eve of the Revolution, and, as the futile attempt to imprison Powell suggests, the upper houses were seldom in a position to chastise printers. The representatives of the people, on the other hand, clearly possessed the power to punish for contempt of their authority, and printers were

[30]Richard Beale Davis, *Literature and Society in Early Virginia, 1608-1840* (Baton Rouge: Louisiana State University Press, 1973) 162; J. A. Leo Lemay, *Men of Letters in Colonial Maryland* (Knoxville: University of Tennessee Press, 1972) 202, 209, 211, 245-46; McMurtrie, *History of Printing in the U.S.,* 116, 346; Walter B. Edgar, ed., *Biographical Directory of the South Carolina House of Representatives,* vol. 1, *Session Lists, 1692-1973* (Columbia: University of South Carolina Press, 1974) 109; Robert B. Zajonc, "Conformity," *International Encyclopedia of the Social Sciences,* ed. David L. Sills, 18 vols. (New York: Macmillan and Co. and The Free Press, 1968) 3:258.

usually most circumspect in dealing with them.[31] Thus Royle's unwillingness to print the Stamp Act resolves of the Virginia House of Burgesses may have been partly due to lack of a specific authorization by the House itself. Being in Maryland made it much easier for Green and Rind to ignore such technicalities. That in 1774 both *Virginia Gazettes* printed the proceedings of the Burgesses protesting the Boston Port Act does not necessarily indicate much greater boldness. This time they were authorized to do so. Furthermore, neither paper commented upon the official resolve, though Purdie and Dixon explicitly praised the unofficial actions of the Burgesses after the House was dissolved by the governor.[32] Moreover, a certain ideological affinity also helped to align printers with the representatives of the people. For the traditional political motto of the press, "Open to ALL PARTIES but Influenced by NONE," corresponded to the politicians' equally traditional credo eschewing partisanship. Only where a party was clearly committed to the public welfare—as in the case of its opposition to tyranny—could such behavior be condoned, and then, as Lord Bolingbroke observed, the party became not a party but the united voice of the country. And that was increasingly the role in which most members of the lower houses saw themselves. Fortunately, English libertarian thought also defined a free press not merely as one open to all persuasions but, more important, as one that could be counted upon to keep a watchful eye on the encroachments of executive power.[33] Thus it appeared that the press and

---

[31]*Virginia Gazette* (Purdie), 3 February 1775; Bernard Bailyn, "Politics and Social Structure in Virginia," in *Seventeenth-Century America: Essays in Colonial History*, ed. James M. Smith (Chapel Hill: University of North Carolina Press, 1959) 111; Greene, *Quest for Power*, 4-7; David C. Skaggs, "Editorial Policies of the *Maryland Gazette*, 1765-1783," *Maryland Historical Magazine* 59 (1964): 345, 346; *South Carolina Gazette*, 20 July 1769; *Virginia Gazette* (Pinkney), 2 February 1775; *South Carolina and American General Gazette*, 25 August 1775; Leonard W. Levy, *Freedom of Speech and Press in Early American History: Legacy of Suppression* (New York: Harper and Row, Torchbooks, 1963) 74-76. See also Harold L. Nelson, "Seditious Libel in Colonial America," *American Journal of Legal History* 3 (1959): 163-64, 172.

[32]29-30 May 1765, *Journals of the House of Burgesses of Virginia, 1761-1765*, ed. John P. Kennedy (Richmond: Colonial Press, E. Waddy Co., 1907) 356-60; 24 May 1774, *Journals of the House of Burgesses of Virginia, 1773-1776*, 124; *Virginia Gazette* (Purdie & Dixon), 26 May 1774; *Virginia Gazette* (Rind), 26 May 1774.

[33]*Virginia Gazette* (Rind), 14 April 1768; Quentin Skinner, "The Principles and Prac-

the lower houses had complementary roles to play.

This did not mean, however, that they were equal partners in the enterprise. The printers had started out as the voice of the whole government; prudence and ideology combined to dictate patriotism and align most of them with the most powerful branch. Doubtlessly, the evolution was a natural one that would have occurred in any event, but the Stamp Act crisis greatly accelerated the process. Aware of the hardships experienced by English printers because of similar taxes imposed in 1712 and 1757, American printers almost to a man opposed the Stamp Act. But equally aware that the penalties for violations were substantial, many in the Southern colonies suspended their newspapers. That action, however, tended to make the individuals whom they sought to emulate and upon whom they were most dependent doubt their commitment to the "right principles." Nothing, one suspects, would have been more apt to make the printers cooperative in the future. Thus, contrary to a recent assertion, it is a mistake to try "to relate the situation of the colonial press before the Revolution to our own times" by imagining "that the student radicals of the late sixties had gained control of the nation's leading newspapers, and were using them to attack the establishment."[34]

Printers were the voice of the local political establishment. Like the colonial agents in London (who had been one of the prizes in the struggle for power between different branches of the governments), they became the spokesmen of colonial leaders. While the agents spoke to imperial officials, the press addressed American constituents. Unfortunately, however, the more accurately the agents reflected the views of the colonial assemblies the less chance for compromise there was as the incompatibility of British and American constitutional positions became increasingly obvious. Better communications among Americans, on the other hand,

---

tice of Opposition: The Case of Bolingbroke versus Walpole," in *Historical Perspectives: Studies in English Thought and Society in Honour of J. H. Plumb,* ed. Neil McKendrick (London: Europa Publications, 1974) 108; "A Dissertation upon Parties," in *The Works of Lord Bolingbroke,* 4 vols. (Philadelphia: Carey and Hart, 1841) 2:48; *South Carolina Gazette and Country Journal,* 31 December 1765; Botein, " 'Meer Mechanics' and an Open Press," 200-25; Clark Rivera, "Ideals, Interests and Civil Liberty: The Colonial Press and Freedom, 1735-1776," *Journalism Quarterly* 55 (1978): 50.

[34]Cranfield, *Development of the Provincial Newspaper,* 42-47; Mott, *American Journalism,* 71-72; Morgan, *Stamp Act Crisis,* 241-42; Tebbel, *Media in America,* 35-36.

unified and strengthened their opposition to imperial policies. Moreover, once resistance had destroyed royal government in the colonies, the creation of efficient substitutes required the assistance of the press. Consequently, the *Maryland Gazette* became, as one historian has noted, "an organ of the Anne Arundel committee of correspondence"; and after Johnston fled, members of the Council of Safety in Savannah frantically begged their compatriots in Charleston to send them a printer. Thus, the "semiofficial role assigned the press by the First Continental Congress" was the logical outgrowth of its previous relationship with the lower houses. No wonder a Loyalist traveling through Virginia soon discovered that "freedom of speech . . . is now a stranger in the Land. The boasted liberty of the press is as a tale that was told."[35]

II

Being the medium of the leadership, colonial newspapers normally contained what its members wanted said. And this, it appears, was a very mixed bag indeed. Advertisements, literary essays, political polemics, and news-filled pages studded with everything from an account of violence in Britain over a "buxom country wench," to a locally composed elegy on the death of a favorite cat, to the proceedings of the Continental Congresses. Such a "superabundance of jumbled, disparate and mainly trivial details," as Allan Nevins once remarked, imposes "on the writer a burden of assortment and synthesis under which most men break down." Worse yet, successful attempts at assortment frequently confront a historian with one of the central dilemmas of a craft that sometimes seems to demand rational explanations for the effects of chance. And there is reason to believe that the vagaries of wind and weather possessed an especially potent influence in determining the contents of colonial newspapers which, like their provincial English counterparts, contained much material reprinted from

---

[35]Greene, *Quest for Power,* 266-96; Michael G. Kammen, *A Rope of Sand: The Colonial Agents, British Politics, and the American Revolution* (Ithaca: Cornell University Press, 1968) 314-15; Skaggs, "Editorial Policies of the *Maryland Gazette,*" 348; Georgia Council of Safety to South Carolina Council of Safety, 8 March 1776, Sparks Collection, 59:506-507, Houghton Library, Harvard University, Cambridge MA; Schlesinger, *Prelude to Independence,* 208; entry of 19 July 1777, *The Journal of Nicholas Cresswell, 1774-1777* (New York: Dial, 1924) 262. See also Rollo G. Silver, "Aprons Instead of Uniforms: The Practice of Printing, 1776-1787," *Proceedings of the American Antiquarian Society* 87 (1977): 111-94.

the London gazettes. Unlike their counterparts in England, though, American printers often failed to credit the specific source of their materials, and the most obvious explanation for the difference in practice would seem to be the greater effect of unforeseen contingencies on the longer communications route. Compiling colonial newspapers, one therefore suspects, was such a haphazard process that American printers probably felt that any regular attempt to identify even major London sources would prove more bewildering than enlightening to readers over the long run. Accordingly, systematic classification of the contents of these newspapers tends to be inherently misleading.[36]

Nevertheless, because there is virtually no other way to cope with this miscellaneous information, scholars have usually sought to isolate and study specific aspects of it. Most recently, they have found advertisements for runaway slaves to be a rich source of otherwise elusive data about the black population; more traditionally, students of colonial literature have derived much of our current knowledge about the subject from the newspapers.[37] That the same has been true with regard to political developments scarcely needs to be pointed out. To be sure, no one has yet done with the newspapers what Bernard Bailyn recently did with the political pamphlets of the period. But for the moment at least indications are that his work makes a full-scale analysis of the rhetoric and ideology of the newspaper essays superfluous. This is, of course, not to claim that specific investigations of selected aspects might not prove fruitful; rather, it is to suggest that, given the nature of the press in the Southern colonies, there is little reason to ex-

[36]*Virginia Gazette* (Purdie & Dixon), 3 September 1767; *Maryland Gazette,* 16 April 1772; *South Carolina Gazette and Country Journal,* 15 November 1774; Allan Nevins, "American Journalism and Its Historical Treatment," *Journalism Quarterly* 36 (1959): 413; R. M. Wiles, *Freshest Advices: Early Provincial Newspapers in England* (Columbia: Ohio State University Press, 1965) 199; Botein, " 'Meer Mechanics' and an Open Press," 196 n. 66.

[37]Darold D. Wax, "The Image of the Negro in the *Maryland Gazette,* 1745-1775," *Journalism Quarterly* 46 (1969): 73-80, 86; Gerald W. Mullin, *Flight and Rebellion: Slave Resistance in Eighteenth-Century Virginia* (London: Oxford University Press, 1972) 39-40; Daniel E. Meaders, "South Carolina Fugitives as Viewed through Local Colonial Newspapers with Emphasis on Runaway Notices, 1732-1801," *Journal of Negro History* 60 (1975): 288-319; Lemay, *Men of Letters in Colonial Maryland;* Davis, *Literature and Society in Early Virginia.* See also Gillian B. Anderson, *Freedom's Voice in Poetry and Song* (Wilmington: Scholarly Resources, 1977), for an inventory of "political lyrics" in colonial newspapers, 1773-1783, that will greatly facilitate future research.

pect to find great differences in the content—or even in the expression—
of political ideas embodied in different formats, though each possessed
unique advantages.[38] As George Mason observed in thanking a friend for
some pamphlets that had previously appeared "in detach'd Peices [*sic*] in
the public papers[,] . . . there is no judging of such Performances by
Scraps"; pamphlets were obviously better for developing extended argu-
ments. But as Mason's comment also indicates, newspapers usually provided a quicker means of wide geographic distribution, and later pamphlets
embodying the same material sometimes proved to be a drug on a saturated
market.[39] Nevertheless, the two forms of publication were frequently employed interchangeably. Published first in the newspapers, Arthur Lee's
"Monitor's Letters" were later collected in a pamphlet; reversing the se-
quence, Jefferson's pamphlet, *A Summary View of the Rights of British
America,* was later carried by the newspapers.[40]

For present purposes it is therefore necessary to mention only two features of these essays that may have been especially characteristic of the
Southern press. One is the relative prominence of Henry St. John, Viscount Bolingbroke; the other is the virulent hatred of Scotsmen. Scholars
have long known that in attacking the English ministry under Sir Robert
Walpole (1721-1742), Bolingbroke and his associates—who included the
most popular poet of the eighteenth century, Alexander Pope—contributed to the body of opposition thought termed "country ideology" that, as
we have recently recognized, permeated the political culture of the colo-

---

[38]Bailyn, *Pamphlets of the American Revolution.* But for the contention that different
literary styles were sometimes associated with different formats, see Schlesinger, *Prelude
to Independence,* 46; Davidson, *Propaganda and the American Revolution,* 210; and Jensen, *Founding of a Nation,* 128.

[39]Mason to [George Brent], 6 December 1770, in *The Papers of George Mason, 1725-
1792,* ed. Robert A. Rutland, 3 vols. (Chapel Hill: University of North Carolina Press,
1970) 1:127; Clinton Rossiter, *Seedtime of the Republic: The Origin of the American Tradition of Political Liberty* (New York: Harcourt, Brace, 1953) 329; Gadsden to Thomas
Bradford and William Bradford, 28 March 1775, in *The Writings of Christopher Gadsden,*
ed. Richard Walsh (Columbia: University of South Carolina Press, 1966) 101-102.

[40]Rossiter, *Seedtime of the Republic,* 329; Davidson, *Propaganda and the American
Revolution,* 241; Schlesinger, *Prelude to Independence,* 125. For Arthur Lee's [?] dedi-
catory address "To the King" prefacing the London editions of Jefferson's *Summary View,*
see also the *North Carolina Gazette,* 24 March 1775, and *The Papers of Thomas Jefferson,*
vol. 1, 1760-1776, ed. Julian P. Boyd et al. (Princeton: Princeton University Press, 1950)
673-75.

nies. But students of the subject have hitherto usually assumed that two less highly placed popularizers, John Trenchard and Thomas Gordon, were the most frequently quoted source of libertarian ideas.[41] It therefore comes as something of a surprise to discover that—at least in Virginia and South Carolina during the late colonial period—more explicit use was made of Bolingbroke's works. Furthermore, his ideas and phrases were almost certainly subject to more silent plagiarism.[42] For the works of Trenchard and Gordon were sufficiently respected—at least in New England—for Josiah Quincy, Jr. to list them along with those of Bacon, Locke, and Algernon Sidney in a bequest to his son upon whom, his father hoped, "the spirit of liberty [might] rest." Bolingbroke, on the other hand, was widely known to have been a man of shady reputation and unorthodox religious views. Thus a few years after his death an English reviewer, whose comments were reprinted in the *Virginia Gazette,* claimed that Bolingbroke's posthu-

---

[41]Isaac Kramnick, *Bolingbroke and His Circle: The Politics of Nostalgia in the Age of Walpole* (Cambridge: Harvard University Press, 1968) 11; Agnes M. Sibley, *Alexander Pope's Prestige in America, 1725-1835* (New York: King's Crown, 1949) 1; Jack P. Greene, "Changing Interpretations of Early American Politics," in *The Reinterpretation of Early American History: Essays in Honor of John Edwin Pomfret,* ed. Ray A. Billington (San Marino CA: Huntington Library, 1966) 172-75; Bernard Bailyn, *The Ideological Origins of the American Revolution* (Cambridge MA: Belknap Press of Harvard University Press, 1967) 35-39; Rossiter, *Seedtime of the Republic,* 141; Gary Huxford, "The English Libertarian Tradition in the Colonial Newspaper," *Journalism Quarterly* 45 (1968): 677-86.

[42]Perhaps a less-wealthy colonial gentry and the relatively fresh memory of Bolingbroke's misdeeds limited references to him prior to his death in 1751; thereafter, increasing prosperity (at least in South Carolina), waning awareness of his career, and the increased availability of his writings resulting from the several collected editions published in London after 1752 partially account for his increased prominence. Thus the works of Trenchard and Gordon figure in the *South Carolina Gazettes* of 12 June 1736, 16, 29 July, 8 August 1748, 20 March 1749, 17 October 1754, and the *Country Journal,* 19 October 1773; whereas explicit reference to Bolingbroke appears in the *South Carolina Gazettes* of 26 March 1763, 20 August 1770, and the *Virginia Gazette* (Dixon), 18 February 1775.

Plagiarism of *Cato's Letters* occurs in the *South Carolina Gazette* of 14 September 1769 (cf. "The Important Duty of Attendance in Parliament Recommended to the Members"), whereas covert borrowings from Bolingbroke occur in the *Virginia Gazette* (Rind), 12 July 1770 and *South Carolina Gazette,* 7, 14 September 1769, and 13 June 1774 (cf. *Freeholder's Political Catechism,* "Dissertation upon Parties": Dedication to Robert Walpole and Letter 17).

Without doubt, the use of Trenchard and Gordon, as well as Bolingbroke, was far more frequent than these examples indicate. My point is merely that a reasonably careful search reveals that after mid-century the latter had probably replaced the former as the most quotable authority in these newspapers.

mously published works had excited more attention than they deserved. For having expended the "Vigor of his Youth in every Species of Riot and Debauchery . . . , he became the Partisan of a Cause [the Jacobite] which he condemned, and which could not be supported without deluging his Country in Blood, merely that he might gratify the Vices of a Man. In his Life, indeed," the reviewer continued, "there is no less Absurdity than in his Writings; nor was there any Difference between his Life and his Death, but that the Folly of Vice was then complicated with the Horrors of Impiety."[43] As a Jacobite and a libertine, he was a somewhat tarnished champion of liberty.

Nevertheless, he was a master stylist, and his eminently quotable writings embodied ideas about the abuse of political power that appeared especially relevant to Americans during the prerevolutionary controversy. It is, therefore, understandable that the note in Rind's *Virginia Gazette* of 12 July 1770, introducing more than a full page of extracts from Bolingbroke's *Freeholder's Political Catechism,* which was described as containing "*a short but judicious Summary of the Duty, as well as Rights, of every English Freeholder,*" attributed the work to the Earl of Bath. Probably much more common than such erroneous attributions, which camouflaged the extent of Bolingbroke's contribution to the ideas expressed in these newspapers, was the entire omission of his name. Crediting only "a celebrated Politician" for a few words, a leading South Carolina planter, John Mackenzie, quietly borrowed extensive passages from Bolingbroke in the course of advocating the nonimportation association. And, though difficult to identify with certainty unless they are as conspicuous as the Americanized versions of Bolingbroke's stirring declaration that "the friends of liberty" would "rather choose, no doubt, to die the last of British freemen, than bear to live the first of British slaves," the phrasing of common beliefs often seems briefly to echo Bolingbroke. For this reason, it is impossible to be sure that a South Carolinian signing himself "THE CRAFTSMAN" intended to adopt the title of Bolingbroke's famous journal for his pseudonym. But that he did not call himself a "mechanic" or "tradesman"—terms then much more common in the area—suggests that he was not an artisan. Furthermore, if his magisterial advice to vote for a

---

[43]H. Trevor Colbourn, *The Lamp of Experience: Whig History and the Intellectual Origins of the American Revolution* (Chapel Hill: University of North Carolina Press, 1965) 78; *Maryland Gazette,* 4 July 1754; *Virginia Gazette,* 4 April 1755.

planter in the pending election does not positively confirm this inference, it indicates that his ideas at least were remarkably similar to Bolingbroke's, for they both believed that independent men of landed property were the most reliable guardians of freedom. This notion, with its special appeal to the planting classes of the Southern colonies, was a fundamental element in the political culture of the region.[44]

Ironically, therefore, a man whose support of the Stuart Pretender involved him in the Scottish Rebellion of 1715 may have indirectly contributed to an equally conspicuous feature of these political essays—that is, a hatred of Scotsmen in general and Scotch merchants and politicians in particular. His Tory misgivings about the political effects of financial intrigue and mercantile manipulation fused easily in the colonial environment with later Whiggish denunciations of the presumed insidious influence at court of John Stuart, earl of Bute, and his Scottish cohorts.[45] No doubt the desire to keep abreast of London fashions partly accounts for the occasional appearance of this invective even in papers owned by Scotsmen; and it is worth noting that *"May the light of Liberty never be put out by a* Scotch *Extinguisher!"* was, according to the *North-Carolina Gazette,* a toast common "in the most polite companies" among the supporters of John Wilkes. Nevertheless, increasing Scottish domination of the Chesapeake tobacco trade, as well as the prominence of Scotch placemen farther south, made

---

[44]David Lundberg and Henry F. May, "The Enlightened Reader in America," *American Quarterly* 28 (1976): 271ff. For the quotations and their sources, see n. 42 above under the *South Carolina Gazette* of 7, 14 September 1769 and 13 June 1774.

"THE CRAFTSMAN" appeared in the *South Carolina Gazette* of 4 April 1774, while more remote echoes of Bolingbroke may also appear in the *South Carolina Gazette* of 14 September 1769 (cf. "Dissertation upon Parties," concluding paragraph), 26 October 1769 (cf. ibid., Letters 3 and 8 on "passive obedience and non-resistance"), 12 December 1774, and 7 September 1775 (cf. ibid., Letter 17). For the contrary supposition that "The Craftsman" was an artisan, see Richard Walsh, *Charleston's Sons of Liberty: A Study of the Artisans, 1763-1789* (Columbia: University of South Carolina Press, 1959) 27.

Jack P. Greene, "The Growth of Political Stability: An Interpretation of Political Development in the Anglo-American Colonies, 1660-1760," in *The American Revolution: A Heritage of Change,* ed. John Parker and Carol Urness (Minneapolis: Associates of the James Ford Bell Library, 1975) 47.

[45]For anti-Scottish prejudices in British politics, see John Clive and Bernard Bailyn, "England's Cultural Provinces: Scotland and America," *William and Mary Quarterly* 3d ser. 11 (1954): 212; M. Dorothy George, *English Political Caricature to 1792: A Study of Opinion and Propaganda* (Oxford: Oxford University Press, 1959) 119-40; and John Brooke, *King George III* (New York: McGraw-Hill, 1972) 145.

the Southern colonies fertile ground for the growth of prejudice. The riots in 1769 against the Scotch merchants of Norfolk, Virginia, are therefore perhaps the most accurate indication of the emotion underlying these diatribes.[46]

Manifestations of the widespread hatred and fear took many forms. "*Irish impudence* is of the downright, genuine, and unadulterated sort," Pinkney's *Virginia Gazette* declared. But "a *Scotchman,* when he first is admitted into a house, is so humble that he will sit upon the lowest step of the staircase. By degrees he gets into the kitchen, and from thence, by the most submissive behaviour, is advanced to the parlour. If he gets into the diningroom, as ten to one but he will, the master of the house must take care of himself; for in all probability he will turn him out of doors, and, by the assistance of his *countrymen,* keep possession forever." Again and again, the same themes reappeared. Timothy's hostility to the combination of Wells and Stuart, which often forced him to reprint news about Indian affairs from the *South-Carolina and American General Gazette,* made him especially sensitive to the "*Scratch me, Countryman!—and I'll scratch thee*" syndrome reputed to be common among Scots.[47] (Their supposed clannishness, however, was a proverbial lament.) So, too, was their corrupting influence which, paraphrasing Pope, Arthur Lee later described as spreading as insidiously and pervasively as "a low-born mist, a Scottish mist." Accordingly, "THE CRAFTSMAN" warned fellow South Carolinians, "You are soon, my Countrymen, to have a *Scot* Governor. If you have a *Scot* Assembly . . . the Lord have Mercy on you!" The outcome, he declared, "would be worse for this Province than it was for Sodom and Gomorrah." Equally alarmed, Christopher Gadsden thought he detected an

---

[46]*Georgia Gazette,* 9 May 1770; *Virginia Gazette* (Purdie), 6 October 1775; *North Carolina Gazette,* 24 June 1768; J. H. Soltow, "Scottish Traders in Virginia, 1750-1775," *Economic History Review* 12 (1959): 83-98; Robert M. Weir, "Who Shall Rule at Home: The American Revolution as a Crisis of Legitimacy for the Colonial Elite," *Journal of Interdisciplinary History* 6 (1976): 689; William M. Dabney, "Letters from Norfolk: Scottish Merchants View the Revolutionary Crisis," in *The Old Dominion: Essays for Thomas Perkins Abernethy,* ed. Darrett B. Rutman (Charlottesville: University Press of Virginia, 1964) 111.

[47]*Virginia Gazette* (Pinkney), 20 October 1774, conveniently available in "Trivia," *William and Mary Quarterly* 3d ser. 11 (1954): 291; J. Ralph Randolph, "The End of Impartiality: *South-Carolina Gazette,* 1763-1775," *Journalism Quarterly* 49 (1972):706-709, 720; *South Carolina Gazette,* 30 May 1774. For an attempt to counter some of this prejudice, see *Virginia Gazette* (Pinkney), 30 December 1775.

unusually elaborate conspiracy. "Dear *Charley* [the Young Pretender] is THEIR object," he told readers of the *South-Carolina Gazette*. Scotsmen, he claimed, promoted oppressive measures in order to provoke a rebellion against the House of Hanover. Posing as a champion of the oppressed in England as well as in America, the Stuart Pretender would then appear to come to the rescue. But after he was firmly seated on the throne, Americans could, Gadsden once privately prophesied, bid "good (or rather bad) night to the English liberties." Although this scenario elicited a "Great God!" from someone with a less fevered imagination, Gadsden was only one of many who believed that Scotsmen were at the bottom of a conspiracy against American liberty. And some polemicists, at least, were certain that they saw further proof of it in the supposedly pusillanimous and self-serving conduct of Scottish merchants during the crises over the Stamp Act and Townshend Duties.[48]

Thus, as those who bore the brunt of these attacks would have been quick to point out, historians might do well to view these newspapers as organs of the local establishments and to view their contents with commensurate skepticism. Although not always readily identifiable, omissions were frequently significant. "No Newspapers the last week," a Tory in Virginia shrewdly observed in 1776, "I suppose the rascals have had bad luck of late and are afraid it should be known." Reports of slave insurrections appear to have been regularly suppressed until the danger was apparently over.[49] And potential insurgents, such as the Regulators of South Carolina, often found the press "shut against them." According to their

---

[48]Arthur Lee to Chairman of Committee for Foreign Correspondence, 30 November 1777, in Richard Henry Lee, *Life of Arthur Lee, LL. D.,* 2 vols. (1829; rpt., Freeport NY: Books for Libraries Press, 1969) 2:30; *Pope, Poetical Works,* ed. Herbert Davis (London: Oxford University Press, 1966) 306; *South Carolina Gazette,* 1, 22 June, 13 July 1769, 4 April 1774; Gadsden to William S. Johnson, 16 April 1766, in Walsh, ed., *Writings of Christopher Gadsden,* 73-74.

[49]Entry of 9 October 1776, *Journal of Nicholas Cresswell,* 163. For reports of insurrection scares that did not appear in the *Country Journal,* see Henry Laurens to John L. Gervais, 29 January 1766, in *The Papers of Henry Laurens,* vol. 5, 1 September 1765-31 July 1768, ed. George C. Rogers, Jr. and David R. Chesnutt (Columbia: University of South Carolina Press, 1976) 53-54; and "Extracts from the Journal of Mrs. Ann Manigault, 1754-1781," ed. Mabel L. Webber, *South Carolina Historical and Genealogical Magazine* 20 (1919): 209. See also Winthrop D. Jordan, *White over Black: American Attitudes toward the Negro, 1550-1812* (Chapel Hill: University of North Carolina Press, 1968) 395; and *North Carolina Gazette,* 12 May 1775.

spokesman, Charles Woodmason, "the Printers said, *They dar'd not*[,] being (as supposed) inhibited and afraid to affront the Commons House." Less blatant but no less real was the censorship of public opinion that apparently prompted an Anglican clergyman in Maryland, Thomas Bacon, to abandon a political allegory that he feared would be too moderate for the tastes of his "Dear Fellow Planters and Country-men" to whom it was addressed.[50]

Evidence of such stillborn items also raises questions about much of the material actually printed. A careful study of the *Virginia Gazette* published in 1773 and 1774 found that "about 9% of all political articles were manifestly erroneous or significantly distorted" in favor of the Whigs. Particularly dubious are the numerous accounts that depict popular protests as decorous demonstrations. According to the *Virginia Gazette*, the exercise of force in North Carolina was so well organized in 1766 that "few instances can be produced of such a number of men being together so long, and behaving so well; not the least noise or disturbance . . . neither was there an injury offered to any person, but the whole affair [was] conducted with decency and spirit, worthy the imitation of all the Sons of Liberty throughout the Continent." Although this report may have been more accurate than many, the *South-Carolina Gazette* described activities in Charleston, which unquestionably included looting, in remarkably similar terms.[51] In short, because they reflect a desire to make the American cause appear righteous and irresistible by emphasizing its orderliness and unanimity, these reports can seldom be read literally.

Faced with such often misleading and intractable materials, scholars have recently turned to the computer in the hope of providing a solid statistical basis for inferences that would otherwise remain impressionistic. The results, however, have been rather uneven. Among the most successful, Richard Merritt's work has revealed an enormous growth in "the amount of intercolonial news carried by the newspapers" which, he found,

---

[50]Richard J. Hooker, ed., *The Carolina Backcountry on the Eve of the Revolution: The Journal and Other Writings of Charles Woodmason, Anglican Itinerant* (Chapel Hill: University of North Carolina Press, 1953) 210; Lemay, *Men of Letters in Colonial Maryland*, 341-42.

[51]Willard C. Frank, Jr., "Error, Distortion and Bias in the *Virginia Gazettes, 1773-1774*," *Journalism Quarterly* 49 (1972): 739; *Virginia Gazette* (Purdie & Dixon), 21 March 1766; *South Carolina Gazette*, 31 October 1765; 19, 21 October 1765, S.C. Council Journals, 32:628-30.

"increased sixfold and more from the late 1730s to the early 1770s." Certainly such findings are illuminating enough for many purposes to warrant application of similar techniques to the contents of the more important newspapers omitted from Merritt's study. Nevertheless, problems arise in interpreting the data. Merritt's discovery that the *South-Carolina Gazette* gave an unusually large amount of attention to local attitudes may reveal more about Timothy's competitive position vis-à-vis Wells, whose ties to royal officialdom frequently gave him priority in acquiring imperial news, than about the interests of subscribers who probably read both papers. Valid generalizations about the attention patterns of individuals in any area served by more than one newspaper would, therefore, require an examination of all the papers involved. But even then the meaning of the findings would not necessarily be clear because, as Stephen Botein has recently pointed out, increasing coverage of American affairs might merely have reflected changes in the British press from which American printers borrowed. It is quite conceivable that in some cases more frequent use of ''American symbols'' indicated not a growing sense of American community but the continuation of unusually close ties to Britain. After all, imperial officials were the first to refer consistently to America in a collective sense, and a Tory (Wells) was the only Southern printer to use the term on the masthead of his newspaper. Even if Merritt is correct in concluding that changes in symbol usage did in fact ''suggest aroused expectations about group membership in a distinctly American political community,'' the reason for the change (as he was the first to admit) remains elusive.[52]

Given these considerations and our present interest in understanding the role of the newspapers in the social context of the Southern colonies, how can one usefully examine their contents? Perhaps the question can best be answered by inquiring what contemporaries considered the special function of the newspaper to be. That some were named after Mercury, the speedy messenger of the gods, and many bore some variant of the motto ''Containing the freshest Advices, Foreign and Domestick'' suggests the

---

[52]Richard L. Merritt, *Symbols of American Community, 1735-1775* (New Haven: Yale University Press, 1966) 56, 97, 131, 180. For indications of the printers' competitive positions, see *South Carolina Gazette*, 4 May 1765, 22 June 1767, 1 August 1768, 17 August 1769; *South Carolina and American General Gazette*, 8 July, 30 December 1774. Botein, '' 'Meer Mechanics' and an Open Press,'' 196 n. 66; Oliver M. Dickerson, ''England's Most Fateful Decision,'' *New England Quarterly* 22 (1949): 388-94.

answer. Their special purview was the prompt reporting of news. Furthermore, several recent studies have demonstrated that the speed with which news travels possesses important social and political consequences. In particular, I. K. Steele has explored some of the relationships between community cohesiveness and the speed of communications within the Empire at the beginning of the eighteenth century; and Allan Pred has shown a connection between the flow of information in antebellum America and the ability of the largest metropolitan centers to maintain their dominant positions.[53] Because similar effects were probably even more pronounced during the revolutionary crisis when the prompt knowledge of events was especially important, we err if we overlook significant variations in times that perhaps now seem to have been almost equally sidereal.

An examination of the speed with which Southern colonial newspapers delivered the news is, therefore, in order. First, a word about the composition of the sample. Practical considerations limited it to approximately 200 issues, selected by randomly drawing one item per quarter from the newspapers published in each of the Southern colonies between 1763 and 1775. The importance of Virginia and the large gaps in the extant files led us to draw from the gazettes of all publishers. In North Carolina, on the other hand, Davis's greater professionalism and established contacts dictated the choice of his *North-Carolina Gazette*. For South Carolina, Crouch's *Country Journal* proved preferable because it was the only local paper regularly published on the nominal date of issue.[54] The last point suggests a caveat. Some news circulated for days before being confirmed by the weekly press, while the practice of predating delayed issues gives a misleadingly foreshortened impression of elapsed time. Although these

---

[53]Thomas, *History of Printing in America*, 2:157, 163, 166, 169, 173; I. K. Steele, "Time, Communications and Society: The English Atlantic, 1702," *Journal of American Studies* 8 (1974): 1-21; Pred, *Urban Growth and the Circulation of Information*, 3, passim. For some earlier, unsystematic attempts to deal with speed in this period, see Crittenden, "N.C. Newspapers before 1790," 26-27; and Schlesinger, *Prelude to Independence*, 283.

[54]Lathem, comp., *Chronological Tables of American Newspapers*, 9, 13; Crittenden, "N.C. Newspapers before 1790," 20; Thomas, *History of Printing in America*, 2:168, 170, 172, 173. In the 25 December 1770 issue, Crouch apologized for failing to put out the *Country Journal* on the day it was dated—the first such failure, he claimed, in its history. Even though the other printers were not as punctual in publishing, trial samples of the *South Carolina Gazette* and the *South Carolina and American General Gazette* suggest that there was little difference in the speed with which each of the Charleston papers delivered the news.

two sources of distortion tend to cancel each other out, their net effect may make the average transit times given here a bit high. Furthermore, despite the possibility of seasonal and perhaps long-term variations, no regular pattern emerged for either. Perhaps enough of the news from Britain arrived via the regular monthly packet service to camouflage seasonal irregularities, and the lack of technological innovation during the period certainly precluded much acceleration except under unusual circumstances. Finally, because in a few cases (for example, North Carolina items in the *Georgia Gazette*) the sample yielded only one or two usable datelines, some of the figures should be regarded as being very tentative.

Nevertheless, despite limitations imposed by the preliminary nature of the present sample and the elusiveness of much of the data, analysis of the nearly 600 datelines reflected in Table 1 clearly reveals several points. Most striking is the magnitude of the difference between the speeds with which

TABLE 1

THE COMPARATIVE SPEED (IN ELAPSED DAYS) WITH WHICH LEADING SOUTHERN COLONIAL NEWSPAPERS REPORTED THE NEWS[55]							
NEWS FROM	Md. Gaz.	Va. Gaz. (Royal, P&D, D&H)	Va. Gaz. (Rind, Pinkney)	Va. Gaz. (Purdie)	NC Gaz.	SC Gaz. & CJ	Ga. Gaz.
British Isles	84	80	78	77	83	71	69
Mass.	21	22	22	24	27	26	31
R.I.	22	18	30	X	16	24	X
N.Y.	16	21	19	15	28	23	40
Pa.	12	19	15	16	23	23	28
Md.	—	X	14	X	X	24	X
Va.	19	—	—	—	19	33	15
N.C.	49	30	4	X	—	20	11
S.C.	43	35	44	X	25	—	15
Ga.	48	65	X	X	X	13	—

[55]The figures in Table 1 are numerical averages, rounded off to the nearest day, derived from the items that appear to have been treated as current news. X indicates that the sample yielded no reports permitting computation of elapsed time. For the range of times involved and a complete tabulation of the number of items in each category, consult the Appendix.

news arrived from North America and Great Britain. On the average, news from even the remote corners of New England was published in all of the Southern colonies in less than a third of the time required for that from London. In fact, the latter often took more than ten to twelve weeks, whereas items from New York and Philadelphia normally arrived in two to three. Equally significant, these two cities obviously served as important distributing centers for news originating elsewhere. Although indirect transmission was probable considerably more common than the datelines indicated, nearly a tenth of the items permitted positive identification of the routes involved; and, as Table 2 indicates, approximately two-thirds of these were through Philadelphia and New York.

TABLE 2

VIA	Md. Gaz.	Va. Gaz.	N.C. Gaz.	S.C. Gaz. & C.J.	Ga. Gaz.	TOTAL
INDIRECT ROUTING OF NEWS ITEMS IN LEADING SOUTHERN COLONIAL NEWSPAPERS[56]						
Mass.	4 Brit.	1 Brit. 1 N.Y. 1 S.C.				7
R.I.	1 Mass.	2 Mass. 1 N.Y.	2 Mass.			6
N.Y.	5 Brit. 1 Mass. 1 Pa.	1 Brit. 1 Mass. 2 S.C.	1 Brit.	1 Mass. 1 Pa. 1 Va.	2 Pa. 1 S.C.	18
Phila- delphia	2 Brit. 1 Mass. 1 N.Y. 1 S.C.	6 Brit. 1 N.Y.	1 Brit. 2 Mass.	1 N.Y.	1 N.Y.	17
N.C.	1 Va.	1 N.Y.				2
S.C.		1 Ga.			1 Va.	2

Being both the western terminus of a transatlantic packet line and the headquarters of the British Army in America, New York was in an especially favorable position to relay news from Canada and the military outposts in the Mississippi Valley as well as from Britain itself.[57] Proximity

---

[56]Of the 584 datelines in the sample, 52 (or nine percent) indicate indirect routing.

[57]William Smith, ''The Colonial Post-Office,'' *American Historical Review* 21 (1916): 271-72; John Shy, *Toward Lexington: The Role of the British Army in the Coming of the American Revolution* (Princeton: Princeton University Press, 1965) 96, 158, 268. For interesting examples of items routed through New York, see *Maryland Gazette,* 30 June 1763,

to New York, strong ties with the West, and good trade connections with the Southern colonies meant that Philadelphia was nearly as well situated. Both of these cities appear to have been quite efficient distributors of the news, and the fastest route from London to Annapolis and Williamsburg was frequently by way of Philadelphia or New York.[58] But if links between the Northern and Southern colonies appear to have been surprisingly strong, ties among the Southern towns seem to have been quite weak. Hence the frequency as well as the speed of reports indicate that Charleston was connected more closely to New York than Wilmington, North Carolina, was to Savannah, Georgia. Furthermore, Savannah seems to have been unusually close to London and relatively isolated from everything north of Charleston. Elsewhere in the Southern colonies communications appear to have been mediocre at best. Even between towns as close as Savannah and Charleston, trading information usually took two weeks.

Although the significance of these figures will become more apparent after we discover who read the newspapers, some observations can be made at this point. First, because the datelines indicated a positive correlation between the amount of news and speed in transit, it seems reasonable to suppose that both were partly a function of the volume of trade between the areas concerned. This, however, is not to say that relatively weak economic links might not have been associated with good communications or vice versa. Thus, the regular coastal trade between the middle and Southern colonies could have been more important in some respects than the larger but seasonal transatlantic commerce in manufactured goods and agricultural staples.[59] But to conclude that such was in fact the case requires

---

1 March 1764, 27 June 1765, 13 March 1766, 5 March 1767, 13 September 1770, 13 April 1775; *Virginia Gazette* (Purdie & Dixon) 21 May 1767; and *Georgia Gazette*, 2 June 1763, 7 February 1765.

[58]Joseph A. Ernst and H. Roy Merrens, "The South Carolina Economy of the Middle Eighteenth Century: A View from Philadelphia," *West Georgia College Studies in the Social Sciences* 12 (June 1973): 16-29. Thus, on 5 November 1772, for example, the *Maryland Gazette* reported an item from London by way of Philadelphia in only sixty-seven days, or twenty percent less than the average time.

[59]David Klingaman, "The Development of the Coastwise Trade of Virginia in the Late Colonial Period," *Virginia Magazine of History and Biography* 77 (1969): 29, 32, 38; Klingaman, "The Coastwise Trade of Colonial Massachusetts," *Essex Institute Historical Collections* 108 (July 1972): 217-34; Francis C. Huntley, "The Seaborne Trade of Virginia in the Mid-Eighteenth Century: Port Hampton," *Virginia Magazine of History and Biography* 59 (1951):298, 302; Walter F. Crawford, "The Commerce of Rhode Island with the Southern Continental Colonies in the Eighteenth Century," *Rhode Island Historical Society Collections* 14 (October 1921):99-130; James F. Shepherd and Gary M. Walton, *Shipping, Maritime Trade, and the Economic Development of Colonial North America* (London: Cambridge University Press, 1972) passim.

knowing that contemporaries considered the quality of communications to be important. That someone was careful to indicate that an item published in the *Maryland Gazette* arrived via the packet service from Britain to New York, that Adam Boyd planned to use express riders to distribute the *Cape-Fear Mercery,* and that Rind began his *Virginia Gazette* by observing, *"a well conducted* NEWSPAPER *would, at any Time, be important, but most especially at a Crisis, which makes a quick Circulation of Intelligence particularly interesting to all the* AMERICAN COLONIES,*"* all suggest that printers believed their readers did indeed want the "freshest Advices." And that some citizens in South Carolina privately supported a rider who presumably made regular runs from Charleston to Pocataligo reveals that the printers understood their customers.[60]

III

Like the men who employed the *"Pocataligo Private Rider,"* most of those who were exposed to the colonial press will never be known with certainty. Nevertheless, they can be divided into two categories. One, containing the individuals who had direct access to the newspapers, was most likely quite small; the other, composed of men and women who received their news from members of the first group, was probably much larger. Furthermore, despite the bias inherent in the survival of such records, there is considerable evidence to indicate that social class played a large part in determining how an individual received information. Almost all of the surviving testimony indicating readership comes from members of the upper classes.[61] Subscription agents for both the *South-Carolina*

---

ciety Collections 14 (October 1921): 99-130; James F. Shepherd and Gary M. Walton, *Shipping, Maritime Trade, and the Economic Development of Colonial North America* (London: Cambridge University Press, 1972) passim.

[60]*Maryland Gazette,* 1 March 1764; Boyd to "Sir," 16 November 1772, in *The Colonial Records of North Carolina, 1662-1776,* ed. W. L. Saunders, 10 vols. (Raleigh: State of North Carolina, 1886-1890) 9:356; *Virginia Gazette* (Rind), 16 May 1766; *South Carolina and American General Gazette,* 22 May 1776.

[61]R. H. Lee to William Lee, 19 June 1771, in *The Letters of Richard Henry Lee,* ed. James C. Ballagh, 2 vols. (New York: Macmillan Co., 1911) 1:58; Knight, ed., *Documentary History of Education in the South,* 565; Lemay, *Men of Letters in Colonial Maryland,* 233; Land, *Dulanys of Maryland,* 190; Farish, ed., *Journal and Letters of Philip Fithian,* 64; H. Laurens to J. Laurens, 26 September 1775, in "Letters from Hon. Henry Laurens to His Son John, 1773-1776," 75.

Gazette and the *Cape-Fear Mercury* were among the most prominent men in their areas;[62] and the same was clearly true of subscribers to the *Virginia Gazettes*.[63] In addition, published personal polemics, like duels, sometimes seem to have been governed by rules of honor which would have required that they be conducted only with and before peers. Stylistic characteristics also confirm that these bouts were usually intended to be in-group affairs. The common, but by no means invariable, use of pseudonyms seldom concealed the identity of writers who were often immediately known to their intended audiences; the abundant use of satire depended on common knowledge and assumptions; and the Latin quotations would have been unintelligible to anyone without at least a rudimentary classical education.[64] Furthermore, frequent mention of the "vulgar," the "lower Class," and so forth indicates that the authors addressed themselves mainly to a restricted audience. Although such public displays of arrogance some-

---

[62]The *South Carolina Gazette*, 25 August 1764, listed 3 subscription agents in the Floridas, 17 in Georgia, 5 in North Carolina, and 122 in South Carolina. Among the latter, 28 can be identified as public officials, 9 as militia officers, 9 as professional men, 10 as merchants, and 23 as prominent planters. Of the others, 16 were also sufficiently important to receive miscellaneous mention in standard sources, while 27 cannot be readily identified. The 11 subscription agents listed in the *Cape Fear Mercury*, 22 September 1773, included 8 public officials, 1 militia officer, 1 prominent South Carolina merchant, and 1 who proved unidentifiable. (Men occupying more than one category were counted under the first mentioned here.)

[63]A sample of forty customers taken from *The Virginia Gazette Daybooks, 1750-1752 & 1764-1766*, Microfilm Publication 5, University of Virginia Library (Charlottesville, 1967), yielded fifteen public officials, one militia officer, and five professional men; ten others may have fallen into one of these categories but could not be positively identified. Nine could not be traced through Swem's *Virginia Historical Index*. The *North Carolina Gazette*, 18 July 1777, listed twenty-four subscribers to the *Virginia Gazettes* presumably resident in North Carolina. Of these, ten were public officials, two were militia officers, one a merchant, four received miscellaneous mention in the *Colonial and State Records of North Carolina*, and seven cannot be readily identified.

[64]Entry of 12 February 1774, Farish, ed., *Journal and Letters of Philip Fithian*, 65; Land, *Dulanys of Maryland*, 302; *South Carolina Gazette*, 21 September, 26 October 1769; Drayton, "To the Public," in William Henry Drayton and Others, *The Letters of Freeman, Etc.* (London, 1771); rpt., ed. Robert M. Weir (Columbia: University of South Carolina Press, 1977) 3; Jack P. Greene, "The Gadsden Election Controversy and the Revolutionary Movement in South Carolina," *Mississippi Valley Historical Review* 46 (1959): 482; Wood, "The Democratization of Mind in the American Revolution," in *Leadership in the American Revolution*, 65, 68-70.

times proved to be mistakes, it is clear that newspaper polemics tended to remain the sport of the relatively wealthy and prominent.[65]

How much wider the readership was is uncertain. News and information were the commodities conveyed; consumers needed physical access, the resources, and the motivation to take advantage of them. In the towns, inns and public houses might have solved the problem of access while perhaps complicating that of motivation. Though out of the financial reach of many individuals, newspapers were almost certainly available in many taverns where it seems that they were sometimes used by men learning to spell. But such activity required the necessary leisure. That few men possessed it is suggested by Isaiah Thomas's attempt to change the traditional format when he began the *Massachusetts Spy*. Smaller amounts of information, more frequently published, would, he believed, reach a new audience of "mechanics, and other classes of people who had not much time to spare from business." That he believed that he was thereby innovating illuminates the situation in the Southern colonies as well as in Massachusetts, for Thomas had worked in Charleston and knew the Southern papers.[66] Nevertheless, men from the North often considered Southerners dilatory, if not lazy, and it is possible that even the working classes took life easier there than farther north. The existence of more than 100 retail liquor outlets in Charleston (then a city of about 1,300 houses) seems to confirm reports of a good deal of conviviality among all classes. And, though this conviviality unquestionably helped to disseminate the news, it also militated against serious reading. So did poor lighting, crude spectacles, if any, and cramped pages frequently printed with worn type. The reading aloud and discussion of important items, such as resolutions of the Continental Congress, occurred in taverns; much silent reading is more doubtful.[67]

---

[65]*Virginia Gazette* (Purdie & Dixon), 20 January 1774; *South Carolina Gazette,* 21 September 1769. For an apparent and certainly delightful exception to the general rule, see the letter in which some mechanics of Charleston suggested that William Henry Drayton, who had termed them the "*profanum vulgus,*" suffered from having had "his upper works" damaged at birth, *South Carolina Gazette,* 5 October 1769.

[66]Charles Shepheard, for example, intended to make the latest newspapers available at his coffee house. *South Carolina Gazette,* 16 May 1743. Alice M. Earle, *Stage-Coach and Tavern Days* (1900; rpt., New York: Dover, 1969) 91-92; Thomas, *History of Printing in America,* 1:xxvii-xli; 2:61.

[67]"Diary of Timothy Ford, 1785-1786," ed. Joseph W. Barnwell, *South Carolina His-*

Outside of the relatively few towns, physical access to the newspapers also presented a formidable problem to all but those wealthy enough to subscribe. Stores and taverns were normally located on the main roads, usually a day's ride apart; militia musters were infrequent and often irregular; and church congregations were easily far larger than the number of subscribing members.[68] Nevertheless, multiple readership is still most common in rural areas, and some newspapers obviously circulated beyond the original recipient. For example, John Harrower, who tutored the family of Col. William Daingerfield of Belvidera, near Fredericksburg, Virginia, borrowed old copies from his employer. But their relationship was a close one; and many subscribers were no doubt unwilling to make indiscriminate loans of relatively fragile items that they often regarded as permanent records.[69] And, had they been willing to lend or give newspapers to acquaintances, distance would have remained an obstacle to potential readers. Even if one grants the unlikely assumption that per capita circulation was the same in the Northern and Southern colonies, geographic distribution—and therefore the possibility of physical access—was far different. Population density in Massachusetts, not including Maine, was approximately thirty-five people per square mile at the end of the colonial period; that of Rhode Island about forty-five. Virginia and Maryland, which

torical and Genealogical Magazine 13 (1912): 142-43; H. Roy Merrens, "A View of Coastal South Carolina in 1778: The Journal of Ebenezer Hazard," South Carolina Historical Magazine 73 (1972): 186; Bridenbaugh, Cities in Revolt, 358; Bull to Hillsborough, 30 November 1770, Trans., S.C., 32:388, SCDAH; Worth, The Colonial Printer, 66: entry of 1 November 1774, Journal of Nicholas Cresswell, 45.

[68]In fact, as late as the 1820s stores and taverns were often still as much as ten to twenty miles apart. See Robert Mills, Atlas of the State of South Carolina (1825; rpt., Columbia: Bostick and Thornley, 1938). Don Higginbotham, The War of American Independence: Military Attitudes, Policies, and Practice, 1763-1789 (New York: Macmillan Co., 1971) 10; Presentments of the Grand Jury, in South Carolina Gazette, 7 February 1771.

[69]Richard L. Merrit, "Public Opinion in Colonial America: Content-Analyzing the Colonial Press," Public Opinion Quarterly 27 (1963): 363 n. 17; Harrower to his wife, 14 June 1774, in The Journal of John Harrower, ed. Edward M. Riley (New York: Holt, Rinehart and Winston, 1963) 56; Davis, Literature and Society in Early Virginia, 220-21; Lemay, Men of Letters in Colonial Maryland, 233; Jensen, Founding of a Nation, 360; Cranfield, Development of the Provincial Newspaper, 259; 29 November 1765, S.C. Commons House Journals, 37:31.

were the most heavily populated Southern colonies, averaged only about half the latter figure; and the area in South Carolina most thickly settled by whites contained less than eight persons per square mile as late as 1790. The only substantial concentrations of population were at Baltimore, Norfolk, and Charleston; Williamsburg and the other cities were scarcely more than villages. The majority of the populace was, therefore, sparsely scattered over an immense area. So, too, of course were the newspapers; Timothy's subscription agents for the *South-Carolina Gazette* stretched from Brunswick, North Carolina, to Mobile, West Florida, while the *Virginia* and *North-Carolina Gazettes* penetrated the interior of their own and neighboring provinces.[70] But given prevailing methods of transportation, it is unlikely that most individuals were within personal reach of a copy.

In any case, access to the newspapers would not necessarily have implied the ability to read them. Literacy in the colonial period is currently the focus of some scholarly interest if not agreement; and it is impossible to be very positive about its level. But by using signatures on recorded wills as an index, Kenneth Lockridge has recently estimated that about eighty-five percent of the adult males in Massachusetts were literate by the end of the colonial period; the comparable figure in Virginia was approximately sixty-six percent. Although the latter seems to be a bit low in view of a long-standing guess (based on evidence drawn from land records) that would "place illiteracy between ten and twenty percent" in the interior of South Carolina, it is compatible with the findings of some of Lockridge's critics, who have questioned other aspects of his work. However debatable his contention that perhaps no more than fifty percent of the men among the poorer classes in Virginia were literate, Lockridge is almost certainly correct in arguing that the correlation between literacy and relatively high social status remained much greater in Virginia than in New England, if only because the more complex urbanized economies of the North de-

---

[70]Stella H. Sutherland, *Population Distribution in Colonial America* (New York: Columbia University Press, 1936) 37; Bridenbaugh, *Myths and Realities*, 3; Julian J. Petty, *The Growth and Distribution of Population in South Carolina* (Columbia: State Council for Defense, Industrial Development Committee, 1943) 69; Bridenbaugh, *Cities in Revolt*, 216-17, 416; *South Carolina Gazette*, 25 August 1764; *North Carolina Gazette*, 18 July 1777; Crittenden, "N.C. Newspapers before 1790," 20.

manded a higher level of skill from the average man than the relatively traditional rural and agrarian patterns of the South.[71]

But all of this is not to imply that the press failed to influence individuals who neither received nor read the newspapers. On the contrary, their wide geographic distribution among militia officers, ministers, and other leading men facilitated the verbal dissemination of newspaper content, while the prerevolutionary controversy increased the demand for news among all elements of the population. Henry Laurens was not an average man, but his changing interests probably represented a fairly typical pattern. "I am," he claimed in 1764, "never very eager in the pursuite of newes unless it be in my proper way of business & then my duty requires me to be both watchfull & vigilant to learn what is going forward & to improve upon the earlyest intelligence." By 1775 the erstwhile merchant, who had become president of the South Carolina Council of Safety, observed that he regularly spent Saturday nights "conning" the only gazette still regularly published in Charleston for a considerably wider range of information. Although the Revolution failed to augment the duties of everyone so dramatically, individuals in all walks of life found the news to be increasingly relevant to their own affairs. Ironically, however, the exigencies of the era may have "escalated the demands" upon individuals to the point where, as Lockridge has suggested, most were "relatively less literate than ever before." Under the circumstances, they naturally turned to leading men not only for the news itself but also for assistance in interpreting it. In the 1740s an educated woman like Eliza Lucas Pinckney drafted wills for her neighbors. More than a century later William Gilmore Simms provided a fictional but essentially accurate description of what probably had been a common occurrence: "Stephen," one backcountry man addressed a more informed associate, "every body knows you to be

---

[71]Kenneth A. Lockridge, *Literacy in Colonial New England: An Enquiry into the Social Context of Literacy in the Early Modern West* (New York: W. W. Norton, 1974) 21, 73, 78; Robert L. Meriwether, *The Expansion of South Carolina, 1729-1765* (Kingsport TN: Southern Publishers, 1940) 177; Kevin P. Kelly's review of Lockridge, *Literacy in Colonial New England,* in *William and Mary Quarterly* 3d ser. 32 (1975): 638-40. It seems reasonable to assume that prevailing economic and demographic conditions offset the tendency of Scotch-Irish immigrants, who were probably more literate than less geographically mobile individuals of similar social status, to raise the overall rate of literacy. See Lockridge, 46, 78-83.

a mighty smart man, with a head chock full of books, . . . and I want you
to tell me something to . . . set my mind at ease, and put me in the reason
and the right of every thing in this quarrel [with Great Britain]."[72]

In these semitraditional societies prominent men were expected to be
teachers, and neither Stephen nor his counterparts in real life could have
discharged their responsibilities without the aid of the newspapers. Revolutionary leaders appear to have been especially conscious of their role in
the communications system. "It is our Duty to inform you," the committee of intelligence wrote to district committeemen in South Carolina, "and
through you, the Public at large." A few months later John Rutledge em-
phasized the point in addressing members of the South Carolina legislature
who were about to return to their constituencies: "If any persons therein
are still strangers to the nature and merits of the dispute between Great
Britain and the Colonies, . . . explain it to them fully and teach them, if
they are so unfortunate as not to know, their inherent rights." And so, as
Edmund Pendleton later recalled, "By a free communication between those
of more information on political subjects, and the classes who have not
otherwise an opportunity of acquiring that knowledge, all were instructed
in their *rights* and *duties* as freemen, and taught to respect them."[73]

---

[72]H. Laurens to Richard Baker, 25 January 1764, in Rogers, *Papers of Henry Laurens,*
4:146-47; H. Laurens to J. Laurens, 26 September 1775, in "Letters from Hon. Henry
Laurens to His Son John, 1773-1776," 75; Lockridge, *Literacy in Colonial New England,*
87; E. L. Pinckney to Miss Bartlett, [c. June 1742], *The Letterbook of Eliza Lucas Pinckney, 1739-1762,* ed. Elise Pinckney and Marvin R. Zahniser (Chapel Hill: University of
North Carolina Press, 1972) 41; *The Writings of William Gilmore Simms,* vol. 16 of *Jos-
celyn, A Tale of the Revolution,* intro. and notes by Stephen E. Meats (Columbia: University of South Carolina Press, 1975) 34.

[73]*South Carolina Gazette,* 7 September 1775; 11 April 1776, *Journals of the General
Assembly and House of Representatives, 1776-1780,* ed. William E. Hemphill, Wylma
Wates, and R. Nicholas Olsberg (Columbia: University of South Carolina Press, 1970) 53;
"Address to the Citizens of Caroline," in *The Letters and Papers of Edmund Pendleton,
1734-1803,* ed. David J. Mays, 2 vols. (Charlottesville: University Press of Virginia, 1967)
2:650. Interestingly enough, recent studies indicate that those whose prestige depends most
directly upon their ability to interpret information for constituents and subordinates still tend
to be the most avid readers of organizational newsletters. See Elisabeth Noelle-Neumann,
"Mass Communication Media and Public Opinion," *Journalism Quarterly* 36 (1959): 408-
409; and Frederick Williams and Howard Lindsay, "Ethnic and Social Class Differences
in Communication Habits and Attitudes," *Journalism Quarterly* 48 (1971): 678.

IV

Because the influence of the Southern colonial newspapers extended far beyond their readers, questions about the nature of their impact supersede questions about the character of the primary audience. Thus, having considered who said what to whom, we now turn to inquire with what effects under the prevailing social conditions.

First, we will consider the case of the initial readership, composed primarily of men of property. These individuals were not always in complete agreement among themselves, and it is possible to exaggerate the political homogeneity of newspaper content. Yet, as Richard Oswald observed, in most of the Southern colonies, "Government has no Party. Being left to themselves, they are all of a Side." Thus with the exception of the *South-Carolina and American General Gazette* and (to a lesser extent) the *Georgia Gazette,* the political news and views were biased in favor of the Whigs. As a result, there can be little doubt that standard interpretations of the role of the newspapers in the coming of the Revolution are substantially accurate in describing their effect on members of the upper classes, to which they were initially addressed. Like the pamphlets of the period, the newspapers embodied a heritage of English libertarian thought that predisposed Americans to perceive a conspiracy against liberty in the actions of the British ministry. In fact, the discovery that Bolingbroke may have been a more important source of this thought for leaders in the Southern colonies than had hitherto been realized demonstrates once again how widespread and deeply rooted this ideological pattern was. For if Bolingbroke and his associates popularized a form of country ideology that possessed special appeal to the landed gentry of the area, their basic ideas about the inherently expansive nature of political power and the proper means of checking it differed little from those of Trenchard and Gordon.[74]

It is also clear that reports of measures taken in one colony stimulated emulation in others. William Henry Drayton's contention that South Carolina patriots hesitated "till in the Northern hemisphere, a *light* appeared,

---

[74]Oswald, "Plan," enclosed in Oswald to Dartmouth, 9 February 1775, in Stevens, ed., *Facsimiles,* 24: document 2032, p. 2; Bailyn, *Pamphlets of the American Revolution, 32, 60-89.*

to shew the political course we were to steer" was therefore accurate enough to rankle. In addition, George Grenville was probably correct in attributing some American protests to factious speeches of the Opposition at home. For the invective of British politics, as well as the violence of the London mob, caused Americans to overestimate their support in England, while the apparent contrast in behavior reinforced a belief in their own moderation and reasonableness. Thus when British authorities proved impervious to argument and the Opposition failed them, the disillusionment of Americans was correspondingly complete. Many therefore came to believe with George Mason—and Junius—that corruption was indeed rampant in Britain and "North America" was "the only great nursery of freemen now left upon the face of the earth." Given the premise, the conclusion was almost inevitable: "Let us cherish the sacred deposit."[75] In sum, the content of colonial newspapers helped to unify American leaders and to estrange them from Britain.

What is equally probable, though more difficult to demonstrate, is that the speed with which this content was transmitted accelerated and reinforced these developments. Correlation does not imply causation, but it is worth observing that allegiance and relatively good communications accompanied each other. In both respects, it seems, Georgians remained comparatively close to London while other Southerners increasingly turned toward Philadelphia and New York, which would eventually become the first two capitals of the new nation. Exploring this line of reasoning a bit further, we find that the classic picture of the British Empire as a rimless wheel with London at the hub holds true only in part for the volume of communication; when the map is redrawn to depict elapsed time, the hub for North America becomes the middle colonies, and a rudimentary rim even connects New England with the South. The possible significance of these findings depends partly on the plausible assumption that American leaders, being accustomed to dominating affairs in their own provinces,

---

[75]*South Carolina Gazette,* 16 June 1766, 28 December 1769; Brooke, *King George III,* 148-50; Ian R. Christie and Benjamin W. Labaree, *Empire or Independence, 1760-1776: A British-American Dialogue on the Coming of the American Revolution* (New York: W. W. Norton, 1976) 281; Mason, "Remarks on Annual Elections for the Fairfax Independent Company," c. 17-26 April 1775, in Rutland, *Papers of George Mason,* 1:231-32. For experimental confirmation that manipulating the ends of the political spectrum can change the perception of the midpoint, see Eleanor L. Norris, "Perspective as a Determinant of Attitude Formation and Change," *Journalism Quarterly* 50 (1973): 11-16.

would, like citizens in modern democracies, tend to identify more closely with communities in which they felt able to influence the course of public events. Furthermore, though by no means entirely dependent on the speed of communications, their political effectiveness was partly related to it. Given the tempo of life in the eighteenth century, reports from Philadelphia or New York arriving in Williamsburg or Charleston within a few days permitted a response, and even these relatively speedy times could be shortened to meet emergencies.[76] Given the nature of British policies and the prerevolutionary debate in which, as one colonial agent observed, "the Ground of yesterday is no longer tomorrow[']s," prompt news from Britain was even more important. But because oceans rolled and months elapsed before reports arrived from London, neither speed nor much flexibility was possible. That the ship chartered by London merchants to rush news of the repeal of the Stamp Act foundered off the bar at Charleston more than two months later, whereas express riders were able to speed reports of the battles of Lexington and Concord to Williamsburg in just over a week are therefore facts of some importance.[77]

To find that the communications and political systems of the embryonic nation were developing while those of the empire were deteriorating should perhaps not be very surprising in view of the recent examples of the rise of modern nationalism under the aegis of better communications.[78] But some other aspects of the contribution made by the press to the development of the new nation may not be so immediately obvious. Take the matter of the Scots. Because national groups normally identify themselves by rejecting others, the presence of a hostile ethnic group facilitates the de-

[76]Cletis Pride, "Content Analysis of Seven Commonwealth Newspapers," *Journalism Quarterly* 49 (1972): 753; Gabriel A. Almond and Sidney Verba, *The Civic Culture: Political Attitudes and Democracy in Five Nations* (Princeton: Princeton University Press, 1963) 230-57; Arthur H. Cole, "The Tempo of Mercantile Life in Colonial America," *Business History Review* 33 (1959): 277-99.

[77]Charles Garth to South Carolina Committee of Correspondence, 14 August 1768, Garth Letterbook, 61, SCDAH; Garth to Committee of Correspondence, 19 January 1766, in Joseph W. Barnwell, "Hon. Charles Garth, M.P., The Last Colonial Agent of South Carolina in England, and Some of His Work," *South Carolina Historical and Genealogical Magazine* 26 (1925): 92; Frank Luther Mott, "The Newspaper Coverage of Lexington and Concord," *New England Quarterly* 17 (1944): 502.

[78]Karl W. Deutsch, *Nationalism and Social Communication: An Inquiry into the Foundations of Nationality,* 2d ed. (Cambridge: Massachusetts Institute of Technology Press, 1966).

velopment of internal solidarity. Until the end of the Seven Years' War, Frenchmen served as the most important outgroup for both Englishmen and Americans. Later, as the United States came to be defined as a white man's country, Winthrop Jordan's work implies, blacks were the most relevant negative reference group. During the revolutionary era, however, Englishmen would seem to have been the logical candidates for the position. Nevertheless, a wholesale rejection of British cultural traditions would have been painful for most Americans and perhaps impossible for members of the Southern upper classes. To be sure, the belief that they remained more English in character is part mythical, but the notion was common among contemporaries, and at least one historian has found that the Southern colonial newspapers appeared to reflect less hatred of the British than their Northern counterparts. Were it not for the Scots, Southerners would have faced a particularly acute problem of self-definition during the Revolution.[79]

But the economic and political power of the numerous Scotch merchants and placemen made them especially unpopular in the Southern colonies. In fact, a Carolina planter went so far as to stipulate that his daughter would inherit less in the event that she married a Scotsman, and Fithian heard one of the young Lees fulminate "that if he ever Shall have a Daughter, if She marries a Scotchman he shoots her dead at once!" Such exclusion from the ties of family suggests that Scots, like blacks, appeared to embody culturally proscribed traits. Thus when the newspapers depicted them as fawning, miserly, devious, and slavish tools of the ministry, the press was helping to construct an anti-image against which Americans could define themselves as brave, generous, open, honest, free, and virtuous. Unattached to the American soil but addicted to trade, Scotsmen seemed

---

[79]Leonard W. Doob, *Patriotism and Nationalism: Their Psychological Foundations* (New Haven: Yale University Press, 1964) 259; Paul A. Varg, "The Advent of Nationalism, 1758-1776," *American Quarterly* 16 (1964): 170-71; Jordan, *White over Black,* 579, 581, passim: Bridenbaugh, *Myths and Realities,* 94-95; "Journal of Lord Adam Gordon," in *Travels in the American Colonies,* ed. Newton D. Mereness (New York: Macmillan Co., 1916) 397-98; Paul Smith, *Loyalists and Redcoats: A Study in British Revolutionary Policy* (Chapel Hill: University of North Carolina Press, 1964) 18-19; Davidson, *Propaganda and the American Revolution,* 143. This is not to imply that residents in the Northern colonies did not share the hostility to Scots, but merely to suggest that it was probably more intense in the Southern colonies. See, for example, John J. Waters, Jr., *The Otis Family in Provincial and Revolutionary Massachusetts* (Chapel Hill: University of North Carolina Press, 1968) 177.

to constitute a subversive group in the colonies and an insidious influence in London. Consequently, as Douglass Adair was one of the first to observe, the "theme of 'Scotch influence' " linked tyranny at home and abroad.[80] And for Southerners especially, this meant that the Scots provided an explanation of events, as well as a means of defining oneself as an American, that enabled Southerners to retain allegiance to their British political heritage while separating from the British nation itself. From this perspective, neither the willingness of Southern patriots to educate children in England during the Revolution nor the rather sudden appearance of a pronounced disdain for the merchant's calling appear quite so puzzling.[81] Insofar as the upper classes are concerned, it is therefore clear that the newspapers helped to make Scotsmen the unwitting midwives of a distinctive brand of American nationalism in the Southern colonies.

At first glance, the impact of the newspapers upon men beyond their immediate reach would appear to have been weak. Yet, the restricted circulation of the newspapers may have actually had the paradoxical effect of increasing their influence upon the population at large. Even in modern societies, students of the communications process have found a phenomenon known as the "two-step flow" of information whereby individuals in contact with the mass media gather and relay items of importance to their acquaintances. Especially intriguing is the discovery that the interpersonal contact involved in the second phase of transmission may be more effective in influencing attitudes and behavior than the direct transmission of information by impersonal means. Although explanations of this experimental finding differ, students of the subject seem to agree that it depends

[80]Will of Adam Daniel, proved 6 February 1767, Charleston County Wills, 11 (1767-1771): 130, Works Progress Administration Transcripts, SCDAH; Farish, ed., *Journal and Letters of Philip Fithian*, 179; Bertram Wyatt-Brown, "The Ideal Typology and Ante-Bellum Southern History: A Testing of a New Approach," *Societas* 5 (1975): 28; John W. Blassingame, "American Nationalism and Other Loyalties in the Southern Colonies, 1763-1775," *Journal of Southern History* 34 (1968): 66; Douglass Adair, "The Stamp Act in Contemporary English Cartoons," *William and Mary Quarterly* 3d ser. 10 (1953): 538.

[81]George C. Rogers, Jr., *The Evolution of a Federalist: William Loughton Smith of Charleston, 1758-1812* (Columbia: University of South Carolina Press, 1962) 79, 90-92; Rosser H. Taylor, "The Gentry of Ante-Bellum South Carolina," *North Carolina Historical Review* 17 (1940): 116-18; Edmund S. Morgan, "The Puritan Ethic and the American Revolution," *William and Mary Quarterly* 3d ser. 24 (1967): 5; Pred, *Urban Growth and the Circulation of Information,* 278. See also George C. Rogers, Jr., *Charleston in the Age of the Pinckneys* (Norman: University of Oklahoma Press, 1969) 52-53.

in part on the relative social status and presumed expertise of the individuals involved. Thus in traditional societies the impact of news and information is often directly proportional to the authority of the man who transmits it. One scholar has plausibly concluded that the two-step flow is perhaps most common and most effective in developing societies where those first reached by the "mass" media tend to be the established leaders.[82]

Clues as to how the indirect dissemination of newspaper content augmented its impact in the Southern colonies appear in Edmund Randolph's almost classic description of the two-step flow. "Many circumstances," he observed, "existed favorable to the propagating of a contagion of free opinion, although every class of men cannot be supposed to have been aided by extensive literary views." Among these he enumerated two of special relevance to the present discussion. In the "convivial circles" of the gentry, he seemed to imply, "a certain fluency of speech, which marked the character" of hospitable Virginians, "pushed into motion many adventurous doctrines, which in a different situation of affairs might have lain dormant much longer and might have been limited to a much narrowed sphere." "Furthermore," he continued, the process also operated across class lines, for "even if the fancied division into something like ranks, not actually coalescing with each other, had been really formed"—which he was reluctant to admit—"the opinions of every denomination or cast would have diffused themselves on every side by means of the professions of priest, lawyer, and physician, who visited the houses of the ostentatious as well as the cottages of the planters."[83]

Equally idyllic, this picture provides a significant contrast to Deane's description of well-read Americans of all social classes discussing politics

---

[82]Morris Janowitz, "The Study of Mass Communication," *International Encyclopedia of the Social Sciences*, 3:50-51; Elihu Katz, "Diffusion: Interpersonal Influence," ibid., 4:179-82; Katz, "The Two-Step Flow of Communication: An Up-to-Date Report on the Hypothesis," *Public Opinion Quarterly* 21 (1957): 61-78; William J. McGuire, "The Nature of Attitudes and Attitude Change," in *Handbook of Social Psychology*, ed. Gardner Lindzey and Elliot Aronson, 2d ed., 5 vols. (Reading MA: Addison-Wesley, 1968-1969) 3:179, 226; Ithiel de Sola Pool, "The Mass Media and Politics in the Modernization Process, in Pye, ed., *Communications and Political Development*, 242; Lloyd R. Bostain, "The Two-Step Flow Theory: Cross-Cultural Implications," *Journalism Quarterly* 47 (1970): 109-17.

[83]Edmund Randolph, *History of Virginia*, ed. Arthur H. Shaffer (Charlottesville: University Press of Virginia, 1970) 193-94.

as equals. Idealized as it was, Randolph's account nevertheless reflected the realities of a social setting especially conducive to augmenting the effects of the two-step flow. Because "People of fortune" were, as Fithian remarked, "the pattern of all behaviour" in the Southern colonies, a leading local figure added his prestige and presumed expertise while passing along news to less prominent associates. Furthermore, if Benjamin Harrison's recall was accurate, an incident in which he was involved indicates that the incremental effect could reach proportions astonishing to even the most patriotic of modern Americans. When the Virginia delegation was about to depart for Philadelphia and the Continental Congress, it seems that some "respectable but uninformed inhabitants" called upon Harrison and his colleagues, saying, "You assert that there is a fixed intention to invade our rights and privileges; we own that we do not see this clearly, but since you assure us that it is so, we believe it. We are about to take a very dangerous step, but we have confidence in you and will do anything you think proper."[84]

By reminding us that superior knowledge usually sanctions leadership, this story also suggests that the press bolstered the local political establishments in subtle as well as obvious ways. Like the possession of a radio, which in the twentieth century might confer additional prestige on the headman of a remote village in a developing nation, receipt of the newspapers was in that era a badge of social distinction. Equally important, greater access to the relatively restricted channels of communication from the outside world contributed to presumptions about the possession of knowledge that even the most arcane information would support. Thus the apparently irrelevant accounts of European royalty, etc., which filled much of the colonial papers, were not entirely unrelated to local politics. This, of course, is not to say that the resolves published by "the Representatives of the People" to demonstrate their "just Sense of Liberty" were not more relevant, and it seems fair to assume that messages reflecting favorably on the communicator were the most apt to be disseminated. Virtual control of the press, therefore, paid multiple dividends to patriot leaders who could

---

[84]Fithian to Rev. Enoch Green, 1 December 1773, in Farish, ed., *Journal and Letters of Philip Fithian*, 27; entry of 26 April 1782, in *Travels in North America in the Years 1780, 1781 and 1782 by the Marquis de Chastellux*, ed. Howard C. Rice, Jr., 2 vols. (Chapel Hill: University of North Carolina Press, 1963) 2:429. For a similar assessment of the influence of the wealthy, see Gadsden in the *South Carolina Gazette*, 9 November 1769.

thereby sanction their own measures, document the inequities of their opponents, and lend credibility to the leadership of the American cause at all
levels. How the process worked in areas where a large part of the populace
had direct access to the newspapers is perhaps clear enough merely from
Peter Oliver's bitter observation that "the Press . . . groaned with all the
Falsities that seditious Brains could invent, which were crammed down the
Credulity of the Vulgar." But in other areas, like the Southern colonies,
where newspapers circulated among the relatively few, the mechanism was
more complex. How it operated there appears perhaps most plainly in the
words of Richard Furman. In addressing himself to a number of politically
doubting Thomases in the South Carolina backcountry, Furman, who was
a Baptist minister as well as a Whig, invoked the "public Gazettes" which,
he noted, "may be seen" to support what his audience had already been
told by patriot leaders. Although he referred to British as well as to American newspapers, his argumentative technique clearly reveals that print
could be—and was—used to reinforce the authority of the speaker as well
as of the spoken word.[85] Obviously, men with a relative monopoly of the
latest information and the ability to interpret it were in a key position to
maintain their own influence.

To make this observation is not to claim that receipt of the newspapers
always gave leading men the first or even the best report of events; it is,
however, to contend that in the long run the press provided them with the
most timely and accurate accounts then consistently available. Important
news still often travels fastest by word of mouth, and Colonel Daingerfield
of Belvidera first learned that the Declaration of Independence had been
adopted by sending an overseer to investigate sounds of distant celebration. Errors, too, are not unknown to the modern press, and earlier printers
sometimes admitted their guilt with a humerous twist. "It is well known,"
the *South-Carolina Gazette* noted in 1772, "that Printers are not INFAL-
LIBLE, and are often misinformed." But, significantly, the advertisement
continued, if the present publishers should ever be "found guilty of mar-
rying Persons contrary to their Inclinations, no *Pope* shall be more indul-

---

[85]Schramm, "Communication Development and the Development Process," in Pye,
ed., *Communications and Political Development,* 53; *Peter Oliver's Origin & Progress of
the American Rebellion: A Tory View,* ed. Douglass Adair and John A. Schutz (Stanford
CA: Stanford University Press, 1961) 105; Furman to "Gentlemen," November 1775,
Furman Family Papers, Baptist Historical Collection, Furman University, Greenville, South
Carolina.

gent, for a Divorce shall be instantly granted."[86] Furthermore, leaders, such as Henry Laurens (who received more than one local paper) and Edmund Pendleton (who requested that friends send him gazettes from other areas), were in the best position to verify or correct reports. Thus, greater access to information about current affairs elsewhere complemented more active involvement in local politics to make men of property the most effective interpreters of contemporary events. Consequently, for those who sought to acquire, maintain, and discharge the responsibilities of leadership, the current history furnished by the provincial papers was as important as the ancient history provided by their education. If, as Edmund Morgan has argued, the American Revolution was "an intellectual movement" in which politics replaced religion as the chief concern of the colonial intelligentsia, newspapers became the equivalent of secular Bibles.[87] No wonder that in the Southern provinces the local political establishments often appear to have constituted a revitalized priesthood whose members became the special custodians of the "word."

The similarity between this development and the temporary strengthening of customary lines of authority that sometimes occurs with the advent of mass communications in the developing societies of the twentieth century suggests that it might have been an ephemeral phenomenon.[88] Yet, the traditional structure of authority appears to have remained remarkably intact in the Southern states well into the nineteenth century. To be sure, as Rhys Isaac has observed, the evangelical movement in eighteenth-century Virginia involved an element of rebellion against the literary culture

---

[86]Karl Erik Rosengren, "News Diffusion: an Overview," *Journalism Quarterly* 50 (1973): 90; entry of 10 July 1776, in Riley, ed., *Journal of John Harrower,* 158; *South Carolina Gazette,* 7 May 1772.

[87]Laurens to Peter Timothy, 6 July 1768, in Rogers and Chesnutt, eds., *Papers of Henry Laurens,* 5:730; Henry Laurens, Account Book, 1766-1773, 44, 184, 294, Robert Scott Small Library, College of Charleston, Charleston; Pendleton to William Woodford, 6 June 1778, in Mays, ed., *Letters and Papers of Edmund Pendleton,* 1:257; R. H. Lee to Samuel Adams, 4 February 1773, in Ballagh, ed., *Letters of Richard Henry Lee,* 1:82; Edmund S. Morgan, "The American Revolution Considered as an Intellectual Movement," in *Paths of American Thought,* ed. Arthur M. Schlesinger, Jr., and Morton White (Boston: Houghton Mifflin, Sentry Edition, 1970) 11-33.

[88]See, for example, James N. Mosel, "Communication Patterns and Political Socialization in Transitional Thailand," in Pye, ed., *Communications and Political Development,* 228; and J. Mayone Stycos, "Patterns of Communication in a Rural Greek Village," *Public Opinion Quarterly* 16 (1952): 59, 60, 70.

of the gentry, and backcountry men in South Carolina often doubted that anyone from the coast could tell the truth. "Democratic Gentle-Touch" and others in urban areas like Charleston also attacked the traditional system of politics in general and specific members of the old political establishment in particular during the 1780s.[89] But the political position of the wealthy in South Carolina, like that of the gentry in Virginia, was probably more secure a decade after the war than before it. And, in fact, similar men of property, though occasionally challenged, maintained control throughout most of the South during the entire antebellum period.[90]

A full-scale attempt to account for the resiliency of this pattern would obviously go well beyond the confines of the present topic, but the most relevant elements can be quickly sketched. In the long run, of course, mass communications undermine traditional leaders by short-circuiting the hierarchical flow of information. In the South, however, such short circuits appear to have been relatively rare; and the antebellum press, like its primary audience, remained strikingly similar to its colonial counterpart. As late as 1850 the combined per capita circulation of periodicals and newspapers among whites in the South was only eight copies per year—a figure less than one-third that of the North. Accordingly, the newspapers continued to be organs of the upper classes, and "the great economic prize for

---

[89]Rhys Isaac, "Preachers and Patriots: Popular Culture and the Revolution in Virginia," in Alfred F. Young, ed., *The American Revolution: Explorations in the History of American Radicalism* (DeKalb: Northern Illinois University Press, 1976) 139; "Fragment of a Journal Kept by the Rev. William Tennent Describing His Journey, in 1775, to Upper South Carolina. . . ," *City of Charleston, S.C., Year Book, 1894,* 299; [Unknown] to "Sir," n.d., filed first in November-December 1775 box, Clinton Papers, William L. Clements Library, Ann Arbor, Michigan; Furman to "Gentlemen," November 1775, Furman Family Papers; Pauline Maier, "The Charleston Mob and the Evolution of Popular Politics in Revolutionary South Carolina, 1765-1784," *Perspectives in American History* 4 (1970): 192-93. For further discussion of the relationship between an "elitist typographic culture" and more popular oral cultures, see Rhys Isaac, "Dramatizing the Ideology of Revolution: Popular Mobilization in Virginia, 1774-1776," *William and Mary Quarterly* 3d ser. 33 (1976): 357-85; and Harry S. Stout, "Religion, Communications, and the Ideological Origins of the American Revolution," ibid., 34 (1977): 519-41.

[90]George C. Rogers, Jr., "South Carolina Federalists and the Origins of the Nullification Movement," *South Carolina Historical Magazine* 71 (1970): 17-32; Gordon S. Wood, "Rhetoric and Reality in the American Revolution," *William and Mary Quarterly* 3d ser. 23 (1966): 27-30; Richard Buel, Jr., *Securing the Revolution: Ideology in American Politics, 1789-1815* (Ithaca: Cornell University Press, 1972) 79-82; Weir, "Who Shall Rule at Home," 679-700; David M. Potter, *The Impending Crisis, 1848-1861,* ed. Don E. Fehrenbacher (New York: Harper and Row, 1976) 31 n. 16, 455-57.

editors," as Clement Eaton has observed, remained the post of government printer. Hence, a British correspondent visiting the South on the eve of the Civil War discovered neither much enthusiasm for freedom of the press nor the "dread of its power" which prevailed further north. Newspapers, it seems, were still performing many of the same functions in behalf of the local establishments as they had during the late colonial period.[91]

Although one would prefer to believe that the Southern press reverted to a captive position under the pressures of the sectional controversy, there are reasons for doubting that it ever fully escaped dependency. Much of the population in the area remained poorly educated and sparsely distributed, and publishers therefore continued to be responsive to a restricted market. Ironically, too, the Revolution itself may have helped to perpetuate some of these conditions. For if the heightened relevance of political events increased the importance of the newspapers, the disruptions of the war reduced their availability and thereby placed leading men with access to rare copies in an even more strategic position than before. Thus, at least as long as hostilities continued, the press tended to reinforce rather than undermine the position of local leaders. Furthermore, at the end of the war conscious attempts were made to maintain or reestablish the old relationship between the government and the press. Members of the Georgia legislature reappointed James Johnston as the public printer in 1783. This reappointment indicated that the legislature fully understood his past role, which included publication of the *Royal Georgia Gazette* under British authority during the occupation of Savannah. In like manner, some of the shrewdest individuals in public life south of Virginia—John Rutledge, John Matthews, and Nathanael Greene, respectively successive governors of South Carolina and commander of the Continental Army in the South—cooperated with the newly reconstituted state legislature to foster newspapers published at Jacksonborough and Parker's Ferry while British forces still held Charleston.[92]

---

[91]Clement Eaton, *The Freedom-of-Thought Struggle in the Old South* (1940; rpt., New York: Harper, 1964) 78; Eaton, *The Growth of Southern Civilization, 1790-1860* (New York: Harper and Row, 1961) 266; William H. Russell, *My Diary North and South*, 2 vols. (London: Bradbury and Evans, 1863) 1:147.

[92]Lawrence, *James Johnston,* 19, 25-26; John Rutledge to Gen. Marion, 13 August 1781, and John Matthews to Gen. Marion, 19 July 1782, in *Documentary History of the Ameri-*

Consequently, postwar stability and the renaissance of institutional legitimacy depended in part upon the reestablishment of the old symbiotic relationship between the press and the personal influence of leading men which, Greene believed, "must supply the defects of civil constitution" in the war-torn land. Perhaps the best testimony to his success and to the durability of the relationship can be found nearly 100 years later in the words of a Union officer from Connecticut stationed in South Carolina. "Every community," he observed, "has its great man, or at least its little great man, around whom his fellow citizens gather when they want information, and to whose monologues they listen with a respect akin to humility." A press that not only helped to carry the Southern colonies successfully through the Revolution but also contributed to the perpetuation of social patterns that would characterize the region for decades to come was indeed as mighty as the sword.[93]

can Revolution, ed. R. W. Gibbes, 3 vols. (1853-1857; rpt., Spartanburg SC: Reprint Company, 1972) 3:126 and 2:201; 26 January 1782, *Journal of the House of Representatives of South Carolina, January 8, 1782 to February 26, 1782*, ed. A. S. Salley, Jr. (Columbia: Historical Commission of South Carolina, 1916) 27; Jacksonborough Imprints, South Caroliniana Library, University of South Carolina, Columbia: Speech of John Rutledge to the General Assembly, 18 January 1782, and the addresses of the House and Senate in reply, n.d.; List of Laws Passed by the Legislature, printed by David Rogers, 1 March 1782; Proclamation of John Mathews [*sic*], 14 March 1782; *South Carolina Gazette* (Parker's Ferry), 15 May 1782, printed by Benjamin F. Dunlap. Account of Dunlap, Accounts Audited, Stub Entries, W238, SCDAH.

[93]Theodore Thayer, *Nathanael Greene, Strategist of the American Revolution* (New York: Twayne, 1960) 289; John William De Forest, *A Union Officer in the Reconstruction*, ed. James H. Croushore and David M. Potter (New Haven: Yale University Press, 1948) 195.

APPENDIX

In the table below, N^1 represents the total number of datelines in the sample; N^2 the number providing sufficient information for calculating transit time; and R the range in days between the slowest and fastest reports.

NEWS FROM	Md. Gaz.	Va. Gaz. (Royle, P&D, D&H)	Va. Gaz. (Rind, Pinkney)	Va. Gaz. (Purdie)	NC Gaz.	SC Gaz. & CJ	Ga. Gaz.
British Isles N^1/N^2	65/63	71/68	17/15	3/2	28/28	55/55	22/22
R	55-321	53-142	63-108	69-85	54-124	59-137	46-134
Mass. N^1/N^2	20/17	19/19	18/16	2/1	15/10	20/20	10/8
R	14-179	14-52	13-76	24-24	20-51	19-90	23-116
R.I. N^1/N^2	5/3	3/3	2/2	0	3/3	7/7	0
R	18-27	18-54	26-33		13-35	19-49	
N.Y. N^1/N^2	14/11	10/9	6/5	2/1	6/6	17/17	5/5
R	10-36	11-40	15-24	15-15	21-43	15-64	28-57
Pa. N^1/N^2	12/8	10/9	6/5	3/2	9/8	12/12	11/11
R	8-32	8-38	10-21	11-21	18-60	14-77	14-186
Md. N^1/N^2	—	0	1/1	0	0	4/4	0
R			14-14			24-58	
Va. N^1/N^2	4/3	—	—	—	9/8	4/4	1/1
R	13-34				13-49	24-49	15-15
N.C. N^1/N^2	2/1	4/3	1/1	0	—	8/8	1/1
R	49-49	23-41	4-4			12-82	11-11
S.C. N^1/N^2	5/4	6/5	4/2	0	1/1	—	8/7
R	38-52	25-65	38-49		25-25		12-45
Ga. N^1/N^2	2/2	2/2	0	0	0	9/9	—
R	44-51	64-66				6-34	

The South Carolinian
as Extremist ──────────────────────────

*The continuity in leadership of the Southern states during the
revolutionary era, like the similarities between the local political
rhetoric of the colonial and antebellum periods, suggests that the
"problem of South Carolina" before the Civil War had eighteenth-century roots. What some of them were and how they developed in the changing moral and political climate of the
nineteenth century is the subject of this essay, which seeks to bring
together some themes introduced earlier in this book. First given
as a paper at the annual meeting of the Southern Historical Association in 1972, the present version is reprinted by permission
from Robert M. Weir, "The South Carolinian as Extremist," South
Atlantic Quarterly 74 (1975): 86-103. Copyright ©1975 by Duke
University Press.*

Why the blood of South Carolinians ran "so hot" in the antebellum period has long been an intriguing question.[1] But in addressing themselves to it, historians have generally overlooked an inconsistency in their
assumptions about the history of South Carolina. Three propositions have
made up the commonly accepted picture: during the late colonial period
local leadership was usually moderate and conservative; nineteenth-century South Carolinians retained much of the eighteenth-century political

---

[1]Frank Vandiver, "The Southerner as Extremist," in *The Idea of the South,* ed. Frank
E. Vandiver (Chicago: University of Chicago Press, 1964) 48. See esp. Charles Grier Sellers, Jr., "The Travail of Slavery," in *The Southerner as American,* ed. Charler Grier Sellers, Jr. (Chapel Hill: University of North Carolina Press, 1960) 40-71; and Richard Maxwell Brown's unpublished paper, "Back Country Violence (1760-1785) and Its Significance for South Carolina History."

style; and the antebellum fire-eater was typically, though not exclusively, a Carolinian. Juxtaposition of these statements raises the possibility that the political culture of the eighteenth century contained latent impulses that the nineteenth century unmasked.[2] Although testing this hypothesis here in its entirety promises to be a major undertaking, examining one aspect of it is feasible. To do so by looking at political behavior as a form of symbolic action is the purpose of this essay.

Certainly, if a reckless disregard for the consequences of his actions was one of the most conspicuous characteristics of the antebellum fire-eater, then upon occasion South Carolinians of the colonial and revolutionary periods could sound like fire-eaters. Christopher Gadsden, the famous revolutionary patriot from Charleston, left "all New England Sons of Liberty far behind," Silas Deane reported from the First Continental Congress, "for he is for taking up his firelock and marching direct to Boston." Indeed, Deane continued, Gadsden maintained "that were his wife and all his children in Boston, and they were there to perish by the sword, it would not alter his sentiment or proceeding." William Henry Drayton, whom British authorities described as "one of the most virulent Incendarys" in South Carolina, declared, "Now that the liberty and property of the American is at the pleasure of a despotic power, an idea of *a risk of life itself* in defence of my hereditary rights, cannot appal me, or make me shrink from my purpose."[3] And William Wragg, a respected Loyalist, defied a revolutionary committee in 1775, telling it, "Let justice be done though the heavens fall." Nor were these statements merely rhetoric. For all he knew, Wragg's steadfast adherence to the Crown jeopardized his life as well as his property. Gadsden was equally self-sacrificing. When captured at the fall of

---

[2]Robert M. Weir, " 'The Harmony We Were Famous for': An Interpretation of Pre-Revolutionary South Carolina Politics," *William and Mary Quarterly* 3d ser. 26 (1969): 498-99; David Duncan Wallace, *South Carolina, A Short History, 1520-1948* (1951; rpt., Columbia: University of South Carolina Press, 1966) 344, 404.

[3]Silas Deane to Mrs. Deane, 7 September 1774, in *Letters of Members of the Continental Congress,* ed. Edmund C. Burnett, 8 vols. (Washington: Carnegie Institution, 1921-1938) 1:18; Alexander Innes to Lord Dartmouth, 16 March 1775, in "Charleston Loyalism in 1775: The Secret Reports of Alexander Innes," ed. Bradley D. Bargar, *South Carolina Historical Magazine* 63 (1962): 128; "A Letter from 'Freeman' of South Carolina . . . ," in *Documentary History of the American Revolution,* ed. R. W. Gibbes, 3 vols. (1853-1857; rpt., Spartanburg SC: Reprint Company, 1972) 1:12-13.

Charleston in 1780, he considered himself to be on parole under the terms of the capitulation. But British authorities, wishing to counter the influence of local leaders who refused to exchange their status as prisoners of war for that of subjects, soon rounded up a number and shipped them off to St. Augustine. There Gadsden refused to accept appropriately modified terms of parole on the grounds that the British command had broken faith by violating the terms of the surrender agreement. As a result of his quixotic gesture, he spent nine months imprisoned in the castle.[4]

Because Wragg, Gadsden, and Drayton were highly emotional individuals, one might attribute their behavior to quirks of personality—were it not for men like Henry Laurens. A rich and conservative merchant who professed to have felt more sorrow over the Declaration of Independence than over the recent death of a son, Laurens epitomized the reluctant revolutionary. Yet, in the spring of 1775, he wrote that Americans "must prepare to meet poverty, imprisonment, Death or all of them, with the dignity becoming a Man who has resolution enough to forego Self gratification, to Stake his Estate, his Life, upon the prospect of Securing freedom and happiness to future Generations." Indeed, South Carolinians in general appeared equally ready to risk their all when, on 3 June 1775, the Provincial Congress adopted an oath pledging signers to defend South Carolina against "every foe" at the expense, if need be, of their "lives and fortunes."[5] At the time, these words hardly distinguished Carolinians from other Americans. What did set them apart in the eyes of contemporaries, however, was the greater danger to which a willingness to rebel exposed them. Weakened by the threat of internal slave revolt to the point of being apparently incapable of defending themselves against external attack, they had sought the assistance of British regulars as recently as 1761 merely to

----

[4]David Ramsay, *History of South Carolina*, 2 vols. (1809; rpt., Spartanburg SC: Reprint Company, 1959, 1968) 2:276; "Reasons Given by William Wragg to the General Committee for His Refusing to Sign the Association, July 22d, 1775," *Southern Quarterly Review* 4 (1843): 144; Christopher Gadsden, *The Writings of Christopher Gadsden, 1746-1805*, ed. Richard Walsh (Columbia: University of South Carolina Press, 1966) xxv.

[5]David Duncan Wallace, *The Life of Henry Laurens* (New York: G. P. Putnam's Sons, 1915) 224; Henry Laurens to Rod. Valtravers, 22 May 1775, Laurens Papers, South Carolina Historical Society, Charleston; *Extracts from the Journals of the Provincial Congresses of South Carolina, 1775-1776*, ed. William E. Hemphill and Wylma W. Wates (Columbia: South Carolina Archives Department, 1960) 36.

cope with the Cherokee Indians. However much they hoped that British authorities would back down, many South Carolinians in 1774 approached the impending hostilities in a mood of reckless desperation. They were determined, whatever the cost, to maintain a posture of moral righteousness. As one polemicist put it, they should be "resolved rather to die the *last of American Freemen,* than *live the first of American Slaves.*"[6]

That these words closely paraphrased those written a generation earlier by Henry St. John, Viscount Bolingbroke, suggests why even conservative South Carolinians could at times sound like radical extremists. By the mid-eighteenth century Bolingbroke's work had become one of the fountainheads of country ideology, a body of related beliefs and assumptions that formed the basis of the local political culture. Based upon the assumption that men were at best unreliable and easily corrupted by power, country ideology depicted political life as the arena in which public-spirited members of the social and economic elite preserved freedom by combating incipient tyranny.[7] To eschew the lure of office and the blandishments of faction and to be ever vigilant were sacred duties incumbent upon the representatives of the people. Because liberty could be undermined by seemingly innocuous steps, all threats to it—even the apparently trivial—demanded the most vigorous countermeasures. Ordinary political action, mob violence, and revolt were, therefore, merely different stages of the eternal battle in behalf of freedom.[8] These conceptions meant that prudence was the chief, if not the only, brake upon extreme action. But the very fact that men conceived of politics as the life-and-death struggle to defend liberty tended to render prudential considerations irrelevant. Thus during a controversy with the royal governor over who was to control the composition of the Commons House, Gadsden could declare

---

[6]Richard Oswald, "Mem[orandu]m with Respect to So. Carolina," 21 February 1775, Dartmouth Papers, 3, Staffordshire County Record Office, Stafford, England; M. Eugene Sirmans, *Colonial South Carolina: A Political History, 1663-1763* (Chapel Hill: University of North Carolina Press, 1966) 338; *South Carolina Gazette* (Charleston), 13 June 1774.

[7]"A Dissertation upon Parties," *The Works of Henry St. John, Lord Viscount Bolingbroke,* 4 vols. (Philadelphia: Carey and Hart, 1841) 2:153; Weir, " 'The Harmony We Were Famous for,' " 474-79.

[8]Richard Buel, Jr., "Democracy and the American Revolution: A Frame of Reference," *William and Mary Quarterly* 3rd ser. 21 (1964): 165-90; Pauline Maier, "Popular Uprisings and Civil Authority in Eighteenth-Century America," ibid., 27 (1970): 3-35.

"that he would rather submit to the distruction of one half of the Country than to give up the point in dispute."[9]

Under the circumstances, public virtue became nearly synonymous with the willingness to risk private interests; above all, politicians were expected to be "disinterested." Wragg's actions in 1769 illustrate how this imperative influenced behavior. Having been the champion of the Crown in the Commons House for most of the preceding decade, he was rewarded by being offered the chief justiceship of the colony. At this point Gadsden charged that the reasons for Wragg's previous conduct now became clear. Wragg then declined the position in order to give the lie to his detractors. "It gives me great pleasure," he declared, "to have the opportunity of making this sacrifice, as it is the fullest confutation of every illiberal and malevolent suggestion propagated to my disadvantage."[10] Similarly, Gadsden's wild rhetoric about attacking the British in Boston, as well as his choice of imprisonment at St. Augustine, enabled him to demonstrate selfless commitment to virtuous principles. "Don Quixotte Secundus" Gadsden once aptly termed himself; Wragg with equal perception earlier noted that Gadsden's patriotism was as "romantic" as his own.[11] In short, cultural imperatives dictated that a member of the political elite respond to a crisis by demonstrating his utter disregard of self. It therefore seems scarcely a coincidence that a man rendered suspect by an abrupt metamorphosis from Crown supporter to revolutionary agitator, William Henry Drayton, was one of the most reckless firebrands of the Revolution in South Carolina.[12]

---

[9]Henry Laurens to Christopher Rowe, 8 February 1764, Laurens Papers, Historical Society of Pennsylvania, Philadelphia; Jack P. Greene, "The Gadsden Election Controversy and the Revolutionary Movement in South Carolina," *Mississippi Valley Historical Review* 46 (1959): 469-92.

[10]Lord Hillsborough to Lord Charles Montagu, 23 March 1769, Transcripts of Records Relating to South Carolina in the British Public Record Office, 32:75, South Carolina Department of Archives and History, Columbia (hereafter cited as Trans., S.C., SCDAH); *South Carolina Gazette*, 9 November 1769; "Rough Draft of Mr. Wragg's Address to the Gentlemen of the Bar," *Southern Quarterly Review* 4 (1843): 135, 124-25.

[11]Gadsden to William Henry Drayton, 15 June 1778, in Walsh, ed., *Writings of Christopher Gadsden*, 132; Wragg to Thomas Boone, 2 February 1769, *Southern Quarterly Review* 4 (1843): 124.

[12]Henry Laurens to George Appleby, 10 April 1775, Laurens Papers, South Carolina Historical Society; William Dabney and Marion Dargan, *William Henry Drayton and the American Revolution* (Albuquerque: University of New Mexico Press, 1962).

Social conditions facilitated such behavior. As Richard Dunn has recently suggested, West Indian sugar planters may well have helped to settle South Carolina partly in the vain hope of being able to escape the perils of the islands where "they grew rich fast, spent recklessly, played desperately, and died young."[13] Ultimately, they found prosperity in the new colony, but at the risk of similar dangers. Throughout the colonial period lowcountry South Carolina remained a notoriously unhealthy place. "In the spring a paradise, in the summer a hell, and in the autumn a hospital" was the contemporary description. And until well into the middle of the eighteenth century, the colony often appeared to be the target of imminent French or Spanish attack. Furthermore, Carolina planters quickly inundated themselves in a sea of blacks who, it constantly seemed, threatened to revolt, or so it seemed. So precarious did life and property appear under these conditions that in 1757 Charles Pinckney resolved to transfer his assets to "a more secure tho' less improvable part of the world." Not surprisingly, in Carolina as well as in the Caribbean men spent money lavishly, drank much, and all too often aged early.[14] To be careless of all worldly goods—even of life itself when such behavior appeared meritorious—was relatively easy in this environment. And once the tradition became established, it tended to perpetuate itself.

Nevertheless, despite its occasional visibility, the wild streak in South Carolina politics remained generally hidden during the late colonial period; normally members of the local elite preferred compromise and conciliation to do-or-die heroics. Their preference reflected a society unusually at peace with itself. Irretrievably committed to slave labor in the rice and indigo fields, South Carolinians appeared to be immune to the doubts and tensions rampant where the institution was less firmly entrenched, and fear of revolt tended to make them cautious. Equally important, by the mid-eighteenth century a remarkably prosperous economy had fused potentially competing interest groups into a single, relatively harmonious unit.

---

[13]Richard S. Dunn, "The English Sugar Islands and the Founding of South Carolina," *South Carolina Historical Magazine* 72 (1971): 92.

[14]Carl Bridenbaugh, *Myths and Realities: Societies of the Colonial South* (1952; rpt., New York: Atheneum, 1963) 69, 112-13; Weir, " 'The Harmony We Were Famous for,' " 482-83; Eliza Pinckney to Lady Carew, 7 February 1757, in *The Letterbook of Eliza Lucas Pinckney, 1739-1762,* ed. Elise Pinckney and Marvin R. Zahniser (Chapel Hill: University of North Carolina Press, 1972) 87.

Great and easy wealth without the price of social conflict helped lowcountry South Carolinians avoid many of the qualms of conscience that plagued other Americans over their apparently general commitment to materialism.

The same was equally true of the highly developed, even strident individualism of the Carolina elite. Whereas in the early days of the colonies this characteristic appeared to imply the triumph of solitary selfishness over a sense of community, by the mid-eighteenth century the dominant assumptions of local political life rationalized individualism as patriotism. Only the self-reliant, financially and intellectually independent individual could meet his public responsibilities. Furthermore, experience seemed to confirm these reassuring notions. Independent men of property, who shared a consensus about the nature of man and political life, actually did respond to prevailing imperatives by uniting in opposition to what appeared to be aggressions on the part of the Crown; moreover, their freedom from factionalism seemed to testify to their disinterested commitment to the public welfare. Thus the realities of local political life corresponded closely to the prevailing theoretical ideal.[15] While the success of the political system helped to perpetuate deference to the elite, pride of accomplishment made its members self-confident enough to be tolerant of their own imperfections. As young planter-patriot John Mackenzie phrased it in 1769, "ALL of us have a little original Sin sticking to our Frames." Seldom challenged, satisfied with themselves and their world, these men could cultivate a neoclassical fondness for calm rationality. Wragg's personal motto, for example, was a phrase by the Roman poet Horace extolling the virtues of maintaining one's mental equilibrium.[16] Only in rare moments of individual or collective crisis did eighteenth-century South Carolinians have

---

[15]Winthrop D. Jordan, *White over Black: American Attitudes toward the Negro, 1550-1812* (Chapel Hill: University of North Carolina Press, 1968) 399-401, 409; Jack P. Greene, "Search for Identity: An Interpretation of the Meaning of Selected Patterns of Social Response in Eighteenth-Century America," *Journal of Social History* 3 (1970): 200; Yehoshua Arieli, *Individualism and Nationalism in American Ideology* (Cambridge MA: Harvard University Press, 1964) 193; David Bertelson, *The Lazy South* (New York: Oxford University Press, 1967) 53-59; Weir, " 'The Harmony We Were Famous for,' " 473-501.

[16]John Mackenzie, "A Second Letter to the People," *South Carolina Gazette,* 14 September 1769; "American Loyalists," *Southern Quarterly Review* 4 (1843): 124; Horace, *Satires, Epistles, and Ars Poetica,* trans. H. Rushton Fairclough (London: W. Heinemann, 1926) 325.

to jettison caution in order to prove their disinterested commitment to virtuous principles.

The situation changed with the Revolution. Americans in general justified their revolt against England partly by their putative moral superiority; indeed, to many the viability of the Republic appeared to depend upon the continued virtue of the American people. Furthermore, as the nineteenth century wore on, Alexis de Tocqueville noted that Americans north and south came to share "a lively faith in the perfectibility of man."[17] It was a faith that undermined the eighteenth-century tolerance of human imperfection. Everywhere these developments tended to increase the force of the moral imperatives that impinged upon Americans, but the demands upon the South Carolina elite were especially great. In part because of the close correspondence between theory and practice that had prevailed in the late colonial period, the political culture of the eighteenth century survived the Revolution remarkably intact. In fact, nineteenth-century pressures upon upper-class South Carolinians appear to have strengthened their commitment to old conceptions. Seeking to defend an institution under attack, they continued to conceive of politics as the defense of liberty. Attempting to maintain their position of leadership in a political system that grew increasingly anachronistic as the rest of the nation became more democratic, they invoked the colonial ideal of the independent man of property who unselfishly devoted himself to the public weal.[18] Moreover, because virtue alone justified the right to command, demonstrating it was particularly important for rising members of the elite, like those from interior districts such as Orangeburg and Edgefield (the homes of Lawrence Keitt and Louis Wigfall, both archetypal fire-eaters). "Power with me," Keitt wrote, "must be won by superiority. . . . I'll be submissive to one purer than my-

---

[17]Bernard Bailyn, *The Ideological Origins of the American Revolution* (Cambridge MA: Belknap Press of Harvard University Press, 1967) 138-43; Robert E. Shalhope, "Toward a Republican Synthesis: The Emergence of an Understanding of Republicanism in American Historiography," *William and Mary Quarterly* 3d ser. 29 (1972): 70; Alexis de Tocqueville, *Democracy in America,* The Henry Reeve Text . . . , ed. Phillips Bradley, 2 vols. (New York: Alfred A. Knopf, 1958) 1:409.

[18]Harold S. Shultz, *Nationalism and Sectionalism in South Carolina, 1852-1860* (Durham: Duke University Press, 1950) 3-25; Rosser H. Taylor, *Ante-Bellum South Carolina: A Social and Cultural History* (Chapel Hill: University of North Carolina Press, 1942) 41-42; Charles S. Sydnor, *The Development of Southern Sectionalism, 1819-1848* (Baton Rouge: Louisiana State University Press, 1948) 288.

self, never to an equal, much less an inferior."[19] The antebellum leaders of South Carolina had obviously assumed an arduous task.

Slavery immeasurably increased their burden by threatening to compromise them. While few Americans questioned the morality of slavery during most of the colonial period, many—including prominent Carolinians—did during the Revolution. As early as 1770 a spokesman of the backcountry, Charles Woodmason, noted that the presence of slaves undermined both the security of the state and the morals of the people. Others recognized that slaves competed with white artisans. Moreover, the Revolution prompted men who had hitherto been considered rather backward colonials to nerve themselves for battle with the thought that the hardships of rural life promoted military vigor. Nationhood also fostered notions about the moral virtues of republican simplicity.[20] These were ideas that comported somewhat awkwardly with the ownership of slaves. Thus the possibility always existed that some local Hinton Rowan Helper would conclude that the slaveholding elite was subversive rather than public-spirited. Worse yet was the assumption commonly held outside the South that the cause of slavery was avarice. Frederick Law Olmstead was typical. Assuming that the fact was beyond debate, he proceeded to discuss other matters: "There are but two methods of vindicating the habit of depending on the labour of slaves for the development of wealth in the land." Thoughtful Americans everywhere feared the effects of the prevailing materialism upon the national character;[21] members of the South Carolina elite had reason to be more concerned than most.

---

[19]Alvy L. King, *Louis T. Wigfall, Southern Fire-Eater* (Baton Rouge: Louisiana State University Press, 1970) 9; Keitt is quoted in Schultz, *Nationalism and Sectionalism in South Carolina*, 17.

[20]Jordan, *White over Black*, 193, 302; *The Carolina Backcountry on the Eve of the Revolution: The Journal and Other Writings of Charles Woodmason, Anglican Itinerant*, ed. Richard J. Hooker (Chapel Hill: University of North Carolina Press, 1953) 121; Richard Walsh, *Charleston's Sons of Liberty; A Study of the Artisans, 1763-1789* (Columbia: University of South Carolina Press, 1959) 109-10, 124-25; "To the Printer" by "Cleanthes," *South Carolina Gazette*, 3 October 1775; Gordon S. Wood, *The Creation of the American Republic, 1776-1787* (Chapel Hill: University of North Carolina Press, 1969) 413-25.

[21]Frederick Law Olmsted, *The Cotton Kingdom*, ed. Arthur M. Schlesinger (New York: Alfred A. Knopf, 1966) 513; Fred Somkin, *Unquiet Eagle, Memory and Desire in the Idea of American Freedom, 1815-1860* (Ithaca: Cornell University Press, 1967) 20-34; David Donald, "The Proslavery Argument Reconsidered," *Journal of Southern History* 37 (1971): 3-18.

Their heritage, their special political status, and their commitment to slavery meant that for the purposes of the proslavery argument, South Carolina was the South. The state, Olmstead wrote, "affords the fairest example of the tendency of the Southern policy, because it is the oldest cotton State, and because slavery has been longest and most strongly and completely established there." Carolinians agreed. Qualms about slavery in the upper South and the raw materialism of the new Southwest combined to make the state the testing ground for the validity of the peculiar institution. "South Carolina and her offshoots have hitherto given dignity to the position of the South," Senator Robert W. Barnwell remarked. "The greater part of the slaveholders in the other states are mere negro-drivers believing themselves wrong and holding on to their negroes as something to make money out of." A contemporary South Carolina historian, William Henry Trescot, summed up the problem: it was the duty of South Carolinians "to prove to a skeptical and hostile world that [slavery was] compatible with the great interests, the high ends, the purifying and elevating influences of a Christian civilization." These elevating influences were supposed to operate upon white as well as black. The South bred men and women, Edmund Rhett declared, "with some other purpose than to make them vulgar, fanatical, cheating Yankees." The slave system, he continued, permits "us to reap the fruits of the earth by a race which we save from barbarism . . . whilst we are enabled to cultivate the arts, the graces, and accomplishments of life." [22] All the claims to the moral superiority of the South's peculiar institution rested upon the behavior of the South Carolina elite. Yet the very existence of that institution appeared to belie its claim to virtue, for as long as slavery continued and men made money out of it, they were bound to be accused of the grossest kind of selfishness.

One way out of the dilemma would have been to abolish the institution, and there can be little doubt that many Carolinians—even those who publicly defended slavery—wished that it did not exist. "God knows I am not inclined to condone it," was Mary Boykin Chesnut's reaction in the pri-

---

[22]Olmsted, *Cotton Kingdom*, 528. Barnwell is quoted in Steven A. Chaning, *Crisis of Fear: Secession in South Carolina* (New York: Simon and Schuster, 1970) 68; "Oration Delivered before the South-Carolina Historical Society, Thursday, May 19, 1859, by W. H. T. Trescot, Esq.," South Carolina Historical Society *Collections* 3 (1859): 33; William H. Russell, *My Diary North and South,* 2 vols. (London: Bradbury and Evans, 1863) 1:214. Edmund Rhett was the brother of Robert Barnwell Rhett.

vacy of her diary. Trescot prefaced his remarks quoted above by noting that what had been "an experiment" to colonial South Carolinians had become the "corner-stone" of their descendants' social and political life. The tone of sorrowful resignation was clear. Frederick Grimké, a perceptive jurist, was even more explicit: "We are never masters of the circumstances under which we were born. . . . To attempt to beat down an institution because we were not consulted as to its establishment is to arrogate an authority which does not belong to us."[23] Obviously these were men who felt themselves caught in the toils of something beyond their own powers to alter. In view of recent scholarship that correlates feelings of cosmic helplessness with aggressive behavior, as well as Calvinistic theology, one suspects that the ineradicable character of slavery contributed to the propensity of antebellum Southerners for both religious orthodoxy and physical violence.[24] Neither would it be surprising if at times slaveholders hated the possessions that appeared to bear witness to their own sin. Mrs. Chesnut's outburst about "dirty, slatternly, idle, ill-smelling" blacks—who made life in the South a kind of martyrdom "with no reward but the threat of John Brown hanging like a drawn sword over your head in this world, and threats of what is to come to you from blacker devils in the next"—reveals the animus. But the black man was there in numbers obviously too great to send back to Africa; his labor seemed to be essential in the rice and cotton fields; and it appeared necessary to subject him to rigorous external discipline. If the institution could not be abolished, the only thing to do, as Grimké concluded, was to convert it "into an instrument of good."[25]

---

[23]Mary Boykin Chesnut, *A Diary from Dixie,* ed. Ben Ames Williams (Boston: Houghton Mifflin, 1949) 155; Frederick Grimké, *The Nature and Tendency of Free Institutions,* ed. John William Ward (Cambridge MA: Belknap Press of the Harvard University Press, 1968) 436-37.

[24]Daniel Walker Howe, "The Decline of Calvinism: An Approach to Its Study," *Comparative Studies in Society and History* 14 (1972): 306-27; Sheldon Hackney, "Southern Violence," *American Historical Review* 74 (1969): 923-25; Clement Eaton, *The Civilization of the Old South: Writings of Clement Eaton,* ed. Albert D. Kirwan (Lexington: University of Kentucky Press, 1968) 181, 203-207.

[25]Chesnut, *Diary from Dixie,* 163; William Harper, "Harper on Slavery," in *The Pro-Slavery Argument . . . Containing the Several Essays, on the Subject by Chancellor Harper, Governor Hammond, Dr. Simms, and Professor Dew* (Charleston SC: Walker, Richards, 1852) 88-91; Grimké, *Nature and Tendency of Free Institutions,* 437.

But remolding nearer to the heart's desire a world that no longer seemed malleable required imagination. Perhaps here lies one of the origins of the proclivity for fantasy which, some historians contend, has been one of the most persistent characteristics of Southerners ever since. Certainly the imperatives and pretensions of the nineteenth century precluded the kind of clear-eyed appraisals of which South Carolinians were once capable. Henry Laurens's son John, who tried to abolish slavery during the Revolution, believed that if blacks appeared to be debased, it was because white men reduced them to a subhuman status. Why? The answer given by his father, who disliked slavery though he had grown rich on the slave trade, was equally devoid of illusions. "My own and the avarice of my countrymen," he wrote, were the bulwarks of the institution.

Painful as the realization that slavery represented a naked form of human exploitation was, most South Carolinians of the colonial period could live with it; their antebellum descendants could not. As Chancellor William Harper admitted, "It would indeed be intolerable, if, when one class of the society is necessarily degraded . . . no compensation were made by the superior elevation and purity of the other."[26] The point here is not merely that South Carolinians were forced to justify themselves in the face of abolitionist attacks. Neither is it that they necessarily felt guilty about slavery during the antebellum period—how guilty they felt and precisely when they felt guilty is still in considerable doubt. Nor, ultimately, is it even that their peculiar institution seemed to conflict with more universal national ideals to which they too subscribed.[27] Rather, South Carolinians confronted a dilemma that arose from their desire both to be and to appear virtuous in a world that not only ascribed enormous importance to virtue but also associated disinterestedness with it. Antebellum South Carolini-

---

[26]T. Harry Williams, *Romance and Realism in Southern Politics* (Athens: University of Georgia Press, 1961) 1-16; John Laurens to Henry Laurens, 26 October 1776, in "Letters from John Laurens to His Father, Hon. Henry Laurens, 1774-1776," *South Carolina Historical and Genealogical Magazine* 5 (1904): 206; Henry Laurens to John Laurens, 14 August 1776, in *Materials for History,* ed. Frank Moore (New York: Printed for the Zenger Club, 1861) 21; Donald, *The Proslavery Argument,* 66.

[27]See Sellers, "The Travail of Slavery," in Sellers, ed., *The Southerner as American,* 40-71; William W. Freehling, *Prelude to Civil War: The Nullification Controversy in South Carolina, 1816-1836* (New York: Harper and Row, 1965) 49-86; George C. Rogers, Jr., *The History of Georgetown County, South Carolina* (Columbia: University of South Carolina Press, 1970) 342-86.

ans, especially, could not admit even to themselves that the basis of their entire social and political system was their own greed. Thus while Northerners sought perfection in backwoods Utopias, South Carolinians had to believe that they found Utopia at home. Theirs was the most perfect society the world had ever known.[28] Until they changed their ethics or their social system, Carolinians were doomed to an endless cycle of trying to prove their claims.

Their mythology reveals their efforts. Antebellum planters discovered Sambo, a character unknown to their colonial ancestors, and the discovery enabled them to conclude that far from being a form of human exploitation, slavery was the most appropriate form of tutelage. Racism had its uses.[29] Indeed, South Carolinians frequently maintained, slavery was an unprofitable institution that demonstrated their own benevolence. The merchant, the overseer, the slave trader, the Yankee were all creatures driven by the sordid lust for gain. Not so the cavalier. Lavish hospitality, loyalty to kin, and a noble disdain for petty monetary concerns testified to his selfless virtue.[30] To be sure, these images were in part designed to remedy faults revealed by critical self-examination. For men such as the Virginian George Fitzhugh, who detected what he believed to be the "insidious influence of bourgeois values," Cervantes provided the corrective model. In a line that speaks volumes about the ethos of the Old South in general as well as of South Carolina in particular, Fitzhugh wrote, "Don Quixote mad, is the noblest, because the most chivalrous and disinterested of all the heroes of Epic poetry; he is but a drivelling, penitent dotard when he recovers." Similarly, South Carolinians like Alexander Garden published accounts of Gadsden and other revolutionary patriots to portray disinterested patriotism in all its glory. In part, no doubt, the same impulse contributed to the esteem showered upon military men. "The fame of the

[28]See Arthur E. Bestor, Jr., *Backwoods Utopias* (Philadelphia: University of Pennsylvania Press, 1950) and Charles S. Sydnor, *The Development of Southern Sectionalism, 1819-1848* (Baton Rouge: Louisiana State University Press, 1948) 331-39.

[29]William Bull to Lord Hillsborough, 7 June 1770, Trans. S.C., 32:281, SCDAH; Mary A. Lewis, "Slavery and Personality," in *The Debate over Slavery: Stanley Elkins and His Critics,* ed. Ann J. Lane (Urbana: University of Illinois Press, 1971) 82-84.

[30]Kenneth M. Stampp, *The Peculiar Institution: Slavery in the Antebellum South* (New York: Alfred A. Knopf, 1956) 383; William R. Taylor, *Cavalier and Yankee: The Old South and the American National Character* (New York: Anchor Books, 1963) xxi, 89, 110, passim.

soldier,'' Trescot remarked, ''is a high and holy fame. Founded in self-sacrifice and achieved through suffering, it shines from mountain to sea-shore.''[31] The problem, of course, was in translating the selfless ideal into reality. Cotton bales behind his barn revealed that the cavalier possessed feet of clay.

However unobtainable the goal, South Carolinians struggled to achieve it. According to Robert Mills (himself a Carolinian), the residents of Charleston supported more charitable organizations per capita than anyone else in the United States. More speculatively, they may also have scuttled the Protestant ethic in their doomed search for disinterestedness. Certainly, antebellum South Carolinians appear to have done regularly what their colonial forebears did rarely—that is, they raised the pursuit of leisure to a cultural ideal.[32] Laziness became functional, for it demonstrated that one was above the sordid pursuit of gain. It is, therefore, only a slight exaggeration to say that while the rest of the nation nourished an ethic of success, South Carolinians cultivated an ethic of failure. When William Gilmore Simms created his famous fictional character Porgy, he could depict him as a decisive and effective revolutionary soldier (a role in which his disinterestedness was established); as a postwar planter, Porgy had to fail.[33]

Perhaps similar considerations help to account for the changing position of the Southern lady. During the colonial period women appear to have been generally regarded as earthy, competent beings; in antebellum South

[31]Donald, ''The Pro-Slavery Argument Reconsidered,'' 16; George Fitzhugh, *Sociology for the South, or the Failure of Free Society* (n.d.; New York: Burt Franklin, 1965) 288; Alexander Garden, *Anecdotes of the Revolutionary War in America . . .* (Charleston SC: A. E. Miller, 1822) 76, 109, 170-73, passim; William Henry Trescot, *The Annual Address before the Calliopean and Polytechnic Societies of the Citadel Academy* (Charleston SC: Walker and Evans, 1856) 18.

[32]Robert Mills, *Statistics of South Carolina, Including a View of Its Natural, Civil, and Military History, General and Particular* (1826; rpt., Spartanburg SC: Reprint Company, 1972) 428; Edmund S. Morgan, ''The Puritan Ethic and the American Revolution,'' *William and Mary Quarterly* 3d ser. 24 (1967): 3-43; C. Vann Woodward, ''The Southern Ethic in a Puritan World,'' ibid., 3d ser. 25 (1968): 343-70.

[33]Bertelson, *The Lazy South,* 189. William Gilmore Simms, *The Partisan: A Romance of the Revolution,* rev. ed. (Chicago: Belford, Clarke, 1887) and *Woodcraft or Hawks about the Dovecote,* rev. ed. (New York: A. C. Armstrong and Son, 1882); these novels originally appeared in 1835 and 1854, respectively.

Carolina, especially, they were believed to be weak and ethereal.[34] However complex the dynamics of this change were, it is worth noting that the new feminine role served as a foil for a masculine self-image. The more idealized women were, the nearer they approached the character of an abstract principle; the more helpless a woman was, the more selfless a man appeared to be in serving her. Significantly, her weakness also insured her purity. Presumably powerless to exploit others in the selfish pursuit of gain, she could become the custodian of the virtue that South Carolinians so eagerly and futilely pursued elsewhere. Similarly, the ne'er-do-well young aristocrat was a legitimate offspring of his culture. No doubt so was the Hamlet figure, several of whom Simms claimed to know in Charleston. Fascinated by Shakespeare's creation, he analyzed Hamlet's character and predicament in a way that made the prince appear remarkably like a South Carolinian. His dying words, Simms noted, betrayed "one of the prevailing features of his character—his intense love of approbation." Hamlet's last command to Horatio was "report me and my cause aright/To the unsatisfied."[35]

Like Hamlet, the antebellum South Carolinian found the resolution of his dilemma in impulsive action, for it was the impulsive act that most demonstrated heedlessness of self. As long as slaveholding brought material rewards, the slaveholder's claims to disinterestedness were suspect. Protestations of virtue, even systematic effort, proved little. As a writer put it in the *Southern Quarterly Review,* "Truly it would seem that the labour of Sisyphus is laid upon us, the slaveholders of these southern United States. Again and again have we, with all the power and talent of our clearest heads and strongest intellects, forced aside the foul load of slander and villainous aspersion so often hurled against us, and still, again and again, the unsightly mass rolls back." An eternity of that brought no salvation. Only by the most decisive and selfless of acts could the slaveholder vindicate himself. Being unable to demonstrate his disinterestedness in the only really effective way, by renouncing slavery, a member of the Carolina slaveholding elite was compelled to seek substitute activities in which to

[34]Julia Cherry Spruill, *Women's Life and Work in the Southern Colonies* (Chapel Hill: University of North Carolina Press, 1938) chs. 11-14; Anne Firor Scott, *The Southern Lady, from Pedestal to Politics, 1830-1930* (Chicago: University of Chicago Press, 1970) [3]-21.

[35][William Gilmore Simms], "The Moral Character of Hamlet," *The Orion; or, Southern Monthly . . .* (Charleston) 4 (1844): 45, 194.

demonstrate his virtue by reckless disregard of self. And his infatuation with romanticism helped to insure that he would go about it in spectacular ways.[36]

South Carolinians, like other Southerners, were thus particularly fond of gambling in all its forms, and they bet immense sums upon horse racing. Neither the hope of large winnings nor the lure of flush times quite accounts for the inveterate gambler's prominence in fact and fiction. What was admired was not his ability to make money but to lose it—or rather to do both with equal equanimity. Joseph Baldwin's description of the Honorable Sergeant Prentiss of Mississippi makes the point clear: "He bet thousands on the turn of a card, and witnessed the success or failure of the wager with the nonchalance of a Mexican monteplayer."[37]

The ultimate gamble was the duel. Not unknown in the colonial period, stimulated by the example of European officers during the Revolution, it still never became really popular until the antebellum period. But when it did, its habitat was predominantly the South, and the standard manual of dueling practice was written by a governor of South Carolina, John Lyde Wilson. That such was the case indicates that the popularity of dueling was the result of more than frontier barbarism, revolutionary violence, or even the military tradition; moreover, that duelists rarely encountered anything but sympathetic juries also suggests that their activity served a symbolic function for society. How both might have been the case is readily apparent. By being willing to bet his life on a moment over a gun barrel, a man affirmed that principles were more important to him than any material consideration, even life itself. "Something must serve as a sign of honor," a student of the South has noted. "Death in a duel was significantly conclusive: it marked the end of a life played out in accordance with the terms of a myth."[38] Yet it was not only the absoluteness of death that was conclusive; it was also the willingness to risk it. For in that moment

[36]L. S. M., "Review of *Uncle Tom's Cabin . . . ,*" *Southern Quarterly Review* new ser. 7 (1853): 81; Rollin G. Osterweis, *Romanticism and Nationalism in the Old South* (New Haven: Yale University Press, 1949) 111-31.

[37]Taylor, *Ante-Bellum South Carolina,* 52; Joseph G. Baldwin, *The Flush Times of Alabama and Mississippi,* intro. William A. Owens (1853; rpt., New York: Sagamore, 1957) 145.

[38]Guy A. Cardwell, "The Duel in the Old South: Crux of a Concept," *South Atlantic Quarterly* 66 (1967): 67-68; Osterweis, *Romanticism and Nationalism,* 96, 128-29.

of truth, as he saw it, a man demonstrated his disinterested attachment to virtue with a finality that at last gave the lie to the ambiguous circumstances of his daily life. In sanctioning events like these, Southern society made a vicarious gesture toward affirming its moral righteousness. But in the end that was not enough.

The ultimate duel was the Civil War. In being willing to bet the wealth amassed under the overseer's lash upon the fortunes of war, South Carolinians signaled to the world and to themselves that they were not selfish slave drivers bent upon the sordid pursuit of riches by exploiting blacks. In risking all, they gained all, for even to fail was to succeed. It was a wager they could not lose. As Sidney Lanier later recalled, among the attractions of the war was the fact that "to virtue [it held out] purity." Thus the desire to vindicate themselves helped to drive defenders of slavery into what Tocqueville would have called a "great" party, one whose adherents clung "to principles rather than to their consequences."[39] Under such circumstances prudential considerations had no meaning. Robert E. Lee believed that the South could not win without foreign assistance and that prospects for obtaining it were slim. "But such considerations really made with me no difference," he wrote. "We had, I was satisfied, sacred principles to maintain and rights to defend, for which we were in duty bound to do our best, even if we perished in the endeavour." Wigfall, a less heroic man who fled abroad upon the collapse of the Confederacy, at least professed the same idea. If ever the occasion should again arise "to strike for liberty and independence," he wrote from England, "I shall feel it my duty to return to my own country without calculating the chances of success." Because war—like politics, the dueling field, and the race track—was a field for symbolic action, the Draytons and the Wigfalls rushed ahead where the Laurenses and the Lees had no choice but to follow.[40] Both the Revolution and the Civil War summoned men to affirm their moral righteousness, and however foolhardy he might consider the choice of time, place, or mode, a man who took the imperatives of his culture seriously could hardly fail to heed the call.

---

[39]Sidney Lanier, *Tiger-Lilies and Southern Prose*, ed. Garland Greever and Cecile Abernethy (Baltimore: Johns Hopkins University Press, 1945) 96-97; Tocqueville, *Democracy in America*, 1:182.

[40]*Recollections and Letters of General Robert E. Lee by His Son Captain Robert E. Lee* (New York: Doubleday, Page, 1904) 151; King, *Wigfall*, 229.

To say this is not to imply that every South Carolinian took these imperatives with equal seriousness or that those who responded to them were necessarily unique. As the mention of Lee suggests, other Southerners shared much of the same ethos. But antebellum South Carolinians occupied a special status that destined them to be the champions of the pro-slavery argument. They, to a greater extent than other Southerners, were heirs of social and cultural heritages that were mutually contradictory yet mutually reinforcing. The continuation of slavery entailed the ideal of a disinterested elite. But the existence of the former constantly threatened to subvert the latter. To prove their professions genuine, South Carolinians were forced to go to extravagant lengths. In short, their values, no less than those of Puritanism, demanded that they be moral athletes, but their social system denied them the ability to demonstrate their prowess by systematic effort. Neither able to win under the prevailing rules nor change them, South Carolinians could only gesticulate sporadically; as in Russian roulette, the essence of the game came to be its recklessness.

This, one suspects, was part of the travail of Carolina slavery. And this, one can be fairly certain, helps to explain the reaction of contemporaries to a gesture that can only be considered typically Carolinian. A collateral descendant of the last lieutenant governor of the royal period, Colonel William Izard Bull occupied the ancestral mansion beside the Ashley River. When near the end of the Civil War General Sherman's troops approached, Bull himself put the torch to the house and all its contents. His action served little military purpose; perhaps it was merely the pointless expression of his loathing for Yankees. Be that as it may, what is important is that other South Carolinians admired it as a virtuous act to be emulated.[41] Subconsciously, perhaps, they recognized that only such outlandish and luminescent moments of apparently utter selflessness could have made the myths of the Old South and the Lost Cause viable.

---

[41]"The Bull Family of South Carolina," *South Carolina Historical and Genealogical Magazine* 1 (1900): 82-83; Henry DeSaussure Bull, "Ashley Hall Plantation," ibid. 53 (1952): 66; Robert Nicholas Olsberg, "A Government of Class and Race: William Henry Trescot and the South Carolina Chivalry, 1860-1865" (Ph.D. dissertation, University of South Carolina, 1972) 420.

Index

Active (vessel), 40

Adair, Douglass, 203

Adams, Henry, 125

Adams, John, 51, 76

Adolescence, 71-73, 86, 121-22. *See also* American Revolution, and family authority; Colonial family

Allegiance, 118-19

American Revolution, 11, 103, 134-38, 220; as a crisis of legitimacy, 83; effect on colonial elite, 84; and family authority, 108-109, 116, 123-24, 127-28; and individual autonomy, 107-108; irrational component of, 120; as normative, 80; and the press, 160-61; and Puritan ethic, 96-97. *See also* Adolescence; Colonial elite; Colonial family; South Carolina

Americans, develop sense of separateness, 81-82

Andover, Massachusetts, 108, 110

Andre, John, 100

Ann (vessel), 42, 43, 44

Answer to the Considerations on Certain Political Transactions of the Province of South Carolina (A. Lee), 54

Authoritarian Personality, The (Adorno), 107

Backcountrymen, 68-69

Bacon, Francis, 181

Bacon, Thomas, 186

Bailyn, Bernard, 64, 179

Baldwin, Joseph, 228

Baltimore Advertiser, 171

Baptists, 15. *See also* Protestant Dissenters

Barnwell, Robert W., 222

Barrow, Thomas, 69

Battle of Brandywine, 90

Becker, Carl, 86

Bills of attainder, 157. *See also* Confiscation Acts

Blacks. *See* Slavery

Board of Trade, 20

Bolingbroke. *See* St. John, Henry

Boston Port Act, 176

Botein, Stephen, 187

Boucher, Jonathan, 106, 107, 115

Boyd, Adam, 163, 169

Bremar, Francis, 36

Bremar, Martha, 36

Bremar, Mary (Molly), 50

Bridenbaugh, Carl, 173

Brodie, Fawn, 121, 126n

Broughton Island Packet (vessel), 41, 48

Bull, Fenwick, 51

Bull, William Izard, 230

Bull, William, Jr., 10, 22, 118, 150, 167, 230

Burke, Aedanus, 138, 142, 151, 157; and confiscations, 146-47

Burke, Thomas, 123

Burrows, Edwin, 109, 110, 118
Bute, earl of. *See* Stuart, John
Butler, Pierce, 138

Calhoon, Robert, 117
Calhoun, John C., 28, 31
Cape-Fear Mercury (Boyd), 163, 169, 192, 193
Carter, Landon, 113n, 115
Carter, Robert, 113n, 125
Cato the Younger, 96
Cato's Letters (Trenchard & Gordon), 14, 181n
Charleston, 11, 13, 136, 164; as intellectual center, 14; population, 10
Charleston Library Society, 14, 15
Chastellux, Marquis de, 114n
Cherokee Indians, 11
Cherokee War, 23n
Chesnut, Mary Boykin, 222, 223
Cicero, 96
Civil War, 229
Classical figures, 96
Clinton, Sir Henry, 90, 137, 145
Clouds Creek, South Carolina, 135
Colonial agents, 177
Colonial elite, 84, 85; and the British, 68-69, 75, 76; and class, 83; growing sense of unity, 79-80
Colonial family, and discipline, 111-14, 115-16; diversity of, 110-11
Colonial society, instability of, 69
Common Sense (Paine), 64, 81, 119
Commons House (South Carolina), 4, 16, 17n, 20, 53, 168, 175; changes name, 19; membership, 9n, 19, 24-25, 26n, 27n; rivalry with Council, 18-20, 52-53; unity within, 22. *See also* Council
Confiscation Acts, 150; and extenuating circumstances, 154-55; legal problems with, 152-53; and legislative authority, 156-57. *See also* Bills of attainder
Confiscations, opposition to, 146-47; as source of revenue, 144-45
Congregationalists, 15. *See also* Protestant Dissenters
Considerations on Certain Political Transactions of the Province of South Carolina (E. Leigh), 54
Constitutions, 4, 121

Continental Congress, 23, 83, 144, 178, 194
Coosawhatchie, South Carolina, 95
Cornwallis, Charles, earl of, 145
Council (South Carolina Royal), 16, 18, 20-22, 52-53
Country ideology, 1-2, 7, 14, 15-17, 18, 24, 29, 180, 199, 216
Country Journal. See South Carolina Gazette and Country Journal
Courts, 150-52
Craftsman, The 182, 184
Creek Indians, 11
Cresswell, Nicholas, 114n
Crosthwaite, William Ward, 129-30
Crouch, Charles, 168, 169, 188
Crouse, Maurice, 113n
Cultural change, 27-28
Cunningham, "Bloody" Bill, 135
Currency Act of 1764, 66

Dart, John, 5n
Dartmouth, earl of. *See* Legge, William
Davis, James, 169, 174, 188
Davis, Richard, 74
Deane, Silas, 161, 162, 214
DeBrahm, John William Gerard, 9n
Declaration of Independence, 81, 119, 128, 131, 215
Deference, 6, 83, 148
Dickinson, John, 85
Dixon, John, 170, 176
Dobbs, Arthur, 169
Drayton, John, 52, 114, 116
Drayton, William Henry, 114, 194n, 199; character of, 24, 79, 214, 215, 217; in council, 21, 52, 53
Dueling, 228-29
Dunlap, John, 171
Dunmore, earl of. *See* Murray, John

Eaton, Clement, 209
Elections, 19, 35n
Elliott, Barnard, 131
Elliott, Bernard, 130
Emerson, Ralph Waldo, 82
Erikson, Erik, 121
Expectations gap, 84-85
Extracts from the Proceedings of the Court of Vice-Admiralty (H. Laurens), 43, 48
Factionalism, 7, 12, 22, 30
Federalist Papers, The 82

Ferguson, Thomas, 124
Feuer, Lewis, 123
Fithian, Philip, 113, 125, 205
Fitzhugh, George, 225
Florida, 11
Franklin, Benjamin, 77, 79, 91, 174
Freeholder's Political Catechism (St. John), 182
Freemen of the State of South-Carolina, To the (Burke), 147
French and Indian War, 71, 73
Fundamental Constitutions of Carolina, 7-8
Furman, Richard, 206

Gadsden, Christopher, 23, 26n, 118; character of, 214, 215, 216-17; and confiscations, 146-47; political ideology of, 5n, 6, 21, 143; on Scotsmen, 184-85
Galloway, Joseph, 78
Gandhi, Mahatma, 121
Garden, Alexander, 118, 225
Garth, Charles, 39
Gates, Horatio, 137
General Assembly. *See* Commons House (South Carolina)
Georgia, 9n, 11, 120, 178
Georgia Gazette, 172, 189, 199
Germantown, Pennsylvania, 90
Glen, James, 20
Glorious Revolution, 69
Goddard, William, 170
Gordon, Thomas, 14, 15, 181, 199
Grant, James, 23n
Great Awakening, 13
Great Britain, contributes to colonial instability, 65-66; discriminates against Americans, 73-75, 77-79
Green, Anne Catherine, 170, 175
Green, Frederick, 170
Green, Jonas, 170, 174
Green, Nathanael, 91, 95, 123, 137, 143, 144
Grenville, George, 200
Greven, Philip, 108
Grimke, Frederick, 223
Grimke, John Paul, 168n
Guerard, Benjamin, 139, 145, 150
Halifax, North Carolina, 170
Hamilton, Alexander, 91, 100, 101-102
Hammond, LeRoy, 150
Hanger, George, 136

Harper, William, 224
Harrison, Benjamin, 205
Hartley, Roger Peter Handaside, 42
Hartley, Sarah, 129, 130
Hay, Douglas, 157
Hayes, James, Jr., 171
Hayes Station, South Carolina, 135
Hayne, Robert Y., 104
Hemingway, Ernest, 89
Henry, Patrick, 110, 125n
Hewatt, Alexander, 9, 22-23
Higginbotham, Don, 134
Himeli, B. Henri, 97
Hindus, Michael, 112, 116
Hoffman, Ronald, 134, 135
Horace, 96
House of Commons, 4, 16, 18
Housman, A. E., 104
Huger, Benjamin, 130
Huguenots, 10, 15, 97
Hunter, William, Jr., 170
Independent Whig, The (Trenchard & Gordon), 14
Innes, Alexander, 20
Insurrection, 11, 12, 185, 215, 218
Iredell, James, 126n
Ireland, 85
Isaac, Rhys, 207
Izard, Ralph, 54, 77
Jackson, Andrew, 83
Jacksonborough Assembly, 141-42, 209
Jefferson, Thomas, 121, 124, 126, 170, 180
Johnson, Robert, 12
Johnston, James, 164, 166, 209
Jones, Willie, 170
Jordan, Winthrop, 124, 126n
Keitt, Lawrence, 220
King George's War, 26
Kinloch, Francis, 143, 155
Lanier, Sidney, 229
Lasswell, Harold, 163
Laurens, Henry, 12, 14, 23, 24, 25, 26n, 34, 48, 60, 67, 89, 91, 128, 207; admonitions to John Laurens, 97, 99, 101; character of, 44-45, 98, 113n, 119, 126, 197, 215; and the customs service, 41-43; and death of John Laurens, 94-95; and Egerton Leigh, 36, 38, 45, 54; and the Mary Bremar affair, 50-51

Laurens, John, 144, 224; account of his life, 89-92; and black batttalion, 90, 93-94, 102-103; character of, 92, 95-96, 102, 103-104; compared to Hamilton, 100, 101-102; contemporary opinions, of, 95; as egalitarian, 92-93; at fall of Charleston, 90-91; and his brothers, 99; his marriage, 99-100; influences upon, 97-98

Laurens, John, Sr., 113n

Lee, Arthur, 54, 77, 180, 184

Lee, Charles, 90, 138

Lee, "Light Horse" Harry, 135

Lee, Ludwell, 126

Lee, Richard Henry, 79, 118, 126

Lee, Robert E., 229

Lee, Thomas, 126

Lee, William, 120

Legge, William, 58

Legislature. *See* Commons House (South Carolina)

Leigh, Egerton, 21, 36, 50, 54, 58, 99; character of, 46, 49, 58-61; as Council president, 52, 53; early career, 34-38; and Henry Laurens, 34, 43-44, 45, 48; his decline, 45-48; justifies himself, 57; on the law and judiciary, 48-49; and legal cases, 40-42, 46; and the Mary Bremar affair, 50-51; as placeman, 33; and the Powell affair, 53; on South Carolina politics, 54-56; and Stamp Act crisis, 38-39, 46; and Wilkes Fund, 52

Leigh, Peter, 37

Liberty, 2-3

Literacy, 196-97

Locke, John, 111, 124, 181

Lockridge, Kenneth, 196, 197

London Gazette, 171

Love, Robert, 136

Lowndes, Rawlins, 23-24, 26n, 75, 119, 148

Loyalists, 24n, 80, 85n, 142, 166; amnesty for, 155-56; attitudes toward, 143-44, 147-49, 149; personality type of, 118. *See also* Leigh, Egerton; Wragg, William

Lucan, 96

Luther, Martin, 121

Lynch, Thomas, 26n, 33, 51

Lyttelton, William Henry, 18, 20, 38, 165

Mackenzie, John, 182, 219

Madison, James, 30

Magruder, Jeb Stuart, 104

Maier, Pauline, 117, 150

Man Unmasked, The (Leigh), 43

Manigault, Gabriel, 113n

Manigault, Peter, 10, 21, 23, 25, 26n, 168n

Marion, Francis, 135

Marmontel, Jean Francois, 97

Maryland Gazette (Green), 170, 171, 172n, 174, 178

Maryland Journal and Baltimore Advertiser (Goddard), 170

Mason, George, 127, 180, 200

Massachusetts Spy (Thomas), 194

Mazlish, Bruce, 109, 121

Mazyck, Isaac, 26n

Merchants, 13, 26. *See also* Gadsden, Christopher; Laurens, Henry; Mazyck, Isaac

Merritt, Richard, 186-87

Middleton, Arthur, 138, 147

Mills, Robert, 226

Miranda, Francisco de, 114n

Mobs, 67-68

"Monitor's Letters" (A. Lee), 180

Monmouth, New Jersey, 90

Montagu, Charles, 6, 22

Moore, Daniel, 40, 44

Moore, Maurice, 113

Morgan, Edmund S., 97, 120, 125, 207

Moultrie, William, 139

Murray, John (earl of Dunmore), 69, 171

Murrin, John, 79

Nevins, Allan, 178

New Bern, North Carolina, 169

News: indirect influence of, 203-207; speed and route of transmission, 188-92, 200-201; two-step flow of, 203-204

Newspapers, 166-68, 169, 170, 172n; and advertising, 171, 172-73; bias of, 183-86; circulation of, 173; content of, 178-80, 186-87; income of, 171-72; and national consciousness, 201-203; and political pressure, 163-66; and political stability, 207-20; readership, 192-95, 197-99; subsidized, 171-72. *See also* names of newspapers

Niebuhr, Reinhold, 26

Norfolk Intelligencer, 171

Norfolk, Virginia, 184

North-Carolina Gazette (Steuart), 163, 169, 172, 173, 183, 188, 196

Officeholding, 34, 35n, 39, 45. *See also* Placemen

Officers, army, 73-74

Oliver, Peter, 85n, 206
Olmstead, Frederick Law, 221, 222
Oswald, Richard, 120, 162, 199
Otis, James, 76
Paine, Thomas, 108, 119
Parsons, James, 26n
Party, 7, 24, 82, 176. *See also* Country ideology
Pendleton, Edmund, 198, 207
Pendleton, Henry, 151
Pennsylvania Chronicle (Goddard), 170
Pennsylvania Gazette, 172
Pennsylvania Packet (Dunlap), 171
Perroneau, Henry, 52
Personal independence, quest for, 122; and self-discipline, 124-25
Pinckney, Charles, the elder, 19, 26, 218
Pinckney, Charles, the younger, 81
Pinckney, Eliza Lucas, 124, 197
Pinkney, John, 170
Placemen, 20, 34, 74
Planters, 13, 26
Pocock, J. G. A., 1
Political culture, 1, 2, 20, 28, 60, 180, 183, 214, 220; and British, 70-71; and social conditions, 218; of South Carolina, 216-17. *See also* Country ideology
Political morality, 11, 25, 45. *See also* Country ideology
Political stability, 25, 71n, 80, 149-50. *See also* Colonial elite; Confiscation Acts
Pope, Alexander, 180
Population, 10, 11, 195-96
Porcher, F. A., 30
Powell, George Gabriel, 67-68
Powell, Thomas, 53, 167
Pred, Allan, 188
Presbyterians, 15. *See also* Protestant Dissenters
Prevost, Augustine, 90, 137
Pride, 85
Printers, elitist, 162; and government, 177-78; income of, 174; and party, 176; restraints on, 175-76; and the Stamp Act, 177. *See also* Newspapers
Professionals, 13
Professions, and European standards, 70n
Protestant Dissenters, 15, 19n. *See also* names of denominations

Provincial Congress, South Carolina, 215
Public service, 17n
Purdie, Alexander, 170, 175, 176
Quincy, Josiah, Jr., 78, 181
Ramsay, David, 22, 23n, 135, 160, 161
Randolph, Edmund, 204
Rattray, John, 19n
Regulators, North Carolina, 66, 68
Regulators, South Carolina, 27n, 66, 148, 185
Relative deprivation, 75n
Religious toleration, 10
Republicanism, 82, 96
Revolution, and emotion, 64; and marginal groups, 84, 86
Rhett, Edmund, 222
Rind, Clementina, 170
Rind, William, 170, 192
Rochford, Lord (William Henry Zuylestein), 50
Rossiter, Clinton, 14
Roupell, George, 41-42, 45
Royal Council. *See* Council, South Carolina
Royal Gazette (*South Carolina Royal Gazette*), 94n, 166
Royal Georgia Gazette (Johnston), 209
Royal governors, 18. *See also* Bull, William, Jr.; Dobbs, Arthur; Glen, James; Johnson, Robert; Lyttelton, William Henry; Montagu, Charles; Murray, John
Royle, Joseph, 170, 176
Rush, Benjamin, 116
Rutledge, Edward, 53, 102, 115, 145, 147, 151, 154
Rutledge, John, 26n, 119, 127; as governor, 137, 138, 141; on politics, 83, 103, 143, 198
St. John, Henry (Viscount Bolingbroke), 15, 176, 180, 199, 216
Saveth, Edward, 110
Saxby, George, 46
Scots, 75, 184-85, 202
Self-discipline, and institutional support, 125; and resistance to authority, 126-27; and threat of deprivation, 126
Serle, Ambrose, 160, 161
Shaftesbury, earl of (Anthony Ashley Cooper), 7
Shinner, Charles, 38
Shy, John, 77, 133, 134

Sidney, Algernon, 98, 181

Simms, William Gilmore, 104, 197, 226, 227

Simpson, James, 35n, 54, 149n

Sirmans, M. Eugene, 18

Slavery, and disinterestedness, 225-27; effect on South Carolina, 11, 221-23; and filial rebellion, 113; Sambo image, 11, 225. *See also* Insurrection; Laurens, John, and black battalion

Smith, Benjamin, 26n, 36

Smith, Daniel Scott, 112, 116

Smith, Thomas, 10

Society of Supporters for the Bill of Rights in England, 52

Some Thoughts Concerning Education (Locke), 111

Sons of Liberty, 124

South Carolina, 120; and American Revolution, 120, 134-38; changing character of women in, 226-27; Council, 74; economy, 8, 9, 12; elite of, 85; physical destruction in, 139; political achievement of, 27; political harmony of, 28-29, 29, 30, 218-19; population of, 10, 11; post-revolutionary, 134; and slavery, 224-25; unifying factors in, 8-13. *See also* Colonial elite; Commons House (South Carolina); Council (South Carolina Royal); Political culture; Political stability

South-Carolina and American General Gazette (Wells), 165, 172n, 184, 188n, 199

South Carolina Gazette (Timothy), 14, 26, 43, 53, 166, 167, 171, 172, 173, 181n, 185, 186, 188n, 192, 196, 206

South-Carolina Gazette and Country Journal (Crouch), 168, 172n, 188

South Carolina Royal Gazette, See Royal Gazette

South-Carolina Weekly Gazette (Wells). 165

South Carolinians, 45; political character of, 1, 214-16; pride of, 85, 220-21, 222

Southern Quarterly Review, 30, 227

Stamp Act crisis, 26n, 38, 165, 167, 168, 169, 170, 176, 177

Steele, I. K., 188

Steuart, Andrew, 163, 169

Stilwell, John, 135

Stuart, John, 165

Stuart, John, earl of Bute, 23, 183

Summary View of the Rights of British America, A (Jefferson), 180

Tarleton, Banastre, 135

Taxation, 14n, 52

Thomas, Isaiah, 194

Timothy, Peter, 169, 173, 184; income, 171; and politics, 166-68, 174

Tocqueville, Alexis de, 220, 229

Townshend Duties, 167

Trenchard, John, 14, 15, 181, 199

Trescot, William Henry, 222, 226

Tuesday Club, 174

Valley Forge, Pennsylvania, 90

Van Buren, Martin, 82

Vice-Admiralty Courts, 58

Virginia Gazette, 169, 170, 171, 172n, 173, 174, 176, 181, 182, 184, 186, 192, 193, 196

Wallace, Michael, 109, 110

Walpole, Robert, 180

Walzer, Michael, 125

Wambaw (vessel), 41, 48

Washington, George, 79, 95, 122

Weber, Max, 96

Webster, Daniel, 82

Wells, John, 165-66

Wells, Robert, 75, 110, 164-65, 166

Wemyss, James, 137

Wigfall, Louis, 220, 229

Wilkes, John, 52, 183

Williams, Robert, 105, 129

Williamsburg, Virginia, 169

Williamson, Andrew, 144

Wilmington, North Carolina, 169

Wilson, John Lyde, 228

Wolfe, James, 73

Wood, Gordon, 64, 84

Woodmason, Charles, 75, 186, 221

Wormley, Robert, 115

Wragg, William, 30, 219; character of, 18, 24, 215, 217; as Loyalist, 5n, 214; offices held, 20, 26n

Wright, Thomas, 26n

Yorktown, Virginia, 91

Zagorin, Perez, 86